THE PATHFINDER

Finding the Right Path

a memoir

By MARK T. MAHAFFEY

with Meghan Everett

Book Cover Design Artwork: Marcus Thomas

Editors: Brianna Miranda-Solberg & Julia Florey

Book Formatting: Jessie Alarcon

Publisher: Richter Publishing LLC www.richterpublishing.com

ISBN-13: 978-1-954094-40-6 Hardback

Library of Congress Copyright & Registration Number (coming soon)

ACKNOWLEDGEMENTS

I would first most like to express my gratitude to family - my wife, Marianne, and my children, Tom, Kiley and Colleen, who have been encouraging me for many years to write a memoir. They have offered ample support and encouragement throughout the entire writing process, especially in helping me recall many of the important family events. I would also like to extend a thank you to Bob Desautels, Leo Lambert, Bill Bond, and Steve Bettcher for cheering me on as I embarked on this grand endeavor.

I would also like to thank Bob Desautels and Marianne for their help in collecting many of the photographs featured throughout this book. I also appreciate the great talents of the various photographers, many unknown, who have captured much of my life's journey on camera.

I would also like to thank Marcus Thomas for giving me the great honor of displaying his incredible painting of the Pelican in Flight on the front cover of this memoir.

I would also like to thank my assistant, Patty Cole, for all her help in gathering data on company history and managing my busy schedule.

Lastly, I would like to thank the MAC Chief Financial Officer, Austin Everett, for recommending that his wife, Meghan Everett, help me with my memoir writing process. What began as a small favor on her part, evolved into a collaboration that eventually brought the finished work to fruition. Her dedicated efforts in organizing, researching, and writing brought my desire to share the Mahaffey family lore a dream come true. As with every other achievement I reached throughout my life, I would have never succeeded in writing this memoir without the combined efforts of many people in my life. I am eternally grateful for all their support.

For my wife, Marianne,
who has been my rock for over 50 years.

For my children, Tom, Kiley, and Colleen,
and my grandchildren, Ansleigh, Reese, Piper, Colton, and Mackenzie,
who keep me young at heart.

For my father, Tom Mahaffey,
who was my first guidepost on my path of life.

And lastly, for my dearest friends,
Bob, Hugh, Dick, Steve, Carl, Tom, Mike, and Leo,
who make life an adventure.

CONTENTS

PROLOGUE

It is not what we have in life, but who we have in our life that matters.
J.M. Laurence

If I had one wish, just a single wish that a genie could grant me, it would not be for fame or fortune. It would not be to glance into the future or be blessed with infinite youth. What I would humbly request of this magnanimous genie would be two hours of time—one hour to sit down with my father and one hour to sit down with mother—to ask them all the questions I never thought to ask while they were living. What I would give to hear their stories now. Perhaps I was ignorant, or perhaps I was simply focused on the road ahead. Whatever the reason, it appears that I only choose to reflect on the past, when time has gone by. As the wheels in my mind cycle through memories and I remember bits and pieces of my own life, the story begins to unfold. Ironically, the more I remember, the more I realize I do not remember, or perhaps never knew. This awareness entices me to crave even more.

If I were given those two hours of time to visit with my parents again, I would ask them to share with me their memories. I would love to hear as many stories, big or small, as they could remember. I would beg them to enlighten me with as much family history as they knew. I long to discover the narrative of my ancestor's lives—their struggles, triumphs, and journeys to and across America. Coming from Ireland, my grandparents' parents started from scratch and built the American dream. To know all the details that went into creating that whole Mahaffey odyssey would be so fulfilling.

But alas, I am aware of no existing genie to grant me this wish. I must console myself to settle on what I do know. And I say "settle" in no diminishing sense, as I still have a full story to share. I am very blessed to be part of the Mahaffey legacy. I was fortunate to have incredibly involved parents and grandparents who were passionate believers in the strength of family and tradition. My goal is to keep that strong folklore going.

One grand observation I make as I look back on my own life, is that I have been blessed with the presence of an immense network of friendships and partnerships. My parents' and grandparents' devoted efforts to connect with people and build lifelong bonds has supported every aspect of my life, either directly or indirectly, from my childhood to now. Seeing my individual life's success story as a compilation and continuation of that endeavor makes me feel both proud and grateful. I have made it my goal to uphold the principle of maintaining and building new relationships, knowing that each person is a thread in the great Mahaffey tapestry of success. I couldn't feel more blessed to be surrounded by such a vast, interwoven group of special people.

I feel a strong responsibility at this point in my life to pay tribute to those important people—my family and friends of past and present. I offer a great *thank you* to those who inspire me and guide me every day. I also aim to give future Mahaffey generations a glimpse at that portrait, so they can feel the same honor and appreciation for the people that built the vision. And perhaps, just perhaps, I hope to answer some questions that they would have never thought to ask.

1

THUMBS UP

Normality is a paved road. It's comfortable to walk, but no flowers grow.

Vincent Van Gogh

I carefully stepped in my polished brown loafers onto the ice-covered sidewalk. The path, which laid at the threshold of my family's meticulously manicured lawn, seemed to extend as endlessly as the sea in either direction. It was a frigid Monday morning in Indianapolis, Indiana, and the first day back to school after the Thanksgiving holiday. It was unusually cold for this time of year. It was 1958. I was fourteen years old, a proud freshman in high school. My school and my friends were the utmost center of my world, and my life was about as all-American as the typical high schooler in the 1950s. I was lucky to be a part of a generation that experienced a coming of age during an idealistic era, where people had the attitude that life is what you make it. The 1950s suburban culture focused on hard work, leisure, sports and community. Life was good, and as a high schooler, I appreciated the simple freedom of navigating this chapter of my life with some newly acquired independence.

Turning south, I strode purposefully along the tree-lined sidewalk. I felt the warmth of the morning sun extend like a handshake through the clouds, offering a welcoming cordiality despite the bone-chilling air. Snow delicately fluttered and swirled throughout this suburban landscape and reflected the light like an illuminated snow globe. The grand, towering oak trees began to hum and moan in baritone manner as a soprano squall swooped in for her exuberant cadenza. I shivered in its imperious presence. How the season had managed to drop to the mere single digits Fahrenheit after reaching the high seventies only the week before I would never comprehend. The Indiana weather was as enigmatic as the mysteries of the Twilight Zone.

I fastened the top brass button of my heather-gray woolen jacket, hoping the top few inches would offer me the warmth my body craved. I immediately regretted the effort however, as I subsequently reminded myself that I was in high school now, and top buttons were most certainly *not* in vogue. I discreetly unclasped the button and grasped my fingers, numb with cold, tightly around my leather-bound stack of schoolbooks. Tilting my head down to brace against the biting gale, I continued to walk quickly and steadily along North Meridian Street.

"Just a few houses further," I said to myself.

I counted the driveways as I strode.

"One...two...three...four...five."

Meridian Street was the center artery that ran north and south through Indianapolis. It was flanked with mature oak and maple trees that seemed to arc over the road if they were nobly protecting it from the rest of the world. My childhood home, built in 1927, was proudly situated on a one-acre lot at 5300 Meridian Street in the prestigious North Meridian Historic District. It was a beautiful, traditional Jacobean-style home, cloaked in brick masonry and adorned with stoned accents. It was originally built by my maternal grandparents, James and Elizabeth Watson, as a family home to raise their three children. When his daughter, Jane (my mother) married my father, Thomas Mahaffey, they bought a smaller home on the next street over, where they raised their four young children. After my grandfather passed away in 1948, when I was just four years old, we traded houses with my still living Grandmother

2

Elizabeth and my maiden Aunt Lizzie, who had still been living with her mother at the time. It was a reasonable trade, as there had been six of us living in that smaller home, which included my father, mother, my two sisters, my brother, and myself. We were all excited to move into our grandparents' big house.

The Mahaffey family home on North Meridian Street, Indianapolis, Indiana

Even though our new home was just a street over, it was a big deal having an address on Meridian Street. All the residences along this thoroughfare were owned by some of the wealthiest and socially elite individuals in Indianapolis. These grand homes boasted some of the best of 1920s architecture. Old World European design elements, such as masonry, columns, and intricate stone and trim work were on-trend in the 1920s. To walk along the street, one would experience a display of the most romantic and regal of English, Dutch colonial, and Italian designs. Years later, in 1986, that stretch of road where I grew up was officially listed on the National Register of Historic Places as "One of America's Great Streets." Of course, to me at the time, it was simply my home—and my world.

My school, Cathedral High School, was an all-boys school about four miles to the south on Meridian Street. I could have taken the city bus to school. My parents naturally thought I *did* take the city bus. But the city bus was agonizingly slow and a real hassle. I painstakingly rode it perhaps once or twice before I thought to myself, *there has to be a better way*. Gearing my mind in focus, I was on a mission to get to school as efficiently as possible. I decided I needed to find my own path.

Original Cathedral High School building on North Meridian Street

Finally reaching my chosen spot, a half-block south and just out of sight of my house, I watched the blurred line of vehicles zoom by on Meridian Street. I observed the businessmen in their expensive suits drive their cars—their *heated* cars—playing the morning radio that promised the start of a successful day. I held my books tightly with one arm, and with resolute motion, I stretched out the other toward the road. Confidently, I held up my thumb, pointing it high to the sky, like a lighthouse in the fog. Locking it strongly into position, I was determined not to let it shake and succumb to the chill of the wind.

I watched the road carefully. One car went by, and then, another.

Finally, I saw Mr. Adams approaching, driving his new, light tan Mercedes.

Jackpot, I thought.

Grinning and full of hope, I patiently waited as the vehicle began to slow. Like the anticipating sense of watching a golf ball fly through the air knowing that it will sink the hole before it actually does, I observed the gleaming car approach me and stop. Mr. Adams rolled down the window, letting a slight burst of steam escape the confines of the vehicle.

"Good morning, Mark! Hop on in," he said in a cheery, yet deep and sophisticated tone. He wore a gray, woolen coat similar to my own, with the addition of a charcoal-gray felt fedora upon his head. His freshly shaven angular jaw was just about as shiny as his new automobile.

"Thank you, Mr. Adams," I replied gratefully in an equally poised manner.

The sweet and woodsy smell of the ivory leather interior signaled to me that I had made it. I sat up straight, shoulders back and chin up in the passenger seat of that toasty car. I was proud. I felt grown up. I had made my own way.

I continued to hitchhike to school for all four years of high school. If I timed it precisely, there were four or so regulars—some were friends of my parents—who would stop and drive me to my destination. If I was a little late, my chances to get a ride were slimmer, but there was usually some kind commuter who would stop to help me out. I got home that same way too, which was a little more challenging, but I always eventually got home. Cities were much safer back in the 1950s. Hitchhiking was considerably more common at that time than it is now. There was a strong sense of community and togetherness, and people sought out to help one another.

Even still, I did not feel compelled to share with my parents that I did not ride the bus. During all four years of high school, my mother never knew that I hitchhiked to school. I suspect my father might have known, but he never said a word. My three older siblings were all much older than I was and were either in college or moved out by the time I was in high school. My sister Ann was the oldest. She was ten years older than me and already married. My only brother, Jim, was eight years older than me and away at college at Tulane in New Orleans. And lastly, my sister Kate, who was four years older than me, was away at college at Pine Manor Junior College, and later, Michigan State University.

I, Mark Thomas Mahaffey, may have been the youngest of my siblings, but I was not hindered by it. I developed a sort of resilience and an independent attitude that I could figure out things my own way. Little did I comprehend at the time how much this hitchhiking experience would form me. It allowed me to develop the confidence to take charge and the bravery to tread new waters. And most importantly, it taught me the value of trust. Life is a journey, and no one is meant to take that excursion alone. Having trust in people, whether strangers or life-long friends, has been the number one principle moving me forward in life.

In my younger years, neither my parents nor my older siblings ever put their arms around my shoulders to show me the ins and outs of navigating boyhood. I never recall my father or older brother, Jim, teaching me how to throw a football or how to win a girl. I never even shot a basketball until I was in seventh grade. However, I do not fault either one of them for that. We just did not have that kind of relationship. I eventually would form a much closer bond to them in my adult years. But as a child, I leaned on my school mentors, coaches, and friends. I can think back and recognize a few influential people in my childhood who helped me on that journey.

The very first person who comes to mind is Mike Johnson. In middle school, we were best buddies, at least from my point of view. He had an athletic build, slick black hair and charisma enough to make everyone feel like his best friend. He was especially popular in school and an incredible athlete. I am forever grateful to Mike Johnson because he taught me how to throw a football, how to ice skate, and how to play basketball. He had the benefit of several older brothers who also taught him poker and chess, which he, in turn, taught me. We spent a great deal of time together, and I soaked in every minute of it.

Mike's family home was perhaps a mile from my home, and I would ride my bicycle there often. In the 1950s, bicycles were absolutely essential for getting around, especially in Indianapolis—*especially* for a kid. I treasured that green and ivory-striped Schwinn Racer more than life itself. It was my ticket to freedom and my vehicle to life experience. It would not be unusual for us to ride two to three miles into the city to visit a friend's house. Once seventh grade began, we started visiting *girl*friends' houses. We would cruise to midtown and spend a couple of hours with girls whom we met from another parish. The girls from our parish were nice and good looking enough, but it was exciting expanding our territory and meeting new girls. Those were wonderful, carefree days full of excitement and pure enjoyment of life.

Alas, as our middle school chapter began to close, and we entered our high school years, Mike Johnson and I began to drift apart. He became more of what I can only describe as a *wild child*. For instance, I remember him as the first person in our grade to drink alcohol. He did not get into a great deal of trouble, but he had a new set of friends I did not care to join. I would not call us adversaries, but he had his group, and I had my group. I believe that was the first time I truly contemplated, "I am going to go this way." I can think back to many forks in the path of life where I had to choose right instead of left. Reflecting on my journey, I think I did a pretty good job choosing, because I am proud of where I stand today. I can also look back and see how each decision helped me grow in some way.

Looking back, I can see that letting go of Mike Johnson allowed me to develop a close friendship with another fellow schoolmate, Bob Desautels. In my freshman year of high school, Bob quickly became my best friend. Because he had attended a different grade school than I did, I did not know him well before high school. I had perhaps seen him a few times at social gatherings, such as at the ice skate social at the Coliseum on Friday nights—but not much more than that. Luckily, both our grade schools fed into the same high school, and we began to spend a lot more time together. I can recall those early days of our friendship like it was yesterday.

Mark Mahaffey, Sophomore at Cathedral High School, 1959

"Mark! Come on over to my house later. We're playing basketball at seven," I can remember Bob saying persuasively at school one day early freshman year.

"Sure thing, Bob! I'll be there," I said.

Later that evening, after hastily plowing my mother's (well, more specifically, *Swanson's*) chicken pot pie into my mouth and scraping my plate clean within minutes, I patiently waited for my father and mother to finish their meals. Supper time was sacred, and I was not to leave the table until my father directed. My mother gingerly forked a single pea and daintily brought it to her lips. I fidgeted in my chair with eagerness and eyed the clock that hung on the wall behind my father's chair. It was 6:50, and the clock hands seemed to move faster than my parents' forks.

I wanted to give myself plenty of time to ride my bicycle to Bob's house and was hoping to leave about now.

"Gee, Sweetie, you must have been hungry! Would you like some more pie?" my mother inquired. She swooped up my plate to serve me another slice without my answering.

"No, no, mom. Really, I'm full. It was very good."

My father chimed in, "The boy isn't hungry. He's got something else he's wanting to do. What is it, son?" My father spoke in a very matter-of-fact, emotionless tone.

I responded, "Well, you see...I'm meeting Bob Desautels at his house for a basketball game at seven."

My father nodded in approval, "Desautels. Yes, good family." He paused, "You may go."

I leapt out of my chair as quickly as a caged bird being finally released and darted toward the front door.

"Mark." My father sternly called after me.

I turned around to see his eyes signaling toward my mother. I walked back to the table, kissed her cheek and said, "Thank you for dinner, Mom. I won't be late."

She smiled and replied, "Have fun. Tell Mrs. Desautels we say hello."

"Yes, ma'am," I said.

Hurriedly, I slipped on my Converse high-top sneakers and hopped onto my green Schwinn Racer. Having mastered bicycling without holding onto the handlebars, I held my arms at my side and zipped across Meridian Street, following the sidewalks to the east. Bob's house was about ten blocks away, across the street from Saint Joan of Arc Church. It was a crisp, cool day in early autumn. The oak and maple trees were in full color, flaunting vibrant shades of scarlet and gold. The setting sun painted the sky, echoing the hues of the fall foliage. I felt as if I was sailing under a dome of color, as if Van Gogh had painted the route.

Quickly grabbing the handlebars to steer my bicycle onto his street, I was at his driveway in no time. I hopped off my bicycle and walked it up the long driveway. Bob's home was a stately red, colonial-style brick house with tall columns framing the front door and a balcony up top. I veered my bicycle to head toward the front door, when I heard a voice call my name.

"Mark! Over here!"

I shifted my gaze toward the voice and looked up the driveway, which continued past the house. Squinting my eyes into the setting sun, I saw the silhouette of a free-standing garage, a basketball hoop mounted above the garage doors, and five boys playing basketball. I quickly leaned my bicycle against the iron fence that ran along the driveway and ran up to play. Getting closer, I could make out the faces of Bob Desautels, Hugh McGowan, Tom Holland, Joe Tynan, and Jerry Bintz.

Without hesitation, Bob passed the ball to me. I dribbled it a few times and took a shot at the hoop. Whoosh! It went in! I was glad Mike had taught me some moves. I beamed with pride and could not hold back a wide grin. Then, out of the corner of my eye, someone caught my gaze. Peering into the far side of the yard, I saw a girl, perhaps a few years younger than I was, sitting on a chaise lounge chair next to the Desautels's backyard swimming pool. She was Bob's younger sister. It appeared she had been reading a book, but had paused to watch the game. She had wispy black hair, fair skin and a few freckles—and the sweetest smile I had ever seen. Our eyes met, and she nodded in silent applause. My grin stretched even wider in appreciation.

Bob's house was undoubtedly the hub of neighborhood activity. I spent a substantial amount of time at their house, bicycling over there every moment I could. Between the basketball court, swimming pool, and large backyard perfect for football, there was never a shortage of things to do at their house.

I learned that back in sixth grade, Bob had started a basketball competition with his classmates at Joan of Arc School. Teams of guys, three against three, would play in a big tournament every May. They even set up brackets. It was called the DBY, which stood for the Desautels' Back Yard. I joined Bob's team my freshman year in high school. It was amazing how that small backyard tournament turned into a big neighborhood event every year. The tournament at its peak had twenty teams. Friends from school, parents, and neighbors would all gather to watch and cheer us on as the competition heated up in the Desautels' backyard. *"See you at the DBY!"* became a familiar cry throughout our neighborhood as games were played almost daily throughout our four years of high school, and even in college. At one point, we even had one of the stars from the Indiana Pacers come referee for the final game. It was a big deal! The local newspaper, *The Indianapolis Star,* featured an article about the DBY, written by none other than my good friend, Hugh McGowan. Even more than being competitive, it was about having fun.

The relationships that I formed at the Desautels' house changed my life forever. Those five boys, Bob, Hugh, Joe, Tom, and Jerry, became my best friends, and I have continued those friendships to this day. I especially admired Bob's family. His parents were so gracious and kind to me. Our families had known each other for years, even before I was born, and it wasn't before long that the Desautels felt like my second family. Little did I know at the time, they would one day *be* my family. That little girl, who I first saw lounging by the swimming pool, would eventually become my wife.

North Side Teens Have Own Basketball League

By HUGH McGOWAN
Cathedral Reporter

There's more to basketball than just rules, equipment and a court.

And there's more to basketball for many Cathedral High School pupils than the formal Indiana High School Athletic Association sanctioned competition.

It might be called "midway" basketball, a compromise between regular school play and scrub-type competition, and goes on almost daily at the DBY. (Desautel's Backyard Basketball Court).

The DBY league has its own set of rules. Players are a group of North Side boys from Cathedral, Broad Ripple and Shortridge high schools.

Summer action begins on the asphalt court when former DBY boys take on the current crop of high school pupils. This year the Old-timers defeated their challengers, 100 to 96.

GAMES ARE played constantly on the court between 3 and 6 p.m. An intersquad tournament is arranged in March. Teams and players are determined by a drawing.

Following afternoon eliminations of the tournament, the two finalists battle it out for the victor's trophies, which are donated by Mr. and Mrs. Leon Desautels.

THIS TYPE of adult approved and supervised activity provides many hours of thrill-packed recreation for North Side teens, providing them with a constructive outlet for excess energy.

"See you at DBY" is a familiar cry around the North Side

The Indianapolis Star newspaper article, September 30, 1961
Written by Hugh McGowan

12

The Desautels family home on Central Avenue, Indianapolis, Indiana

2

I'VE HAD THE TIME OF MY LIFE

And so, with the sunshine
and the great bursts of leaves growing on the trees,
just as things grow in fast movies,
I had that familiar conviction that life
was beginning over again with the summer.

F. Scott Fitzgerald, The Great Gatsby

"Only an hour further," my mother hollered back to me as I slumped in the rear bench of our family Ford Station Wagon. Our summer expedition took a pause as we refueled at Wilson's Gas Service Station in Gaylord, MI. The friendly gas attendant, in his faded uniform, began to fill our tank as my mother, my sister Kate, and I stepped out of the car to stretch our stiff legs. Despite the lingering dust kicked up by the occasional car driving over the dry, unpaved roads, I breathed in the fresh, oxygen-rich forest air. The sweet, earthy fragrance of the surrounding balsam firs seeped into my body as if I was inhaling life itself. It was a great relief from the usually pleasing new-car scent that we had begun the road trip adoring, but had become stale and resentful after seven hours of travel. My father's automobile financing company blessed us with many new cars over the years, but I was ready to get out of the car and get to our summer cottage at Burt Lake in northern Michigan.

Mahaffey family cottage at Burt Lake, Michigan

It was the summer of 1959. My freshman year in high school had ended just a week earlier, and this getaway was a welcomed break from a long school year. It was an annual tradition for our family to head up to Michigan for the summer, but this year, it was just my mother, Kate, and I traveling. My father would join us a few weeks later.

Back in middle school, when I was ages twelve, thirteen, and fourteen, I had spent my summers at Camp Al-Gon-Quain, located on the same Burt Lake as my family's cottage. Founded by Herb Twining in 1925, it was a private, sleep-away camp with an incredible reputation that drew the more prominent families from around the country. I stayed at this all-boys camp for eight weeks each summer of middle school. Activities included boating, ball sports, horseback-riding, sailing, fishing, and every other northern Michigan outdoor hobby you could imagine. Those summers offered an adventurous experience that was truly unforgettable. Beyond the practical sportsmanship skills, it taught me the importance of comradery and teamwork, as well as the value of tradition and honoring history. At age fourteen, during my final year there, I remember taking a two-week canoe trip to Canada. Our group, which included fourteen campers and two counselors, packed a weeks' worth of supplies and food into eight canoes, and we set off into the rugged Canadian wilderness. It was a tremendous experience living in the wilderness for those two weeks. It is something that I will never forget.

Camp Al-Gon-Quain at Burt Lake, Michigan

After that year, as I was now a freshman in high school, I was offered the position as CIT: *Counselor in Training*. I hemmed and hawed for a bit before deciding to turn it down to take a different fork in the road. I thoroughly enjoyed my time at camp, but I was ready for a change. I longed to spend my summers relaxing at my family's cottage on Burt Lake, exploring the nearby town, and boating and fishing on the lake in my own free time. I can remember that summer just beginning, and I could not have been more excited to get to the cottage and start a new adventure.

Hopping back into the freshly fueled automobile, my mother, Kate, and I continued north. I leaned my head against the glass window watching the wall of dense forest quickly pass, like a stage curtain drawing quickly to open, but never seeming to clear. Finally, a half-hour later, the brilliant stage was revealed—beautiful, glimmering Burt Lake was before us. My mother carefully steered the car to the left and followed the road that traced the shore of the waters. The sun was beginning to settle in the cloudless sky, and the rippling waters glittered like millions of crystals.

Rounding a curve, we finally got to our lakefront cottage. It had never looked so picturesque. Nestled in the trees was our white, wood-clad home that fashioned a Dutch gable roof and a tall stone chimney. A large, screened-in porch, trimmed with scarlet geraniums and snow-white petunias, wrapped around the side of the house like an embrace. Similar to my family home in Indianapolis, this was a historic property. Bought by my maternal grandparents, James and Elizabeth Watson, in the 1930s, it was the pride and joy of Mahaffey generations. My grandparents had first decided to purchase a summer home in Burt Lake, as it was a popular destination for their circle of friends in Indianapolis. Northern Michigan offered the perfect summer escape from the suburban heat and bustle with its cool summers and peaceful wooded landscape. Being comprised of mainly rugged wilderness pre-1900s, Burt Lake was only newly developed and still had that magical forest ambiance. Most importantly, it boasted some of the best fishing around—small mouth bass, trout, and walleye were just a few of the myriad of different fish species in the water. I could not wait to cast my reel into those shimmering waters. I knew this was going to be my best summer yet! What I did not foresee was how the events of that summer would change the trajectory of my life forever.

Soon after arriving at the cottage, I settled into my summer routine fairly quickly. Reading books, fishing, and navigating every nook and cranny of Burt Lake became my everyday pastimes. On special occasions during past summers, our neighbor in the cottage next door would give me rides in his turquoise MG, which was a vintage English-made car. Summer days at Burt Lake were wonderful. However, during this particular summer, the days began to get long and dull, as I craved the companionship that I had at camp the years before. Even my neighbor with the MG was no longer resident on Burt Lake. I found myself bored.

"Come on, Mark. You are coming with me to the yacht club," my sister Kate said to me one evening after dinner. We had three weeks before it was time to head back to Indianapolis, and Kate was determined to set me up with some fun. The yacht club was located on the other side of the lake on Columbus Beach, named by the residents who were primarily from Columbus, Ohio. Kate's boyfriend at the time belonged to this club, and Kate and I enjoyed sailing with him. My family did not own a sailboat, but I had first learned to sail at camp. I was quite good and had even started a crew for Kate's boyfriend, who was a great sailor and a great teacher. We used to race sailboats twice a week. Our class of boats was called *Lightnings*.

I agreed to join Kate, and we set off for the yacht club at once. When we arrived, we quietly walked through the large, dimly lit hall and out the back doors that led to the docks out on Burt Lake. I immediately noticed there was a yacht club meeting about to start with perhaps sixty or so people attending. Most, if not all, seemed well above my age, and I was beginning to doubt my decision to come. Looking at Kate, I saw her scan the scene as if looking for someone.

"There!" she said.

Kate swiftly pranced across the deck, and I followed closely behind her. Much to my surprise, Kate had a friend in mind for me to meet. She introduced me then to Dick deVore, who was the younger brother of a friend of hers. Dick was sixteen years old—a year older than I was. I had remembered seeing him years ago, but I did not know him well.

Dick said to me, "Mark, you are coming with me."

Kate encouraged, "Yes, Mark, go on with Dick."

"Okay." I agreed.

Well, that ended up being the start of one of the best friendships I have ever had. My family barely saw me those last three weeks of summer. Dick and I were inseparable. He was old enough to drive a car, and we explored northern Michigan having the time of our lives. I would also crew for him on his sailboat. Dick is still one of my best friends to this day.

The next summer, when I was sixteen years old, my family returned to our Michigan cottage on Burt Lake. I could not wait to see my friend, Dick. I immediately headed over to the Indian River Inn, which was located on the other side of the lake and owned by Dick's parents. I was hoping to find him there. I adored his parents, who were of French descent. Mrs. deVore was a grand dame with southern charm—kind and generous as could be, but with a spitfire spirit. Mr. deVore, on the other hand, was an ex-racecar driver with a stern exterior, but a kind soul. They bought the inn years ago and had expanded it to double the size.

Dining Room at Indian River Inn, Michigan

Indian River Inn was a first class, thirty-room inn and restaurant, which was truly a rare gem amongst the wilderness in Northern Michigan. It was a white-washed, wooden cottage-type restaurant with flower boxes embellishing the street side windows. The grand dining area was a feast for the eyes to behold. Seating about 150 guests, tables were dressed with white tablecloths, freshly picked flowers, fine China, and artistically folded napkins. The back wall was decorated with seasonal, three-dimensional art pieces, including a massive, back-lit image of a boat cruising through the water. The waiters and waitresses, primarily college students, cruised effortlessly about the tables as if dancing a choreographed routine. The waiters wore tuxedo pants with a cummerbund, a bow tie and a waiter's coat. Waitresses wore light blue dresses with aprons and hairnets. Dick, my friend, worked there as one of the waiters.

"Dick, what time are you off? Let's go sailing!" I said excitingly, under my breath to him as he was rushing to the kitchen.

"Mark, it's going to be a late night. Maybe tomorrow."

I was distraught. I had spent that past year counting the days to come back to Michigan and relive those final weeks of summer vacation that I had spent with Dick. But now that he was working so much, I barely saw him. Week after week went by, and all dreams of summer adventure were starting to fade. I at least cherished the few times I did get to see him, and we tried to make the most of it sailing on the lake.

As the summer chapter was beginning to close, I remember Dick and I sitting on his boat, casts in the water, patiently waiting for a fish to bite.

He popped a Ruffle potato chip into his mouth and said to me, "Mark, I've talked to my mom. What do you think about coming to work for us next summer?"

"Really?" I inquired.

Dick replied, "Look. Here's the deal. You'll be seventeen-years-old next summer, but we're all supposed to be eighteen-years-old, as we serve alcohol. Just lie on the application. My mother will know, but she'll go along with it. My father will never know."

"Deal," I said promptly. I trusted Dick, and I was excited for this opportunity. I knew his father was always one to play by the rules. He would have never allowed me to work serving alcohol at seventeen. Dick's mother also had a very strong personality and ran the restaurant with an iron fist. But she ended up allowing me to work there because she knew I would work hard. Not to mention, Dick could be very persuasive. I could not wait to come back to Burt Lake the next year.

20

The following school year came and went as quickly as the year before, and summer punctually arrived before I knew it. Much to my dismay, my parents decided to stay the month of June in Indianapolis before heading north. I was not about to wait the month, so I decided to head up to Burt Lake without them. To my surprise, my parents did not have a problem with that. Not only did they allow me to travel by myself, but also, my father lent me his Thunderbird car for the trip up north. I was in shock! I was proud they trusted me. My mother arranged with Mrs. deVore for me to stay at the deVore's cottage until my mother and my aunt arrived at the end of June. I knew it was going to be the summer of a lifetime.

Patsy and Jerry deVore greeting their dinner guests at Indian River Inn, Michigan

Feeling like I had the world at my feet, I headed north in that Thunderbird the first week in June. I began working at Indian River Inn and waited tables every day until Labor Day. I worked very hard. The hours were long and serving the guests was tiring, but I loved every minute of it. When I think back to that time—the summer guests, the dinners, the parties—the image is as romantic as the movie *Dirty*

21

Dancing. We would work until midnight, and then we would all party until 3:00 in the morning. It was good, clean fun, and as the theme song of *Dirty Dancing* goes, "I had the time of my life."

One of the best parts of the summer was being able to meet so many new people. I remember most of the girls there were in college. I was going to be a senior in high school, so I was significantly younger. Determined not to let my age hold me back, I confidently told them I was going to be a freshman in college, which in truth, I wouldn't be for another year.

They would ask me, "What's your major?"

I would naively say, "Math."

Of course, one did not just major in *math* in college back then. The girls believed it though; or at the very least, they wanted to believe it. Nevertheless, it was a ball.

The following summer, the deVore family invited me to wait tables again for a second year. Without hesitation, I agreed, as I had enjoyed working for them so much the year before. By this summer, Mrs. deVore had discovered the concept of salad bars, which was a very trendy item for high end restaurants that year. She set out a long table covered in white linens and arranged a beautiful display of lettuces, fresh vegetables, cottage cheese, and most importantly, at least a half dozen varieties of relishes in silver bowls and trays. Indian River Inn was known for their delectable assortment of relishes—most especially their corn relish. My personal favorite was the herring marinated in sour cream. Dick taught me a trick of bringing a fork into the walk-in refrigerator to "steal" a bite. It was scrumptious! The salad bar made our jobs as waiters much easier, as guests were encouraged to serve themselves. We still worked long hours though, and partied on the nearby sand dunes at night. It was another summer to remember.

The next year, however, in 1963, the path of my life took a turn. The deVore family invited me again to work there, which would have been my third summer at the Indian River Inn. They promised to promote me to head waiter, which was very tempting. I had grown a lot since waiting tables there. Most importantly, I learned how to talk to people. Before this job, I would not have considered myself very shy, but I was certainly not overly outgoing. I had learned quickly that the friendlier you were, the more rapport you had with the staff and the customers. Not to mention, the tips were much better. I learned how to dig deep within myself and find the confidence to relate to many different types of people. I was ready to sign on for the third summer, but then, my father suggested a different idea.

At that time, my father had relocated to Saint Petersburg, Florida and had started an apartment company. He was in the process of developing *The Carlton Towers*, which was a ten-story apartment community in downtown Saint Petersburg. It is now a condo development called *The Beacon* and is still standing after sixty years. My father requested I come down to Florida during my summer break and help him and my brother, Jim, rent apartments. He knew I had been invited back to the Indian River Inn. He also had seen the growth that I had experienced communicating with people and felt I would be a great asset to him.

It was in late spring, before the summer had even started, that my father approached me with the idea. He looked at me with his stern eyes and straightened, thin lips. He had a very dominant, commanding character, and without a doubt, I had expected him to say, *Mark, this is what you are going to do*. However, in that moment, my father's face softened. He said, "Mark, I would like you to come work for me in Saint Petersburg. I know you have been invited back to Michigan, and I know you enjoyed working there. But, please consider a change this year. I think you would be a wonderful addition to our family business. The choice is yours however."

I was astonished by my father deference, which made his offer very appealing to me. He could have forced my hand there, but he was smart enough and wise enough to say it was up to me. I took a few weeks to think it over. I judiciously calculated the pros and cons. I loved spending my summers working hard and playing hard at the Indian River Inn on Burt Lake. Dick deVore was my best friend. Summers were as idealistic as if right out of a movie. But then, there was reality. I knew I wasn't going to spend the rest of my life as a waiter at an inn. Working with my father would teach me real tools that I knew I would use in business for the rest of my life. In addition, an adventure to sunny Florida was enticing as well. But more than anything, I yearned to develop a closer relationship with my father. At eighteen years old, I still saw my father as a mystery that still needed solving. Throughout my childhood, he was primarily focused on his business, and I was focused on my school and friends. Now that we were both adults, I saw this as an opportunity to get to know him as more of an equal. With that realization, my decision was made. I turned down the head waiter position at Indian River Inn and hopped on a plane to Florida.

When I arrived, I was overwhelmed by the scenery. Saint Petersburg could not be more different than northern Michigan. The first thing that struck me was the sunshine. *It's about time I invest in some sunglasses,* I thought to myself. Saint Petersburg seemed as if it were right out of a tropical vacation commercial. Palm trees lined the coast and swayed ever so slightly in the breeze. The calm waters of Tampa Bay mirrored the brilliant, bright blue sky. Men and women walked the sidewalks in bathing suits, sundresses, wide brimmed sunhats, and all smiles. This was certainly a happy place.

My father gave me a general tour of the city and a more detailed tour of the construction site. The *Carlton Towers,* being mere blocks from the Tampa Bay, had stunning water views on the upper floors. I definitely could see myself getting excited about this! Next, my father took me to the motel where he was staying—Edgewater Beach Motel, which was located adjacent to the Vinoy Hotel. It was certainly no Indian River Inn. It did not have fine dining with silver and China, nor did it have the country charm of a forest cottage. What it did feature, however, was an incredible waterfront view of Tampa Bay, a refreshing swimming pool, a trendy bar and lounge (called Murph's), and large guest rooms with two twin beds. My father and I shared one of these motel rooms for the two months I worked there. If there was ever a chance for us to develop a relationship, this was it.

Edgewater Beach Motel, Saint Petersburg, Florida; postcard from 1968

That summer of 1963 ended up being better than I could have ever imagined. My father and I got along famously. He taught me all about the apartment development business, and I was an enthusiastic pupil. I listened to his every direction and took note of all his business philosophies. I worked hard for him that summer. The job was not easy, but it was an experience. I remember we had an office trailer on the construction site, where the potential residents would come to inquire about an apartment. As the elevators were not in working order yet, I had to take the stairs each time. It was exhausting, especially in the Florida heat, but I was determined to do my best every day. Fortunately, I was a numbers person, and I memorized the rents. The higher the floor, the higher the rate—because of the bay view. I learned about the business from the ground up, literally and figuratively. And even more than learning about the business, I learned about my father, and he learned about me. We formed a wonderful companionship that I think we both had been craving deep down for many years.

One pastime I distinctly remember enjoying with my father that summer was attending the dog races. At that time, there were greyhound races at the Saint Petersburg Derby Lane, as well as at the smaller venues of Sarasota Kennel Club and the Tampa Bay Downs. With each racetrack open and running cyclically for about four months of the year, there were races to attend year-round. Cheering these dogs on, my father and I bonded in a special way. Those moments meant everything to me.

One evening that summer, a night I recall as if it were yesterday, I was driving home from one of the races in Sarasota. My father was awful behind the wheel, so any opportunity he offered me to drive, I would take. We were driving this particular time over the original Skyway Bridge (that has since been rebuilt), which extended from Sarasota to Saint Petersburg. It was a dark, moonless night, and the waters under the bridge were as black as Cuban coffee. The tall light posts that lined the bridge guided our route. I decided to break the car's silence.

"You know, Dad, I'm not as quiet as you think I am," I declared.

My father replied, "I know more about you than you think I do."

"I know," I responded.

This was my father's way of telling me I did not need to prove myself to him. He had been watching me grow all these years, and despite us not having the closest relationship, he knew me better than anyone else. He had witnessed me develop into a confident young man who had enough experience in life to ease into society as an adult. This moment with my father was very special to me. It gave me the peace and comfort in knowing I could be myself around him, and he was proud of me. He was a man of few words, but he made those words count.

3

IRISH PRIDE

Courage means being afraid to do something, but still doing it...
Build up your weaknesses until they become your strong points.

Knute Rockne, Notre Dame football coach from 1918-1931

PATHFINDER. *Pathfinder* has been my longstanding nickname since my past college days at the University of Notre Dame. A *pathfinder* is generally defined as "a person who goes ahead and discovers or shows others a path or way." Curiously, broadly reflecting on my life as a whole, I deem it rather ironic this praiseworthy identity was granted to me. As my mind's eye scans the clips of events that brought me to where I am today, I cannot overlook all the people that influenced me, led me, and helped me along the way. My mother and father, many profound friendships, as well as several notable mentors, have all shaped my path in some significant way. It does give me great honor, however, to consider that I might have inspired others in a similar manner.

Mark T. Mahaffey, "The Pathfinder"

I cannot recall the precise moment the moniker was birthed into existence, but I *can* remember the person who bestowed it upon me—Matt Dwyer. Of all the nonsensical nicknames I am sure a fellow college peer could invent, *Pathfinder* was a decently respectable choice. It was perhaps branded in witticism or jest, but I wore that name proudly. Matt related the story to me many times that in our freshman year, he noticed me confidently leading others through the labyrinth of dormitory hallways. As he witnessed me guide fellow students to help them find their way, Matt claims he came up with *Pathfinder* on the spot. Although I do not remember this, I can easily imagine myself feeling quite at home at Notre Dame despite it being my first year of college. The Notre Dame campus was like a second home to me, on account of all the football games I had attended with my father throughout my youth.

Even beyond football, Notre Dame ran deep in my family history. My paternal uncle, Fred Mahaffey, graduated from Notre Dame in the late 1910s. My father, Thomas Mahaffey, graduated with a business degree in 1933 mid-term, which was a semester late due to a football knee injury. My father played football under the famous Notre Dame football coach, Knute Rockne. Knute Rockne served as coach for thirteen years, 1918-1931, leading the Notre Dame football team to 105 victories and only 12 losses. He is remembered as a brilliant leader and coaching genius. His passionate team spirit credo was instilled in his teams through inspirational life speeches and sportsmanship pep talks. My father describes the three years he played under this coach as the greatest experience of his life. Many life lessons were learned beyond the field, and he credits Knute Rockne for influencing much of his own philosophies of life and discipline. Teamwork, trust in one another, and confidence in the win were big life principles my father lived by and instilled in me. In gratitude for the impact Notre Dame made on his life, my father maintained continual support to Notre Dame. Until the end of his days, he was a generous donor and hardcore football fan.

Through my father's influence, when it came time for me to choose a college for myself, the University of Notre Dame had become my dream school. As I was pretty good at mathematics in high school, it made logical sense to walk in my father's footsteps and study finance at the school he attended. Especially taking into account football weekends, my Irish heritage connection, and fifteen of my high school peers also planning to attend, Notre Dame could not have been a better match. I was particularity thrilled that my friend Hugh McGowan was also enrolling. After a long, determined period of devotion to my high school studies and a copious amount of planning, I graduated from Cathedral High School in 1962 and was thrilled to be accepted at the University of Notre Dame.

Beyond choosing a college, there was a much more crucial decision I made that year that impacted my life more than I could have ever imagined at the time. When my mother discovered that I had been accepted into Notre Dame, she commanded, "Mark, you must sign up for the NROTC program."

"NROTC? No way!" I replied starkly. "I want to enjoy my time at college and not be buried in work and drills."

I knew what NROTC stood for—Naval Reserve Officers Training Corps. It is true this program had, and still has, a phenomenal reputation. The University of Notre Dame and the United States Navy have had an incredibly close relationship that has spanned almost a century. The Irish and the Midshipmen, their football team names, respectfully, have been playing football against each other annually since 1927, making them the longest continuous intersectional rivalry in the country. They deepened their relationship during World War II when the Navy chose Notre Dame as the primary facility to train their Naval Officers. Despite the ruthless economic grip the war had on other colleges, Notre Dame flourished with rising enrollments and a renewed purpose. This propelled the school to enjoy continued success for years to come. I knew it would be an honor to go through the rigorous and well-esteemed program, but I was also only 18 years old, and the easier route was much more appealing to me.

NROTC posing in front of the "Touchdown Jesus" at the University of Notre Dame

Nonetheless, I was blessed with a very headstrong and determined mother. She was adamant that I signed up for the NROTC program. Not only was she aware of the program's credibility, but she was also worried about the Vietnam War, which loomed in the distance. She had a right to be concerned, as the United States' involvement was initiated just a few years later. I also feared it would be a tremendously dangerous war, and rumors were already circulating that Americans would soon be drafted. My mother believed that the Navy was most likely the safest path if drafted—not necessarily perfectly safe by any means, but better than boots on the ground in combat. Trusting her judgement, I begrudgingly filled out the paperwork for NROTC and was accepted.

Before I left for college, my mother gave me a small gift. It was a paperbound book titled *The Fountainhead*, by Ayn Rand.

"This book is special," she told me. "I hope it inspires you as you make your way in life."

I flipped through the pages—over 700 pages worth. I was not certain whether my classes would allow time for any extra-curricular reading, but I thanked my mother and assured her I would try my best to read it. To my surprise, as soon as I began to delve into the hefty novel, I could not stop. Set in the 1920s and 1930s, the narrative captured my attention as I was immersed into the life of a man named Howard Roark, a fictional, aspiring architect with innovative and radical ideas. Despite his designs being at first shunned by the tradition-bound architectural community, he pushed through, sticking to his principles and carving his own path to success. The book finishes with a triumphant development of one of Roark's designs and him gaining the community's approval and recognition. I was deeply inspired by this book, and it gave me a boost of determination and drive as I began my freshman year.

Nevertheless, as I had initially predicted, my freshman year at Notre Dame proved to be a real challenge. I was the only one of my friends from high school who signed up for an ROTC program. As for most freshmen, college life was naturally tough being an overall new experience. To add a Navy program on top of my general studies was beyond difficult. Fifteen credit hours a semester was the required base for the finance degree program. The Navy program was an additional three credit hours, plus two drill times. Jam-packed with obligations, my schedule was bursting. I was exhausted and nearly flunked my freshman year of Navy courses. I was determined to find a way to succeed. I just had to figure out what I was doing wrong. In high school, I had performed well and was not used to this feeling of proximate failure. The following semester, I decided I would push myself harder. I set my alarm to 5:00 am to wake up before sunrise, hoping to use those early hours to study. Tired as I was, week after week, my grades somewhat improved. But I knew I could do better. I had to somehow work smarter, not harder.

Finally, in my junior year, my saving grace came in the form of a library and dormitory geography. It was during this year that I began to take advantage of the newly constructed Memorial Library, which has since been renamed the Theodore Hesburgh Library, honoring the Notre Dame president who served from 1952-1987. This library was a godsend to the Notre Dame community of students. The old library was small, dingy, and echoey, and not the least conducive to studying. The new library was modern, enormous and masterfully designed. It contained a whole system of libraries and study halls that were quiet and perfect for both individual and group study. My father was a great supporter of this library, which earned him a space in the library after his death—*The Thomas Mahaffey Jr. Business Library.* On the southern elevation of the main library, which faced the football stadium, there is a beautiful mural spanning 134 feet high and 68 feet wide called *The Word of Life*. It was nicknamed *Touchdown Jesus* by my graduating class, which has stuck to this day. The Theodore Hesburgh Library is an incredible and proud asset to Notre Dame.

That September, in 1964, I developed a new routine of walking from my dormitory to the library every day in the afternoon or evening to study. This was a considerable change from my usual habit of early morning cram studying before an exam. Providentially, I began this new habit at the beginning of autumn, when the weather was still mild. Boarding at Alumni Hall, it was a decent trek to the library, perhaps a half mile. A half-mile stroll in beautiful weather is one thing, but trudging that distance in the cold, snowy Indiana winter was another. I believe I would have never committed to studying at the library if I had started in the winter. It would have been too cold and cumbersome. I am thankful for fate for inspiring me to initiate this habit in the beautiful autumn weather. The biggest thing I learned was the importance of filling in my notes the same day as class when it was fresh in my mind. Since studying at the library required that long, intentional expedition, I was motivated to stay and make the most of my time there. This was a game changer for me. When the weather got colder, I continued walking to the library because I saw the benefit. I watched my grades get better and better, not only in my finance courses, but also in the NROTC program. By my senior year, I was getting As and Bs instead of Cs and Ds. Earning better grades gave me a whopping boost in confidence, and I began to enjoy my classes much more. That confidence propelled me during that fundamental time in my life.

I cannot grant the library full credit for my success, however. I also counted it a great blessing to have a wonderful support group of friends on campus. Living on campus afforded me the opportunity to completely embrace college life, form companionships with fellow students, and focus on my studies. I was lucky to room with the same friend three of the four years I attended the university. His name was Stan Colligan from Fort Wayne, Indiana. We were randomly chosen to board together freshman year in Kennan Hall, and we got along famously. At the time, Stan—nicknamed *Pierre Puck* by me—was an avid hockey player and an enthusiastic fan of the Fort Wayne Komets. He became president of the Notre Dame Hockey Club and brought his enthusiasm to the hockey program at Notre Dame. He pushed for hockey to become a major sport at Notre Dame, which it did a few years later. Stan was the ideal roommate—quiet and friendly. We were both finance majors, but we each had our own set of friends, which sometimes intermingled, but overall, we did not get in each other's hair. It was a great setup.

Back in my sophomore year, Notre Dame developed a new system called the *stay hall system*, which allowed students to stay in the same hall their entire time at college. Knowing this, I chose Alumni Hall to be my stay hall, which was one of the oldest and biggest residence halls on campus, centrally located close to the Notre Dame Circle. Since Stan ended up rooming with a different friend that year, I chose to room with

Doug Ford, one of my good friends from Boston. It was a short-lived arrangement, however, as my Boston friend soon decided he preferred a singles room after the first semester. Another acquaintance of mine, Mike (Mickey) Houk from Indianapolis joined me the rest of the year. He was a great roommate, but I surely missed rooming with Stan.

By good fortune, in junior year, Stan was in need of a new roommate. His previous roommate Lenny did not maintain high enough grades to stay on campus. The school had a very strict grade and board policy at that time. If you did not make the grade, you were kicked off campus, which seemed rather counter-productive if you ask me. Stan, on the other hand, was top of his class and had first pick of the rooms. Stan chose a room in Alumni Hall that was at the end of a hallway with a private bathroom, which was unheard of! I was flattered when he asked me to room with him junior and senior year. Though the room was not large, we bunked the beds, which made plenty more space. We had a TV and a telephone in our room, which was truly a rare luxury for a college dorm. We put a sign on the door labeling our room *The Palace – Home of Pierre Puck and The Pathfinder.* Stan and I were famous around school. It makes me smile thinking about all the fun I had.

One story that comes to mind involved one weekend in wintertime when I went to a party at Dayton University, Ohio.

Brrrrriiinnnggggg!!! I startled as my beloved black and white rotary telephone rattled atop my cluttered wooden desk. I had been casually resting on my lower bunk watching the newest episode of the Dick Van Dyke Show in *The Palace.* Quickly dialing down the television volume, I dug through the piles of papers to retrieve the ringing device. As I picked up the receiver, the coiled cord swung, knocking papers off my desk in one fell swoop.

Ignoring the mess, I greeted the caller. "Hello. Mark Mahaffey speaking."

"Hi Mark!" responded an animated young woman. "This is the Mary Ann Galdabini, Hugh's girlfriend at Dayton University."

Another woman chimed in on the phone, "Please tell us you are free next weekend. We would be most delighted if you came to see us!"

Another woman added in a high-pitched squeal, "We are throwing a party on Saturday. We already talked to Hugh McGowan, and he's coming. Bring your other friends too. It will be a great time!"

I was overjoyed to receive their invite. I replied swiftly, "Wow. Yes, I am pretty certain I am available. Thank you for calling. I'll see if Bob Desautels can come as well."

"That would be most wonderful! If you come Friday evening, you all can stay until Sunday!"

"Fantastic. Thank you, ladies. See you then!"

I returned the phone to its cradle, then quickly raised it up again to dial Bob Desautels, as well as a few other friends. Being friends with Hugh had its benefits, as he lived off campus and had access to a car, which was against campus rules at the time. He was just as excited as I was to attend this weekend party, as we had quite a few friends from high school that went to Dayton University. The semester had just ended, exams were behind us, and we were ready to party.

When Friday afternoon finally arrived, Hugh and I, along with a few other friends, all piled into Hugh's mother's car—a 1965 burgundy Oldsmobile 88. After about a four-hour drive, we arrived in Dayton, Ohio and met up with the girls we knew there. Bob, who went to Xavier University in Cincinnati, drove separately and met us there. We all mingled and relaxed that evening, looking forward to the real party on Saturday.

On Saturday evening, the eager party guests began to arrive. I was in utter amazement at all the people coming in. I guess there must have been about 30 or 40 college students at the girls' house. I can distinctly remember the lively music, the people dancing, the food and the drinks—lots of drinks—all amidst a fog of cigarette smoke. It was a wild night!

For this weekend's gathering, the girls had kindly set me up with a blind date. I had recently broken up with another girl whom I had dated for most of high school and the first two years of college. I appreciated having a blind date, but I admit I was not a great escort to her. I had a few drinks, not so much to be drunk, but enough to get a bit carried away and clown around. Throughout the evening, I was moving around quite a bit and working the party, and I imagine she must have been pretty annoyed with me.

Realizing this, I decided I would try to find her again amidst the crowd. I remember squinting and peering through the smoky haze as I meandered through the rooms. To my surprise, I spied an old girlfriend of mine—Rosie Kennedy. She was a cute, Irish gal, originally from Chicago, whom I had met at a Notre Dame football weekend. We dated for my junior year. We had amicably parted ways when she fell in love with another guy at Dayton, but we still remained good friends. Forgetting my blind date, I decided to go over and talk to her. It was wonderful to catch up with Rosie, and hear her voice again. We chatted for a while before she went back to visit with her friends.

Now that I had been at the party for a few hours, the smoke-filled rooms began to become cloudier, and I realized my eyes were beginning to blur. The alcohol was really beginning to hit me, and I needed somewhere to lie down. There must have not been a couch or bed to spare, as I found myself landing in the pink-enameled bathtub located in the main bathroom. I slowly laid my throbbing head again the cold, cast iron sides of the basin. The coolness brought tremendous relief to my pounding headache. I pulled the olive and white, floral shower curtain closed to soften the harshness of the vanity lights. My eyes fell shut as I breathed in the sweet smell of the dial soap that laid on the soap rest. My mind was in a daze thinking about Rosie, my blind date, and how on earth I had ended up here...

The next thing I knew, I heard the bathroom door slowly creak open and someone enter. I froze my thoughts. It was one of the girls from the party. My brain began to rush. *Do I make my presence known and potentially embarrass or startle her? Or, do I continue to hide behind the curtain and hope she does not notice me?* The latter seemed too risky, as I imagined I could get in big trouble if I were found. So, in a split second of panic, I quickly opened the curtain.

"Ahh!" she yelped, as she jumped back in surprise.

"I'm sorry," I muttered. And without another word, I scurried out of the bathroom in a flash. She was a good sport, whomever she was. But I was embarrassed. People began to tease and poke fun at me, so I

36

decided it was time to go. My blind date, by that time, was tired and also wanted to go home. I apologized for not being a great date, offered to walk her home to wherever she lived on campus, and we headed out.

Later on, Rosie told me that as I left the party, I passed by her sitting on the couch in the living room. One of her friends asked her, "Who was that guy?"

She paused a moment, allowing another person to chime in, "I don't know, but they call him *The Pathfinder.*"

The legend lives on.

Another memory that comes to mind from senior year, also involved Rosie Kennedy. It was May, right before graduation, and there was a big senior weekend event at Notre Dame. As all my buddies had girlfriends, it was going to be more of a couples' event. Still being single at the time, I was worried I was going to miss out. Thinking about what good friends Rosie and I still were, I decided to call her up.

"Hey Rosie, how are you? I have something to ask you that you may think is a little unusual."

"What is it?" Rosie curiously prompted.

I told her the truth. "We are having this big couples' Senior Weekend coming up at Notre Dame, and frankly, I'm not going out with anybody. I don't know if you'd be interested in coming up here and just having a good time, but I would love for you to join me. We're such good friends, and you know a lot of the people up here."

She kindly replied without hesitation, "I wouldn't miss that for all the tea in China."

I was thrilled she joined me! Our friendship was special to me, and we had a ball. There was a big senior dance that Friday night with live music performed by the one and only Jerry Lee Lewis. He was wild that night, and we rocked and bopped, having an unforgettable night. The next day, we went out to the dunes on Lake Michigan and had a picnic lunch. That whole weekend is such a happy memory for me.

With good grades, great friends, and my confidence soaring, I graduated with a finance degree on a sunny day in early June, 1966. I also received my Naval commission the following day, which told me where I would be stationed for the next three years. I had requested *a cruiser* and *the West Coast* when submitting my dream scheme, so to speak. I was fortunate to be commissioned as an Ensign on an aircraft carrier (my second choice), which was home ported at Long Beach, California.

Reading my orders carefully, I read that I was to attend a week of weapons school in San Diego, California, before I boarded the ship. I was shocked they wanted me to report to the school just a week after graduation! I thought I would have at least a month to enjoy some time off for the summer. I was invited to stand up in a few friends' weddings, but I had to learn that things do not always go as planned. I followed my orders.

Hopping onto the plane to head to California, I sat and reflected on my journey. I could not believe where my life had taken me. I had worked hard, played hard, and made so many wonderful memories. I knew there was a lifetime of new memories just waiting to be had. I did not know what was in store, but I was ready for it. As the plane landed at the San Diego Airport, I grasped my brand, new luggage and took a deep breath as if breathing in all the strength and assurance that I would conquer this new adventure. I could not help but laugh to myself looking down at that new luggage. It had been the one graduation gift from my parents when I had graduated from college. To think I had been so disappointed that it had not been a car. I suppose the luggage was better use to me now as I was about to be an Ensign on a Navy carrier.

On the first day of weapons school in mid-June, I mentally prepared for a rough week. I knew the course would be short and rigorous, and I would most likely be spending the week studying. I took my seat at a small, metal desk in a stark classroom. The space was minimally decorated having white-painted walls and a black chalkboard at the front of the room. There were about fifteen other men in the class. Most of them were beginning Ensigns, all dressed in the signature khaki Navy uniform, like myself. The teacher, a Lieutenant, stood at the front of the room and began discussing the syllabus. He distributed multiple handouts and discussed the content we would cover over the class period. I started to panic at the volume of the material. There was no way we would cover it all in a week.

At lunchbreak, I walked up to the Lieutenant and said, "Sir, I'm curious. How long is this class?"

He responded, "Eight weeks."

"Eight weeks?!" I could not hold back my surprised reaction. "Maybe I'm in the wrong class. My orders sent me to a one-week course."

"Hmm, let me see your orders," he demanded.

I handed him the papers, and he said, "Let me check on this and get back to you. Go on and have lunch, and I'll let you know what I find out when you get back."

After lunch, he called me up to his desk at the front of the classroom.

"It seems there is a mistake on your orders. This *is* the course they assigned you, and it *is* an eight-week course. You are where you are supposed to be. Your ship will be notified that you will report in eight weeks instead of one."

I was utterly disappointed, but what else could I say but, "Yes sir."

Surprisingly, weapons school in San Diego ended up being a such a fun experience. Yes, it was eight weeks, but, as there was not any homework, I spent my evenings and weekends exploring and enjoying the city with my fellow classmates. We all lived in the Bachelor Officer Quarters (BOQ) right on the base. At the nearby Marine Depot, there was a mixer every Tuesday night. It was a great spot for guys and girls to mingle. There, I met a girl named Cindy Beining that first week, and I dated her for those few summer months. She was visiting her sister who was married to a Navy guy also stationed in San Diego. They lived in Coronado, which is an island just off San Diego and home of the famous Hotel Coronado. Back then, you had to take a ferry there, but now there is a bridge.

I will never forget one night when Cindy and I went out on a date. I had some car trouble with an awful Volkswagen that I had rented from a local dealer. It had a very tricky battery system. If the battery was not functioning, I would have to get someone to push the car while I popped the clutch. Unfortunately, the battery went out during our night out. I was absolutely embarrassed, but luckily, Cindy took it in stride.

I shook my head in humiliation, "You're never going to believe this, but do you know how to drive a stick?"

"No," Cindy said with a worried glance.

"Well, then, I am so sorry, but you get to push," I apologetically stated.

"Okay," Cindy reluctantly agreed.

She did not have to push it very fast or very far, but she did a great job. She had a great sense of humor, and sarcastically said, "What a date you are. I get to push your car!" What a memory! We had a lot of fun that summer.

In August, after finishing the weapons course, my next step was to report to my ship. It was a WWII aircraft carrier named *USS Bennington*. I received a graciously handwritten welcome letter from the Executive Officer, who was an Irish gentleman by the name of Commander Brian Eagan. In the letter, he wrote that he was sorry to hear I had to be in San Diego for longer than I had thought. He added that *USS Bennington* had been out running exercises off the San Diego coast, but would be back just in time when my class ended. I would report to the weapons department on the ship, and very soon afterwards, the ship would depart again. He added that in November, the ship was scheduled to journey to Vietnam and remain there for about six months. Considering we were in the thick of the Vietnam War, I thought to myself, *this is no pleasure cruise.*

I was touched by such a gesture as a handwritten letter and wanted to reply as soon as possible. As I sat with pen in hand, I contemplated his words. The ship would be departing very soon afterwards? And then be in Vietnam for six months?! It would be my first Christmas away from my family. The thought was heartbreaking, and I decided to take a risk. In my letter replying to the Executive Officer, I humbly requested that I take a few days this summer to visit my family before reporting to my ship. I explained how I had only one week after graduation before having to report to weapons school in San Diego and that I missed my family dearly.

By the grace of God (and perhaps the grace of sharing an Irish background), Commander Brian Eagan must have been moved by my letter. He replied, "Permission granted." He arranged for me to report onboard the ship that Friday. After reporting to duty, I would then immediately take my leave for seven days. I could not believe it! In addition, to my luck, *Bennington* was conveniently ported in San Diego, offloading the Air Group's equipment and supplies after their exercises. I appreciated the opportunity to see my family one more time before the long voyage to Vietnam.

That Friday, in my freshly pressed uniform, I reported onboard *Bennington* to the Officer of the Deck. The Officer of the Deck signed me into the log, and then called the Administrative Officer. The Administrative Officer came down promptly, handed me my leave papers and signed me out. This all happened in less than fifteen minutes. I stored my gear on the ship with Tom Cox, a fellow Notre Dame alumnus, and I was off! I am still amazed to this day that I was allowed to take that leave. I had not even made it past the Quarterdeck, which was the greeting deck of the ship, before I turned around to hop on a plane back to Indiana.

It just so happened that my summer fling, Cindy Beining, was also returning to the Midwest that same weekend. Needless to say, we decided to fly together. We had been dating seven weeks at that point and had a splendid relationship. As we settled onto the plane to Chicago, we had the epiphany that we had flown on the same plane from Chicago to San Diego back in June. On the same day and the same plane that I flew on to go to weapons school, she flew on to see her sister. What a coincidence! She remembered that I was in uniform and sat four rows behind her. I told her I remembered a cute girl sitting four rows in front of me. It was too funny to think that now we were flying back home together.

I had to play all my cards right, however, because I knew Rosie Kennedy was coming to the airport to pick me up. I planned to stay at her parents' house that night and spend the weekend with her. I was not sure what she would think of seeing me with Cindy. Knowing Cindy was getting on a connecting flight to Milwaukee, I thought, *I just might have a chance to pull this off.*

We punctually arrived at the O'Hare Airport in Chicago and stepped out of the plane. My heart was beating out of my chest. *Lord, get me through this!*

Cindy and I begin to leisurely walk down the long airport hallway that led to the exit, when suddenly, Cindy stopped.

"I have to turn here to get to my other flight," she said.

I replied, "It was so great getting to know you. I am going to miss you."

I really was. She was a great girl.

"Am I ever going to see you again?" Cindy looked up at me with tears in her eyes.

"Of course," I reassured her, not really knowing what the future held, but wanting to comfort her. "I'll see you when I get back from Vietnam."

I remember hugging her that last goodbye, and we parted ways. Despite being emotional as well, I pulled myself together quickly. I knew Rosie would be right at the end of that hallway. I opened the heavy door to the arrivals waiting area. On the other side, I saw Rosie Kennedy beaming with a big smile and carrying a big bag of all my favorite chocolates. Just seeing her smile brought me such joy. She really was a great friend. I spent that night at her family home and met her parents. It felt good to be home in the Midwest.

The next day, I visited my family, as I was so eager to see them. At that time, my family had sold my childhood home on Meridian Street, and lived in a new house, still in northwest Indianapolis. My mother celebrated my return with a Christmas dinner, despite it being mid-August. She made a roast turkey, mashed potatoes, and more side dishes than I could possibly eat. Being home with my family and the people I loved was like a breath of fresh air. After a week at home, I felt rejuvenated and refreshed as I mentally readied myself for the upcoming tour to Vietnam. I did not know where my life would take me, but I never imagined that trip home would end up being the last time I ever saw Cindy Beining or Rosie Kennedy. They will never know how much our relationships meant to me. I can say with certainty they played a key role in keeping my spirits high during a potentially stressful transitional period of my life. I will always be thankful to them for that.

Hopping on the plane to Los Angeles, I said to myself, *Vietnam, here I come.*

4

BLUE AND GOLD

*Life's roughest storms prove the
strengths of our anchors.*

— Author Unknown

Finally returning to the Long Beach Naval Shipyard, I took in deep breaths as I marched quickly across the blistering concrete pier to *USS Bennington*. I could see its grand outline at the end of the dock, a dark shadowing beast contrasting starkly against the sunny California sky. *Bennington* was first commissioned in 1944 as an aircraft carrier in World War II. This 842-foot ship had traveled from Panama to Pearl Harbor to Japan, where it participated in many successful air attacks against the Japanese. To think of all the things this ship had seen!

USS Bennington off the California coast, 1967

USS Bennington alongside USS Tolovana

Gaining proximity to this hulking, steel giant, I gazed up past its broad, charcoal-shaded girth. I saw dozens of airplanes and helicopters parked on its flight deck. *This vessel is my new home for a while,* I said to myself. I admired the brown pelicans coasting along the glass-like waters just off the Navy port. Surrounded by a world of the concrete and steel, these birds struck me as a thing of natural beauty. I marveled at their air of grace, focus and brotherhood as they shared their home with the Navy base. It was amazing to see man and nature finding balance and accord in the most unexpected of places.

After reporting for duty, I was led to the ship's main office of the weapons department. It was a considerably-sized room with a large, metal desk stationed in the left corner. It just so happened that an Officer meeting was in progress at that exact time, and the 25 weapons department Officers were all together gathered in this space.

The mate who had brought me in said, "Come on, let me introduce you to the Gun Boss."

Commander Ulm, head of the Weapons Department, sat squarely at the desk with a magisterial air. He had a strong, imposing demeanor that was quite intimidating at first. But later on, I would find that he was quite interesting once I got to know him.

Upon introducing myself to Commander Ulm, he quickly exclaimed, "Well, goddamn! You finally showed up! How long is your contract?"

"Three years," I replied.

"Great. Well, let's officially get it started. I'm glad you are here."

"Yes, sir. I'm ready to give my one hundred percent." I said, feeling embarrassed, but trying not to show it.

The Commander subsequently announced to the group, "I want you all to meet Ensign Mark Mahaffey. We were going to mark him as missing because we thought he was coming eight weeks ago. And believe it or not, then, he went on leave!" Half of the Officers smiled, and the other half just raised their eyebrows. Oh boy. What a start.

My role on the vessel began in the Third Division of the Weapons Department as an Assistant Officer of the Division. This deck position demanded much of the grunt work of running a ship, including maintaining deck surfaces and participating in the handling of the ship in entering and departing different ports. After three months of dedicated work, I was promoted to head of that division with about thirty men on my squad. It was not glorious work, but I learned a great deal about running a ship and leading a crew.

About six months into my time on *Bennington*, Steve Bettcher entered my life. He would end up not only being my best friend during our Navy years, but also a close friend for the rest of our lives. On the day I met him, I was working the deck of *Bennington* as it cruised miles out in the Pacific Ocean. A strong breeze whipped though the deck on that cool and misty morning in late February. We received word that a Navy Ensign would be transferred to our ship soon, but we kept our daily routine while waiting.

Before long, I heard the bosun's pipe sing out its shrill tones. *Low......high. Low......high.* The whistling call danced high above the thundering ocean waves that crashed into the hull of the ship. *All hands on deck*—that was the call.

I looked into the distance and observed the profile of another Navy Oiler, a ship used for replenishing fuel to other ships at sea.

"That must be Steve Bettcher," I told my fellow shipmate.

At that time, there was a particular method used to transfer men from ship to ship. It was surely unusual, and most certainly not used anymore as it is very dangerous. As the ship drew nearer, our mission was to align ourselves closely to this vessel matching its speed and direction. It took some tricky maneuvering, but after some time spent positioning, we finally achieved the necessary parallel path. Our ships were no more than fifty feet apart.

The adjoining ship casted to us a long, strong cable.

"Secure the cable!" called the Captain.

We caught hold of the cable and fastened it to a pulley system on our ship. I had heard about these personnel transfers over cables, but had yet to witness one. It was an exhilarating event!

Once attached, the ships had to be driven with perfect synchronization. One wrong move, and the cable could snap. The black sea churned and growled as the two vessels narrowly sliced through it. I observed the men on the smaller ship attach a bosun's chair to the cable with a large hook. The chair was no more than a wood and metal swing apparatus with thin, steel bars that were intended to frame in its rider. A man wearing a bright orange life jacket and helmet, presumably Steve, stepped into the chair and sat down. His fellow shipmates fastened a belt around his waist and secured him to the chair.

After calls of approval and commencement, the bosun's chair, with Steve in it, was set free from the ship and sent down the wire. The chair whipped back and forth as the cable waved in the wind. The ocean spat and rolled as if it was a boiling black cauldron below. Even from my distance, I could see Steve's face pallid with fear and his knuckles white grasping onto the metal bars. This was understandably a very risky and dangerous crossing. Irate, frothing waves soaked Steve's legs as the chair dipped toward the center of the line.

"Pull him in!" I called as we tugged at the cable.

With a great deal of coordination and guidance, Steve was finally pulled up safely onto our ship deck. He looked as if he saw a ghost.

I greeted him, "Welcome aboard. I'm Ensign Mark Mahaffey."

"Thank you. I'm Ensign Steve Bettcher," he replied as we shook hands.

"I'll show you where to put your gear," I directed.

We walked into the corridor of the ship, and I remember asking him about his background.

"I'm from Elkhart, Indiana," he said. "I graduated from Hanover College in Indiana and attended OCS afterwards."

"Elkhart, Indiana? Wow! I'm from Indianapolis, Indiana. I went to Notre Dame. What a small world!"

We became fast friends from that day on. We served together for about two and a half years and formed a brotherhood that we hold close to this day. It is heartwarming for me to think back to our early days of friendship.

After I served on *Bennington* for about a year, the head Officer of the G division, Jack Cannon, was about to finish his term. The G division was the team responsible for storing the ammunition. I was flattered when he recommended that I succeed him. I became his assistant for a couple weeks before he left, and I learned a lot. Taking his place, my new title was Ordinance Handling Officer. It was a huge responsibility. Not only did I keep inventory of the ammunition, but my crew would take the ammunition from the magazines located deep in the bowels of the ship and transport it up to the flight deck. It took a great deal of coordination, but we did a great job.

Another responsibility I acquired was the role of Junior Officer of the Watch (JOOW). In this position, I worked on the bridge in close proximity to the Captain. I was part of a four-man team that manned the bridge, which included the Officer of the Deck (OOD), Junior Officer of the Deck (JOOD), and two JOOWs. The OOD was the top rank, followed by the JOOD, and then followed by the JOOW. I gradually made my way up to OOD, not necessarily by merit, but rather by attrition. I can remember that when I was asked to advance to the OOD position, I was in disbelief. I did not deem myself qualified by any means to take on a role with that much responsibility. However, since I had the most experience of the men there, I accepted the role.

I was surprised that my assigned JOOD, who would be serving under me, was a full lieutenant. He was a Military Officer with *Mustang* ranking and had been enlisted for over 25 years. He had more Navy years under his belt, but less experience on the bridge. My two JOOWs consisted of a Lieutenant Commander/Meteorologist and Steve Bettcher, who was an Ensign like me. Our job was to rotate the watches, manning them every four hours. Little did I know how quickly we would be put to the test.

I can remember my very first watch as OOD. *Bennington* was far out into the Pacific Ocean heading toward Hawaii for scheduled exercises. My shift, supposedly the slowest watch, was 4:00-8:00 in the morning. I stood positioned on the bridge. The ship was quiet, the sea rolled its predictable rhythm, and the slightest hint of sunlight was just beginning to peak above the horizon.

Without warning, I received a call from the Combat Information Center. "We have an unidentified Russian trawler. It seems to be on a collision course with us," they informed me over the intercom. Although it was certainly possible to encounter foreign vessels while on duty, it was a rare occurrence. Whether it was a war ship in disguise or merely a fishing vessel out to harass us, we had to take it seriously.

"We are signaling them to identify themselves, but they will not respond," I was told. "Their vessel is approaching with speed."

I knew my next step was to inform the Captain. The Captain at that time was Captain Graffy. Tall and lean, he was an austere, but very capable ship handler. At this point, he was in the enclosed sea cabin, positioned perhaps twenty feet from me. I picked up the intercom and punched in his number. With conviction, I informed him, "Hello, Captain. This is the Officer of the Deck. We've got a situation out here I think you need to know about."

He replied hastily, "Yes. What is it?"

"Well, we've got a ship out here. We think it is a Russian trawler. It's starting to get a little close to us. It might be just harassing..."

I did not even get through my sentence before I saw the Captain leap out of his cabin like a jack rabbit. He was standing by my side in seconds—and in his bathrobe! For about two hours we watched that vessel. Luckily, it eventually turned around and left us. It turned out that it was just pestering us, curious as to what we were up to. I wrote the event in the log and sighed in relief. What an eventful first watch! To think I had expected my first watch as OOD to be a quiet one.

After a year, when Captain Graffy's line of duty was up, a new Captain took his place who would forever impact my life. His name was Captain Daniel J. Murphy. Originally from Brooklyn, he joined the Navy in 1943 after graduating from the University of Maryland and the Naval War College. He started what would end up being his 37-year Navy career, flying anti-submarine patrols over the North Atlantic during World War II. With prematurely silvery-gray hair, tanned skin, and baby blue eyes, he possessed a charisma unmatched by anyone I had ever met. He reminded me of the Hollywood actor, Cary Grant. He had a calm, confident disposition balanced by a no-nonsense attitude. He was a kind and proficient leader, empowering his men to perform their best.

Captain Murphy assuming command from Captain Graffy

We were out in Hawaii when he first joined our ship. After monitoring me for a few weeks, he told the Navigator, "Ensign Mahaffey really needs to bone up on his knowledge and skills. He is qualified for an independent steaming, but he needs a fleet qualification."

When I heard about this criticism, I took it very seriously. It was a real lesson in humility. I spent the next few weeks hitting the books and undergoing guided experience drills. I knew I made the grade when Captain Murphy handed me a letter and said, "Good job, Mark." I was shocked he used my first name, as they are rarely ever used in the Navy. It was a real boost to my confidence.

Captain Murphy was an excellent Captain and a huge influence in my life. He taught me, through example, the qualities of a great leader. He treated everyone with respect, no matter their rank. He was a great listener, and he was fair. He brought out the best in people, and inspired his crew to do the same. Most importantly, he taught me that the best leaders inspire others to lead.

Captain Daniel J. Murphy, 1968

There was a genuine loyalty between Captain Murphy and me. I had a good rapport with him that allowed me to get away with what nobody else would dare. I remember the other Officers of the Deck teasing, "You get away with more with our Captain than anybody."

I would say, "Yeah, but I know I can only get so far."

I remember one day, as Officer of the Deck, I was inspired with an idea. I decided to meet with Captain Murphy to see what he thought. Walking into his office, I saw him sitting at his desk. He was wearing a freshly pressed Captain's uniform and a red baseball cap embroidered with scrambled eggs and the word *BENNINGTON* written across the front. He adjusted his black-framed reading glasses as he observed me walk in.

Captain Daniel J. Murphy, 1968

I said, "Captain, I have an idea."

He replied, "What is it, Mark?"

I cleared my throat and said, "Well, as you know, when you first came onto *Bennington*, I wasn't quite knowledgeable or qualified. You let me know, which spurred me on and made me realize that myself. I wanted to prove myself to you, so I worked hard."

He cut in, "You are definitely qualified now."

"Well, I'm not looking for a compliment," I said. "What I'd like to do is perform a sort of experiment. I would love to encourage the JOODs to advance to OODs. Here is my plan—I'd like to take a JOOD and make him OOD for a few watches. I will be his JOOD under him. If I need to step in, I will, but I'll let him run the watch. I think by doing this, it will get him qualified and more experienced quicker. That way, he will not have to take that big step to OOD like I did. Of course, you will have to approve when the JOOD officially becomes an OOD. I have two or three men in mind, but would like to start with Steve Bettcher as my first trial run. I'm willing to step down to give him an opportunity to learn."

Captain Murphy was quiet for a moment as he pondered the notion. He tapped his fingers rhythmically on his desk. "Yes. I like that idea. Go ahead and try it out."

"Thank you, sir!" I exclaimed.

Within a week of starting Steve Bettcher in the OOD role, he became qualified. I was proud of him. He was my best friend, and he deserved the rise in responsibility.

My experiment went so well, I decided to try it again with another JOOD. It was successful again. We ended up qualifying about six people. I was so happy Captain Murphy allowed me to do this. It not only boosted my confidence as a leader, but also boosted the confidence of my men. We had a great team. We worked hard and pushed each other to grow.

One day, I approached Captain Murphy and said, "Captain, I've got one more JOOD whom I would like to qualify."

"And who might that be?" he asked.

"Well, you're going to have to take a big breath here," I prepared him.

"Alright, tell me who you've got in mind," the Captain pressed.

I said, "Dorsey Morris."

In shock, Captain Murphy quickly sat up straight in his chair. "Dorsey Morris?!" he exclaimed. "Are you kidding me?"

I understood his reaction. Dorsey Morris was not your typical, dedicated Navy JOOD. He was smart, but he did not have a great work ethic. He was rather laid back and lackadaisical— and just plain slow.

I defended my suggestion saying, "Captain, I know Morris is smart enough, he just needs someone like me pushing him. And believe you me, I will be pushing him. Life will not be that pleasant for Dorsey, but I will encourage him, because I am confident he can do it. However, you are the one who has to approve this. And you are the one that has to say he's qualified. I admit he may never get there, but I'd sure like to try."

Captain Murphy shook his head and said, "Alright. You've been right so far, and I'm trusting your judgement. Let's give it a whirl."

The OOD role was very difficult for Dorsey Morris, and I was very hard on him. Boy, it was a challenge for the both of us. I am sure I became frustrated with him and sometimes a little angry, but I think for the most part I kept my cool. I would tell him, "Doggone it, Morris, you've got to do this and step up. You've got to be a leader and run this team, not me." He struggled at first, but day after day, he seemed to improve. He took a little longer than the others, but he could do it. He just needed to be given a chance.

After several weeks of ample effort and endurance, he had matured and learned so much that Captain Murphy officially qualified him as OOD. When I heard the news, I told him, "Dorsey, hopefully you'll forgive me for being so hard on you. But doggone it, I thought you could do it, and you did! You ought to be proud of yourself!"

I could tell by the beam in his smile that he was proud. It was an astounding thing to witness the change in Dorsey Morris from that day on. That bit of success boosted his confidence so much that he continued to work hard and grow. I am not sure what happened to Dorsey Morris after those Navy days, but I'd like to think I had a positive influence on him. His success not only proved my method of training Officers effective, but also inspired me to implement the concept throughout the rest of my life, even as a business owner. I try to see the best in people and give them the opportunity to learn while giving them more responsibility. It always amazes me what people can do when someone has a little faith in them.

In 1968, with Captain Murphy still in charge, *Bennington* cruised out to the Gulf of Tonkin in the South China Sea to help fight in the Vietnam War. Steve Bettcher, Bill Jones, Lou Raisler, and I formed four

OOD teams that reported to Captain Murphy during this time. We performed our flight operations about 30 miles off-shore in North Vietnam, which was dubbed *Yankee Station* (South Vietnam was accordingly dubbed *Dixie Station*). Our mission was primarily focused on search and rescue and reconnaissance. We had twin prop planes, reconnaissance planes, and helicopters.

Working on the ship and enduring the perils of war, Bettcher, Jones, Raisler, and myself developed a real sense of brotherhood. We all became great friends and are still very close to this day. We all loved and respected Captain Murphy. Any of us would have taken a bullet for him. We knew, by God, we were going to serve this guy, and the ship, and our country. We looked forward to all those watches, even though they were long, tedious, and tiring. We performed our missions well for Captain Murphy, and he treated us well in return.

During those times when the ship was in port for maintenance or R & R, the Captain instructed the Navigator to excuse the four of us from our port watches. Captain Murphy thought that the four OOD's deserved a break. He would say, "My boys need a rest." We certainly appreciated this gesture of concern from our caring Captain. While in port overseas, one of us was required to stay on the ship in case of an emergency, but the three others would usually go into town to the *Officer's Club*, or *O-Club*. We would go and enjoy dinner and cocktails. Captain Murphy would usually join us for a quick cocktail before joining other Senior Officers at the O-Club. It was a small gesture from our Captain, but it was one that we sincerely appreciated and would always remember. He was there for us when we needed him, and we were there for him.

I remember a funny story about Captain Murphy on our expedition in the South China Sea. We were traveling to Hong Kong to take a week for some rest and recouperation. Captain Murphy's wife happened to be in Hong Kong, and he could not wait to see her. To push his anticipation to get to Hong Kong even more, there was a typhoon on our tail. He told the engineering department to execute a high-speed exercise, which was essentially an experiment to see how fast the ship could go without breaking.

"Start at 20 knots," called the Captain. "Now 25 knots....30 knots!"

Cruising at high speed was unusual for *Bennington*, especially considering it was an old, World War II carrier. Luckily, the ship managed well. As we traveled closer to Hong Kong, Captain Murphy commanded the ship to slow down. The typhoon was well behind us, and the sun shone brilliantly in the bright blue sky. The air was still and the deck was quiet. Captain Murphy decided it was the perfect moment to catch some rays in preparation for seeing his lovely wife. He said, "Mark, I am going to change my clothes and get some sun out on the starboard wing."

I acknowledged, "Yes, sir."

Next thing I knew, Captain Murphy came out of his Captain's quarters wearing orange swimming trunks and holding a folded towel. He proceeded to the starboard wing, which was out in the open air. He spread his large blue towel onto the ground and laid himself on it to get a suntan. He had been resting there for about twenty minutes, most likely half asleep, when I received a call from a friend of mine, John Erickson, from the Admiral's Bridge. He told me over the phone, "Hello Mark, I thought I'd give you a heads up. Admiral Weymouth is coming down to have a chat with the Captain in about five minutes. I just wanted to tell you so that you are not surprised." Admiral Ralph Weymouth was the head of the fleet, and therefore, was a big deal.

I calmly said, "Thank you, John. I will pass the word on."

I dashed out to Captain Murphy lounging on the deck.

Trying to catch my breath, I said, "Captain, I just got a call from a friend of mine from the Admiral's Bridge. Admiral Weymouth is coming down in five minutes. He wants to talk to you about something, but I am not sure what."

The Captain leapt up and sprung to his Captain's quarters faster than the cartoon character Road Runner. He came out within seconds in uniform and wearing his red scrambled eggs baseball cap. He flew into his elevated Captain's chair, and in no more than a minute later, the Admiral came down. I waited as they chatted for perhaps ten minutes. After the Admiral left, Captain Murphy slumped in his chair, looked straight ahead, and let out a sigh of relief. I stood next to him, also looking straight ahead. I knew he was going to say something. It was just a matter of time.

He finally looked over and said, "Well, I guess I owe you another one."

Smiling, I said, "Yes, sir."

As an epilogue to that story, I met the Admiral's son, Yann Weymouth, in Saint Petersburg, Florida, almost 50 years later. Yann Weymouth, a world-renowned architect, currently lives in Saint Petersburg with his wife, Susana. We met through our shared appreciation for the arts, as both Yann and his wife are very involved in the arts and culture scene in the Tampa Bay area. In 2016, Susana Weymouth, Executive Director of Tampa Bay Businesses for Culture and the Arts (TBBCA), honored me with the Patron of Culture & the Arts Impact Award for my family's contributions to the arts over the years. I did not connect the dots of the Weymouth name until later, when Yann and Susana visited my home to observe my art collection. I must have mentioned I had been in the Navy to Susana, because at one point, Susana beckoned me, "You must share with Yann some of your Navy stories!" Through conversation, we mutually discovered that Yann's father was Ralph Weymouth—my Admiral—the Admiral in the famed story of Captain Murphy and the orange bathing suit. I told Yann the story, which he subsequently related to his 99-year-old father who resided in Washington DC. Yann later told me that his father got the biggest kick out of my story. What a neat connection to make all those years later.

Captain Murphy remained the Captain of *Bennington* until the latter part of 1968. I remember the farewell party thrown for him at the Officer's Club at Long Beach, California. Captain Murphy was very respected in the Navy community. There must have been one hundred people in attendance. Admirals, Captains, and Senior Officers came, as well as lower ranked Navy men like myself. However, I was the only one of the OOD teams who could make it. I would not have missed it for the world.

At the end of the evening, Captain Murphy stood up and gave an inspiring and moving speech. He spoke of what a privilege it was for him to command such a great ship on our overseas mission. He was proud of how the ship performed and incredibly grateful for all the work the crew put into it. At the end of his speech, he added, "Let me tell you. When you have guys like Mahaffey, Jones, Bettcher, and Raisler, you cannot go wrong."

Mark Mahaffey (center) with fellow G-Division Weapons Department mates, 1968

My eyes filled with tears as I heard his words. It was beyond an honor to hear him tribute our team. Senior Officers came up to me afterwards and patted me on the back saying, "Good job, Mahaffey." They told me they had never heard a Captain thank any of their crew by name. I was speechless. It was such a humble gesture for Captain Murphy to credit the team. I will never forget that.

USS Bennington in Hong Kong, China, 1968

Mark at Honk Kong, China, 1968 (USS Bennington in background)

Fellow Navy officers of the USS Bennington, 1968
Enjoying their time in a suite at the Peninsula Hotel in Hong Kong, China
Steve Bettcher, Mark Mahaffey, Rob Small, and Kevin Gardner

Steve Bettcher, 1968

5

THE FAMILY JEWELS

What the heart knows today, the head will understand tomorrow.

James Stephens, Irish poet

Fate is a curious thing. To some, it is an indisputable truth. The events of our lives are predetermined, and our future destiny is utterly out of our control. To others, the concept of fate is a mystical fantasy, and freewill rules the game. The debate I am sure will go on for eternity because I am certain it is a puzzle too complex to understand.

In the meantime, I stand somewhere rather balanced in the middle. Looking back at my life, I see a road defined by a series of decisions. Most decisions are small, such as choosing what color socks to wear or what type of creamer to put into coffee. However, some decisions are much more life-defining, such as choosing a wife or a career path to pursue. When I came to these crossroads, I put a great deal of thought and intention into my decisions. I also sought the advice of people I loved and respected to help guide me. I take great pride in the path I chose, and I always felt very much in control. However, I also realize that the freedom I possessed was a blessing—a gift bestowed by generations of my hardworking Irish ancestors. I will never know how much the decisions they made in their lives affected me in mine, but I am sure it is substantial. It also gives me the peace of mind knowing that possibly, there was a plan for me from the beginning, and I merely had to choose to accept. Perhaps the plan was crafted by God, or perhaps, just perhaps, many of those bricks beneath my feet were laid by my grandmother.

My paternal grandmother, Katherine (Kate) Louise Kiley Mahaffey, was born in 1869 in the small town of Marion, Indiana. My memory of her is as an elderly, frail woman resting in a recliner knitting. She died at the age of 91 in 1960 when I was only 16 years old. Although I only knew her in her last feeble years of life, I was told she was a much different woman in her younger days. She was a fierce, strong woman with a vibrant personality and contagious energy.

My father and I would visit Grandmother Kate often in her apartment located inside the historic Marott Hotel on Meridian Street in Indianapolis. I recall one Sunday afternoon in particular, when I was about ten years old, my father and I decided to pay my grandmother a visit after attending Catholic mass. My grandmother's apartment was modest, but materialized the sentiments of a woman who cherished the small things in life. Photos of family, crystal trinkets, and fine China were displayed on wooden shelves scattered about the room. Hand-made blankets and doilies spread over the back of the sofa and on the side tables. I will never forget the sweet, pungent smell of rose-scented soaps and powders, which gave the space a distinct scent that could only be Grandmother's.

When my father and I entered the living room, we saw Grandmother sitting in her favorite chair, sipping a cup of hot tea. She was wearing a pink house coat with matching slippers. We were surprised to see that my Uncle Fred, my father's one and only brother, happened to be there as well. He had brought a friend with him, a burly man with combed-back tawny hair. My father and I joined them on the Victorian, floral-printed sofas adjacent to my grandmother's chair.

My Uncle Fred introduced his friend to me saying, "This is my good friend and Irish Hollywood actor, Pat O'Brien. I'm sure you recognize him from his star role in the movie, *Knute Rockne All American*."

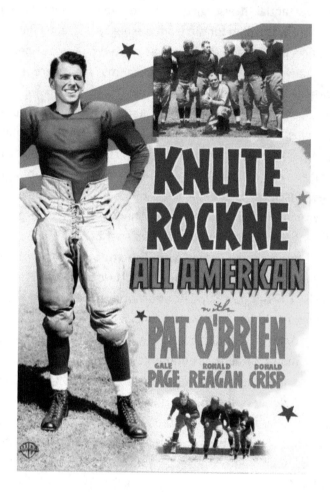

I nodded in amazement. To say I was star stuck would be an understatement. In the movie, alongside young actor Ronald Reagan, Pat O'Brien had portrayed Knute Rockne, the famed Notre Dame football coach. Considering Knute Rockne was my father's football coach, we had watched that film many times. To be standing in the same room as this famous actor was mind blowing.

Pat O'Brien chimed in with a flirtatious wink toward my grandmother. "I could not pass up an opportunity to come visit this fine dame, Mrs. Kate Mahaffey,"

Grandmother blushed at the flattery. "Pat," she beckoned. "Why don't you do the Rock Speech for my grandson? The one Knute gives from the locker room during the big game."

At first Pat O'Brien dismissed the request, but my grandmother insisted. Pat said, "Okay, Kate. I will do it for you." He stood up from the couch, towering over us, as we were still sitting. It was obvious Pat O'Brien had been asked this before and was well-rehearsed. Taking a few deep breaths, he was quiet for a moment. Then, without warning, Pat O'Brien burst into character. In a passionate and captivating spirit, he spoke in speedy, staccato bursts, grabbing our attention at once.

"And when we get 'em on the run, men, we're going to push 'em right down that field— right down that field—and over the goal like that old Notre Dame Spirit. They can't stop us! Nobody's going to stop us! We're going back in there, and from the first kickoff, we're going to drive – drive – drive – drive – get 'em – get 'em – get 'em!"

Applauding at once, we could tell he had just made my grandmother's day, and mine too! Knute Rockne had been well known for his half-time fury, and Pat O'Brien had captured that impeccably. What a privilege it was to be in the private audience of this famous actor!

Visiting my grandmother was always special. I am thankful she lived nearby so that we were able to visit her often while she was alive. Some of my fondest memories with her was when she would tell stories of her past. Every time she spoke, I felt as if I was being transported in time.

"Mark, come closer so I can see you," I remember her telling me on another one of our visits.

"Yes, Grandmother. Please tell me one of your stories," I pleaded.

I remember stepping over to her and clasping her soft, creased fingers. She slowly rested her other hand on top of mine and paused a moment to cherish the closeness.

She began, "Well, dear, you know life was much different when I was a little girl. Life in Marion, Indiana, back in the 1800s, was all about hard work. We went to school, but also had to help my mother at home and my father at the saloon he owned."

I asked, "And your parents were both from Ireland, right?"

My grandmother nodded and said, "Yes. Both my parents, John and Catherine Kiley, were originally born in Ireland and moved to the United States for a better life in 1848. They got married in Ohio in 1858 when my mother was only seventeen years old. They settled in Marion after having my oldest sister. I was one of thirteen children. Sadly, several of my siblings died at a very young age. Life was hard then, but it taught us to be tough."

I asked her, "Didn't your father go to California at some point?"

She said, "Yes. During my mother's sixth pregnancy, my father's spirit of adventure came over him. He told my mother, '*Catherine, there is word of golden mountains in California. More gold than you could ever dream of. I'm going to take this year to travel there, get us some gold, and come back the richest man in Indiana!*' Well, one year turned into nine years. I'm not sure he came back too much richer, but my mother must have forgiven him because I was born early the following year. And they had six more children after me. My father was a strong, determined man."

It is interesting to note that years later, I discovered that my grandmother's stories were very true. My great-grandfather, John Kiley, had traveled to the North Pacific Coast, but not by traversing over the continental United States, but rather, by going the long way. From Marion, he traveled to New York City and boarded a ship that sailed south to Central America. Landing at Panama, he walked across the Isthmus of Panama before the Panama Canal was ever dug. Crossing the country to the Pacific Ocean, he then boarded another ship that took him north to California, where he staked a plot of land. Amazingly, he mined $8,000 worth of gold, and later returned to Marion a rich man. He invested in many local businesses and saloons, and he eventually became mayor from 1902-1904.

Great-grandfather, John Kiley, Mayor of Marion, Indiana
Character sketch by local cartoon artist: Moe H. Baldwin, 1905

My mother, who was sitting quietly next to my grandmother, asked her, "Kate, please tell us again how you and Tom met."

"Oh, my Tom Mahaffey—he was a handsome one! He was from Seneca, Illinois, but came to Marion to start a brewing company with a few friends. They named that brewery the *Indiana Brewing Association*. That's when I met him. We married soon after in 1887. We had our honeymoon in Seneca, but chose to continue to live in Marion where his brewing business was booming. Sadly, with the prohibition on the horizon, the company was forced to shut down 1913. The IRS came and confiscated the remaining 1,800 barrels of beer. And can you believe it— they dumped those barrels into the Mississinewa River! Everyone in town was taking buckets of river water and swimming amongst the drunken fish. It was such a sight!"

Pausing for a minute and smiling at the memory, she then looked at me and said, "Enough about me. Tell me about you. How is school? Are you making any friends?"

I said, "Yes, school is great. I am in high school now, and I have lots of friends. My best friend is Bob Desautels. We play basketball together at his house."

My grandmother's eyes lit up. "Desautels? Oh, what a lovely family. You know, I tried to get your Uncle Fred to marry Bob's mom, Josephine." Her smile faded. "But unfortunately, that Duke Desautels snatched her up instead," she added grumpily.

"Really?" I asked.

My grandmother continued to tell the story I had heard many times before narrating how Duke Desautels swept Josephine Stout off her feet. Duke was a very debonair young lad, and my Uncle Fred was no match to Duke's French accent and fancy Stutz Bearcat car. Josephine was a beautiful young girl and came from a very well-to-do Irish family. They fell in love and eventually got married. My grandmother loved to play matchmaker and was completely bitter that my Uncle Fred had not pursued Josephine.

When it came time for my father to marry, he chose my mother, Jane Watson. She was an Irish/Scottish girl whom Grandmother adored. Although she was not Catholic, as my grandmother would have preferred, Jane's father had an echelon position at Link-Belt, a large crane company. Thus, their family had a "grandmother-approved" high social status.

Years later, at the age of forty, my Uncle Fred finally fell in love with a lovely woman named Elinor Kirby. My grandmother, however, was less than thrilled. Elinor was Catholic and Irish, but she was from the wrong side of the tracks, so to speak. My grandmother was a very stubborn woman and a bit of a snob, and sadly, treated Elinor terribly. My Uncle Fred and Elinor eloped to escape the rage of my grandmother. Despite this lack of support, they ended up having a wonderful marriage with six children.

When my grandmother was nearing the end of her life and dividing her riches, her prejudices became more apparent. Her most prized possession was a beautiful, black velvet pouch filled with her jewelry. It contained an assortment of rings and necklaces, and most importantly, her treasured diamond-studded broaches. I assume they were gifts from my grandfather.

My mother would say to my grandmother, "Kate, you should write down who you want this jewelry to go to."

My grandmother would say, "I'll just leave it all to you, Jane."

My mother would plead, "You can't do that. Your eldest son is married to Elinor. You cannot just slight him. You may not like her, but she is part of the family. You have to get over this."

Finally, my grandmother agreed, "Okay, I will do it."

However, she never did. When she passed away, my uncle and my father put the jewelry-filled velvet pouch in a safety deposit box. Out of sight and out of mind, a decision had not been made.

*   *   *   *   *

Fast forward almost a decade, and I was now an Ensign in the Navy. It was toward the end of May 1967 when I took a ten-day leave to visit my home in Indianapolis. Serving in the Navy for almost a year, I missed my family and friends dearly. Two important events were scheduled that week—the Indianapolis 500 and Bob Desautels' graduation ceremony at Xavier University. He had technically graduated in January, but he wanted to walk during the procession in May. Upon hearing that I would be in town that week, Mr. and Mrs. Desautels cordially invited me to join their family for the ceremony in Cincinnati. I naturally agreed to go, as I wanted to support my best friend. I was especially excited to take the mini road trip south to test out the wheels on my new, British racing-green 1967 Mustang convertible. I decided to drive down Friday and stay until that Sunday.

On Friday night, Mr. and Mrs. Desautels hosted a lavish dinner party for Bob at a restaurant in Cincinnati. It was a formal, yet cozy steakhouse that seated us in a private room toward the back. When I walked into the dimly lit room, I observed a long dining table draped in white linens that seated perhaps twenty people. When Bob's mother,

Josephine, saw me enter, she gestured to me, "Come on over here, Mark. Come sit next to me and Marianne."

Never declining a seat between two beautiful women, I took the empty chair assigned to me between Marianne and her mother. In retrospect, I have no doubt Josephine had a matchmaking plan up her sleeve.

The dinner was delightful, but my real attention was on Marianne. It had been a while since I had seen her, and I could not believe what a beautiful woman she had grown into. I was mesmerized by her rich, black hair that laid delicately on her shoulders and her brilliant hazel eyes, framed by her soft, fair skin. I was captivated by her poise and grace in which she ate her meal and mingled with the other guests. She was perfection.

Following the dinner event, I offered to walk Marianne back to her hotel. It was on this stroll where the sparks really began to fly. We talked and laughed, having a wonderful chemistry from the start. I already could not wait to see her again.

The following day ended up being a whirlwind of events, including the graduation ceremony. I felt disappointed I did not get to spend much time with Marianne. I longed to be with her and to get to know her better. When Sunday came, I decided to ask her if she would like to drive home with me to Indianapolis. I knew I would be leaving Monday to return to California, and I was adamant to make the most of what little time I had left.

I said to her that morning, "Marianne, would you like to ride home with me?"

She said, "Oh, Mark, I would love to! But first, let me ask my parents."

She requested permission from her mother, who was standing nearby. Her mother responded with the biggest smile on her face, "Oh yes, of course. Go ahead, Marianne."

I had never been so thankful to have my own car. Those couple hours driving home were precious to me, and I was really beginning to fall hard in love.

While driving, I decided to invite Marianne to be my date at a going-away party that evening. I asked her, "Marianne, my good friend Jerry is throwing a going-away party for me tonight. Would you like to go to the party with me?"

Marianne responded, "Yes, I really would love to accompany you, but Jerry already invited me to his party to be *his* date."

My stomach sank. I said, "Oh."

Marianne consoled me, "I really would rather go with you though. Let me talk to Jerry."

Well, later, she talked to Jerry, and he was a good sport. I could not have been happier going to the party with Marianne's arm linked in mine. Now, when we tell the story, we tease that Jerry must have been heartbroken—which he really was not—because he didn't get married until he was about fifty.

I kept close to my heart the memories Marianne and I made that weekend as I traveled back to my Navy obligation in California. The next time I saw Marianne was December, later that year. It was a long seven months being separated. Our relationship continued to grow and blossom during that time through many love letters sent back and forth, as well as phone calls. I wish we still had those letters. Marianne is especially devastated they went missing over the years.

On the eight days I was home in December, we especially got hot and heavy, soaking in every minute we were together. Every day and every evening, we spent together. It was pretty obvious to everyone we were getting serious. Luckily, both our parents were very encouraging of our relationship. Bob, my best friend and Marianne's brother, seemed genuinely pleased that we were dating.

A few months later, my parents telephoned me in California and said, "Would you like us to come visit you? We'd love to see your ship and meet your Captain, of whom you speak so highly."

I said, "Oh, that would be great!"

They added, "Would you like us to bring Marianne as well?"

I was ecstatic. "Definitely!" I exclaimed. "I will call her."

As soon as we hung up the phone, I called Marianne and invited her. She was overjoyed, and subsequently asked her parents, who immediately said yes. Our families had been very close for years, thanks to my grandmother, and it gave me such peace having everyone's blessing.

In April, my parents and Marianne came out to California to visit me. They stayed almost a week, and I showed them a little bit about what life in the Navy looked like. There was a Navy dance one of the nights they were in town, and I invited Marianne to join me. She was such a joy in my life, and I was proud to introduce her to my Captain and shipmates. When Captain Murphy met her, he tried to convince her to talk me into staying in the Navy even after my three years were up. I loved the ocean, but not so much to live on it long term, going in and out of port for a good portion of my life. I am certain Marianne agreed with me, as she politely smiled and said, "I am not so sure."

Later that week, Marianne and I took a little trip to Las Vegas with my parents. As one can imagine, we surely took that time to become closer. We dreaded the months we spent apart. Luckily for the letters, we remained close throughout the remainder of the year. Marianne will say to this day, she first fell in love with me through my letters.

The next time we saw one another was later that year on Thanksgiving. I took a leave for Thanksgiving and decided to fly to Indianapolis to see Marianne, as well as my family. Technically, it was an illegal leave, as I was not supposed to travel more than 200 miles. Indianapolis was 2,000 miles from my station at Long Beach, California. I missed Marianne so much though, and I had to see her.

With a bad bit of luck, my connecting flight from Chicago to Indianapolis was cancelled due to a horrible snowstorm. I was determined to get to Indianapolis one way or another, so I rented a car and drove the last leg myself. In the snowstorm, it took me five hours to drive from the O'Hare Airport in Chicago to Indianapolis. I remember driving and thinking, and thinking, and thinking. Marianne was on my mind. It had been a year and a half since her brother's graduation dinner, when we first began to fall in love. Despite me being overseas for most of the time since, we maintained and grew our relationship into something I could have never dreamed of. I had originally planned to propose to her at Christmastime. But as I drove in that car, I thought to myself, "Why wait?" I knew she was the woman I wanted to spend the rest of my life with. I wanted to tell her that. I *needed* to tell her that. I decided I could not wait another day to declare my utmost and undying love to my sweet Marianne.

Finally, on that Thanksgiving eve, I arrived at her home at the very late hour of twelve o'clock midnight. She met me at the front door, and we embraced, cloaking each other in love. We segued to the adjoining, cozy den and sunk into the large, leather sofa. Whispering in the dark, I said, "Marianne, you are my everything. We've known each other since we were just kids, and every day I have grown more and more in love with you. I know maybe this isn't the perfect timing or moment, but I cannot wait a minute longer. I am so completely in love with you. Will you make me the happiest man in the world, and please marry me, Marianne Desautels?"

Silence...

"Marianne?" I whispered a bit louder. Nerves began to take over my body as my heart thumped in fear that perhaps she did not feel the same way. I tried unsuccessfully to read her face in the darkness. It appeared that she had fallen asleep. I laughed to myself. Oh boy. I guess that is what I get for deciding to propose in the middle of the night. I repeated my very important question a bit louder. "Will you marry me, Marianne?"

Well, that seemed to jolt her. "Oh yes!" she cried. She wrapped her arms around me, and we kissed passionately like we had never kissed before.

"I am so sorry I do not have a ring to give you," I apologized. "I was planning to propose at Christmas, but I decided I love you too much to wait another day. I cannot promise too much at this time, but I will promise you that it will not be boring." I am pretty confident that I did fulfill that promise.

"Don't you worry for a second," she replied. "I am so happy. I cannot wait to tell my parents!"

Marianne woke her parents, Duke & Dote (Josephine's nickname), and they came rushing downstairs and hugged us both as they were genuinely happy for us. I remember Duke reminded me the next day that I had not asked him for his daughter's hand. I, in turn, immediately asked my future father-in-law for Marianne's hand, despite it being after-the-fact. He enthusiastically approved with a handshake and a hug.

After first telling Marianne's parents that night, and a few more hugs and tears later, I drove home to my parents' house to awaken them with my big news. They were also very happy for us. My mother could not contain her excitement and said gleefully, "Oh, my goodness! That is such wonderful news. Congratulations! Thank you for waking us." She then added, speaking to my father, "Tom, I think it's about time you talk to Elinor about the jewelry."

"Yes, dear," I heard him mumble half asleep.

My Uncle Fred had since passed away, but my grandmother's jewelry was still in the safety deposit box. My Aunt Elinor, upon hearing that I was engaged, also thought instantly about the jewelry. She, my father, and my mother retrieved the black pouch and gave me the center diamond from my grandmother's favorite broach. I took the diamond to a local jeweler, who made a beautiful ring with a solitaire setting in platinum.

When I returned to Indianapolis at Christmastime, I gave Marianne the dazzling ring. Now, we were officially engaged. Mr. and Mrs. Desautels threw us an engagement party the weekend after Christmas and posted an announcement in the local newspaper, as was the custom at the time. It was such a romantic, festive time of my life, full of excitement, anticipation, and love.

Marianne was honored to wear my grandmother's diamond. Turns out, years later, I would receive a treasure from her side of the family as well. Shortly after the death of Marianne's father in 1981, Marianne's mother met us at a restaurant to speak to us. I remember her seeming quite nervous the whole duration of the dinner, as if she was going to say something important, but waited. Finally, after we finished our meal and the plates were cleared, she pulled a small box out of her purse.

"Mark, I have something for you. You know I have three sons, but Duke and I always felt like you were our fourth son. He loved you dearly," she said.

I replied with gratitude, "I always thought of him as another father. He was a wonderful man, and I miss him."

Marianne's mother handed me the box. She said, "I know he would have wanted you to have this."

I carefully opened the pocket-sized box, and inside was Duke Desautels' ring. It was the ring that he always wore on his right hand for as long as I could remember. It was a blue star sapphire ring engraved with his initials, "LD", for Leon Desautels (his birth name) with diamonds on either side. I was bewildered and honored. I loved Duke and always respected and looked up to him. I appreciated deeply that Marianne's mother would consider me as the recipient of the ring.

Two years later, when Marianne's mother's own days were limited, she said to me one day when we were alone, "Mark, I am counting on you."

"Yes, you can count on me," I reassured her.

"I want you to take care of my three sons," she implored.

I said, "I can do that." And I kept that promise. I helped her sons when I could.

The Mahaffey and Desautels families are like one family. We have been close for years. It is incredible to think how far back in time that bond goes and will continue to span time through our children's lives as well. I am certain if my grandmother were still alive at this time, she would be proud. She perhaps did not get her exact wish of her son Fred marrying Josephine Desautels. However, she did get her grandson to marry Josephine's daughter. Sometimes, I wonder if she has been matchmaking from heaven this whole time.

6

THE PELICAN TAKES FLIGHT

A journey of a thousand miles begins with a single step.

Lao Tzu

My seven-month engagement to Marianne from Thanksgiving until June was a time of anticipation and preparation. Marianne gleefully narrowed her full attention on all things wedding-related. Her world was brimming with floral decorations, cake flavors, and guest lists. She and her mother executed the wedding planning beautifully, and I can take very little credit. I was away in California for most of our engagement, as my Navy obligation was not complete until May. However, that is not to say I did not have any planning of my own to do.

While Marianne focused on the upcoming wedding day, I tried to piece together how our life would look afterwards. I deemed it my utmost responsibility to provide Marianne with the best life I could give. It was just a matter of figuring out what that life looked like. I already knew a life-long career in the Navy was not for me. Instead, I seriously considered attending graduate school to get my Master of Business Administration. I had a bachelor's degree in finance under my belt, and since I saw myself eventually running a business of some sort, an MBA seemed the natural next step. Not to mention, I had formed wonderful memories in my undergraduate years, and continuing that experience was very tempting. I knew I would learn a great deal, and a master's degree would open many career doors in my future. College life was perhaps not Marianne's perfect idea of starting a marriage, but at least we would be close to her family if I chose Notre Dame again.

Nevertheless, when I expressed my thoughts to my father, he had another proposal. "Look, if you want to go to graduate school, whatever one you can get into, do it. I will pay for it. But you obtained a first-class education when you went to Notre Dame for your undergraduate degree. And you had a great experience in the Navy. Come work for me in Saint Petersburg." He then paused, letting the silence coax my thoughts.

I must admit I expected my father to make me an offer at some point. We had worked well together when I had helped him get his apartment company up and running those summers back in my high school and college days. Despite my father's stern and demanding nature, I enjoyed learning a lot about real world finance. My brother, Jim, was presently working for him in Florida full time, but my father had big plans about expanding the company and needed additional cavalry. It was a unique opportunity, and the experience would undoubtably be invaluable. However, appreciating the offer immensely, I could not deny a deep-down drive for independence stewing in my core. I was the *Pathfinder*, and I wanted to pave my own way. Going to graduate school would most assuredly give me the tools I needed to succeed on my own.

"Hmm, thank you, Dad," I replied hesitantly, breaking the stale silence.

He continued, supposedly reading my thoughts. "I'll be the first to admit you will certainly learn a lot in graduate school. But I've been around for a long time, and I can teach you by giving you the experience you need to really understand how business works. I'll teach you more in 90 days than you will learn in two years of graduate school."

It was surely a sweeping statement that caught me by surprise. My father did not lack confidence in himself or his ability to teach others. I still lacked complete conviction, however. "Let me think on it," I answered without committing.

Later the following week, while stationed at Long Beach, I was shocked to receive a letter from my older brother, Jim. I carefully opened the sealed envelope to find a note, three pages long and handwritten. I had never before received a letter from my brother that I could remember. He was not one to pen heartfelt compositions in his free time by any means. He struggled with penmanship and had almost illegible handwriting. To receive a letter from him was very meaningful and significant to me.

I began to read the letter, deciphering the black scribbled rows of script. The content of his message concerned my father's job proposal to me. I wish I still had the letter, but to the best of my memory, it went something like this:

Dear Mark,

I understand that Dad has offered you a job position to work with us in Saint Petersburg, Florida. I wanted to reach out to you to hopefully persuade you to accept it. Dad and I have been working down here for seven years now, and we have two properties in development. We have several more deals in the works and want to begin construction on those soon. Dad and I have been handling it well, but as the company grows, we need more help. You joining our team now would be incredibly valuable to the company.

From what I have heard, I understand you desire to go to graduate school. I am certain the education you will attain there will be advantageous. However, now is the time we need you. I must stress the incredible experience it has been for me working for the company. I have learned more in these past few years than I ever did in a classroom. Please consider joining us now and being a part of this grand vision that we have for the future.

Sincerely,

Jim

Jim's letter truly touched my heart. I knew it would mean a great deal to my father and my brother if I were to join them in the family business. However, was I really ready to sacrifice my graduate education? I had my father's oral argument and my brother's written argument, but it was not enough. I needed some advice.

Still in a quandary, I decided to go see my Captain. There was no individual's opinion I esteemed more than Captain Dan Murphy's. He already knew that I was not going to extend my Navy obligation, so we were beyond that conversation. I was curious to see if he had any insight into which way I should turn in this particular fork in the road of life.

Following protocol, I quickly scheduled an appointment to meet with Captain Murphy as soon as possible. When the day arrived, I punctually walked over to the Captain's stateroom at the agreed-upon time. The stateroom was a sizable suite comprised of a bedroom space, an office space with a large wooden desk, and a living room with two leather sofas, an armchair and a coffee table. Rich, blue carpeting grounded the room, bringing an element of Navy-esque sophistication. Approaching the open doorway, I observed heaps of papers scattered about the room on every possible surface. Captain Murphy and another younger man, Captain Barrow, were seated on the sofas opposite of one another intensely discussing one of the stacks of papers. Captain Barrow was shadowing Captain Murphy, as he prepared to succeed Captain Murphy's position in three weeks' time. I gently knocked twice on the wooden door frame to alert the two Captains I was there.

Captain Murphy slowly glanced up, gently set down the paper he was holding, and greeted me.

"Come on in, Mark. Let's have our chat. If you'd like, I can ask Captain Barrow to leave. Or, perhaps, you would like him to stay?" Captain Murphy knew I was there to seek advice. I liked Captain Barrow from what little I knew of him, and I did not mind his presence.

"Perhaps two heads are better than one," I suggested.

"Okay," said Captain Murphy.

I sat down on the cognac leather armchair and took a deep breath before beginning my prepared monologue. I then explained to them my dilemma, sharing with them the pros and cons of me attending graduate school versus joining the family business in Saint Petersburg. I acknowledged I was blessed to have two great paths laid before me, and perhaps it was this precise fact that contributed to the difficulty of the decision.

Captain Dan and Captain Barrow listened silently and intently. When I finished speaking, they took a moment to ponder my words. Captain Dan slid his thumb and forefinger along his rigid jawline, mentally formulating what his advice might be. They left me in suspense for a few seconds, but it felt more like ten minutes. I was very anxious to hear what they had to say.

"Well, it seems that your father and brother need you *now*." Captain Murphy looked at me directly in the eyes. "If I were in your shoes, I would go down and work for your father as soon as you get married. Give it two years. Not one year, not eighteen months, but a full two years. At the end of those two years, if you find working in Florida is *not* something you want to do, then you can make an alternate decision at that time. I am most certain you will know by that time. But my advice is to work for your father while he needs you. It sounds like a great opportunity to me."

Captain Barrow nodded in agreement. "Yes, that is great advice," he said. "That is what I would do too. You mentioned that you worked there during the summers in your college days. You were a junior employee then. Now, you will be at more of an executive level. I'm sure it will be a great experience. The opportunity is obvious to me. The opportunity is *now*. And I think you'll know for sure after two years."

I graciously shook their hands in gratitude. "Thank you so much for your advice. I think you both are right. I will take those two years as a trial period. What a superb idea. I appreciate your time and your thoughts."

When I returned to my quarters, I sat at my desk and reflected on my father's words, my brother's letter, and my Captain's advice. I picked up the telephone and called my father.

"I'm in," I told him.

He was ecstatic. "You won't regret this, son."

After concluding our phone call, I pulled a blue ballpoint pen and some loose Navy-embossed stationary out of my desk. I wrote:

Dear Marianne,
I hope you are ready for some Florida sunshine!

I continued the letter sharing how I had come to the decision of accepting the job offer from my father. Marianne and I had discussed the options earlier, and she had voiced that she trusted me and would follow me wherever I went. It gave me great peace of mind knowing that she supported me in whatever I chose.

A few weeks later, my father called me and proposed I take a break from the Navy for about a week's time to bring Marianne to Florida to see Saint Petersburg. He suggested it might help Marianne to visualize what life in Florida might be like. I agreed and immediately requested a leave of absence. At this time, my ship *Bennington* was in the shipyard undergoing extensive repairs. In the meantime, I was assigned on Long Beach shore patrol, which was a similar role to the military police on the beaches. My schedule was a cycling four hours on patrol and eight hours off. Luckily, the head of the weapon's department, who was generally a disagreeable fellow, allowed me to take leave.

Around late April, as planned, I flew directly from Los Angeles to the Tampa Airport and eagerly met Marianne there. We spent a delightful week visiting my parents in Saint Petersburg. We explored two of my father's apartment developments, Carlton Towers and Carlton Arms of Saint Petersburg, which was still under construction. We also took a three-day pleasure excursion to visit some family friends at the exclusive Ocean Reef Resort in Key Largo, Florida. The dazzling sunshine, rich tropical landscape, and brilliant water views could not have been more perfect. It was not difficult for Marianne and I to fall in love with Florida. We were very eager and excited to start our lives there.

With plans in place and hearts full of anticipation and love, we got married in Indianapolis on June 28th, 1969, at Saint Joan of Arc Church. After our honeymoon to Bermuda and several weeks packing, we officially moved to Saint Petersburg in August. Our adventure had officially begun, and we were mentally and emotionally ready for it. Unfortunately, the apartment we were planning to live in was *not* ready. We had reserved an apartment at Carlton Arms of Saint Petersburg, and although it was near completion, it was not set for move-in quite yet. My father graciously offered for us to stay with him in his apartment in the Carlton Towers for a few months, while we waited for ours to be finished.

My mother was spending the summer in Indianapolis, so my father told us he would appreciate our company. We humbly accepted his offer.

Mark and Marianne on their wedding day, 1969

Mark and Marianne on their wedding day, 1969

Mark and Marianne on their wedding day
with Marianne's parents (left) and Mark's parents (right)

*Mark and Marianne on their wedding day
with Marianne's sister, Kathleen (Sister Mary Colleen)*

*St. Joan of Arc Church, Indianapolis, Indiana,
where Mark and Marianne Mahaffey married*

Miss Desautels' Wedding Is Held

Miss Marianne Desautels and Mark Thomas Mahaffey were married yesterday in St. Joan of Arc Catholic Church.

Miss Kathleen Sullivan was maid of honor. James Mahaffey of Maitland, Fla., served as best man.

After the ceremony, a reception was held in Highland Golf and Country Club.

The bride is the daughter of Mr. and Mrs. Leon Edmund Desautels, 4232 Central Avenue. Mr. and Mrs. Thomas Mahaffey Jr., 3830 Rue Voltaire and St. Petersburg, Fla., are parents of the bridegroom.

The new Mrs. Mahaffey was graduated from Ladywood School and attended St. Mary-of-the-Woods C o l l e g e. Her husband was graduated from the University of Notre Dame.

The newlyweds will take a trip to Bermuda. They will live at St. Petersburg.

MRS. MARK THOMAS MAHAFFEY

Newspaper article featuring the wedding of Mark and Marianne Mahaffey, 1969

Beginning our married life in Saint Petersburg, Florida, brought more life experience and growth than we ever could have imagined. For me, it brought back nostalgic memories of the summers I spent living with my father at the Edgewater Beach Motel. From Marianne's perspective, however, I am sure it was not so pleasant for her to spend the first few months of marriage living with, and taking care of two men. She persisted without complaint, nonetheless. Every day, my father and I would go to work, and Marianne would have dinner waiting for us when we returned. Once September came around, my father caught a cold, and my sweet

Marianne selflessly nursed him back to health. She had such a cheery, positive attitude throughout it all, but she could not have been happier when the townhouses at Carlton Arms were finally finished. We moved into one of the townhomes while we waited for our long-term apartment to be completed. As the property development was still underway, we were right in the midst of construction. However, we loved having our own space despite the construction mess around us.

My office, which was also at Carlton Arms of Saint Petersburg, had its own series of moves as well. First, it was in a trailer on the construction site. Then, it was temporarily in an apartment on the first floor. Finally, when the clubhouse was finished, my father and I moved into there. However, neither my father nor my brother had put much thought into the office design. My father positioned himself in the card room in the main clubhouse, as he wanted to be where the action was. I was assigned a very small room in the back—a *shoebox*, I called it. My brother, Jim, did not have to deal with the office space problem. He was currently working at the Winter Park location they had built a few years earlier.

I declared to my brother, "You are lucky I did not see this when you tried to lure me down here! Next property we build, I am going to be the one designing the offices."

He laughed and said, "Go right ahead."

That first year was tough to say the least. My father was the sort of man that threw you into the lions' den to fight your own battles. I'd like to think he would have saved me if I was being devoured, but I had to learn on my own. I admit it was a great way of gaining experience. He believed in me and gave me responsibility that I would have never deemed myself ready for.

The following year was much better. After putting my all into working hard and improving myself, I gained essential business skills and found my niche, so to speak, in the financial department. I also honed my communication skills, which I first learned back waiting tables at the restaurant in northern Michigan. I became more and more comfortable talking to people, especially in the financial strata. Over those two years,

I gained confidence in a business sense, and once I had that confidence, I really started to progress and grow.

One contribution I made to the company pretty early on was the institution of assistant managers. Just how I had trained the Junior Officers of the Deck, the managers would train their assistants, letting the assistants run the show. This structure worked fabulously and led to the development of a core group of well-trained individuals managing the properties. I appreciated my father granting me the freedom to make this change.

When reminiscing on those early years working with my father, I must also pay tribute to another huge contributor to my success—Richard Earle, Jr. He was one of my first mentors I had in Florida. The story goes that Richard Earle Jr. represented the Fitzgerald's, who were the original owners of the land on which Carlton Arms of Saint Petersburg now sits. When my father and brother had negotiated purchasing the land—a few years before I got there—they had been so impressed with Richard Earle Jr.'s knowledge and expertise that they had decided to bring him on as their own real estate attorney. It is incredible to note that over fifty years later, his son, Richard Earle III, is our current real estate attorney. The relationship has been not only longstanding, but consistently valuable to our company.

When I first moved down to Florida, Richard Earle, Jr. took me under his wing. He had a bit of a gruff demeanor, but he was extremely intelligent and very kind. He took a liking to me, and I to him. I can remember clear as day him sitting at his large, cherry-stained wooden desk in his office in downtown Saint Petersburg. He had brilliant, white, combed-back hair, unruly eyebrows, and a perpetual frown drawn onto his face, despite whatever his internal emotion may have been. I regularly enjoyed visiting him as he always had some new advice to offer me. I took it all to heart.

"Mark, you need to get involved in the community," I remember him telling me one day as I was settling into my life in Saint Petersburg.

"Alright. Sure," I said.

"Let me make some calls," he insisted.

About a day or two later, Richard Earle Jr. said, "I've got you on the committee at the Saint Petersburg Chamber of Commerce."

"Wow. Thank you!" I replied.

He had been, at one time, the president of the chamber of commerce, among other committee organizations.

He added, "You are also on the beautification committee. Your first committee meeting is a week from Thursday."

I had never imagined myself participating in community meetings, especially not in my late twenties, but it ended up being a meaningful experience for me. It not only helped me connect to the community of Saint Petersburg, but also led to many other influential relationships. Over time, I realized how much I enjoyed participating on boards. Volunteering my time for the betterment of the community was extremely fulfilling. As suggested by Richard Earle Jr., I later joined the Environment Development Commission (EDC). This commission was a great learning experience for me because I was able to gain the city's perspective on development, as opposed to being the developer. I took the EDC meetings very seriously, passionately participating for ten years, five of which as chairman. Another board I joined was Sabal Trust, where I have served for 20 years and met my good friend, Ward Curtis. I was also on the C&S Bank Board, Suncoasters Board, just to name a few. Each board boosted my growth professionally and socially, allowing me to really learn our city and form strong connections with its people. I thank Richard Earle Jr. for his role in getting me started.

It seemed that every day that I lived in Saint Petersburg, I fell in love with the city more and more. I adored the sunshine and the positive spirits of the people who lived there. Also, having been a sailor, fisherman, and Navy man, I felt an undeniable connection to the ocean there. I remember during those first years, I would walk along the shores of the Tampa Bay pondering its beauty. I would watch the brown pelicans glide in their small groups of three or four, carving their path through the salty air with a focused direction. I felt transported back in time to the Navy port in California. I had admired the pelicans there, and I now realized they seemed to be guiding me along my path in life. The pelicans always looked so graceful, unwavering in flight just above the shimmering waters of the Tampa Bay. I loved their concentration, their teamwork, their strength, and their connection with the sea. I envisioned myself having the spirit of a pelican. I always saw myself as a quiet force, humbly flying with my team, focused on my path and direction. As time went on, I decided to adopt the pelican as my symbol, as it represents a guiding force on my path in life. My brother adopted the Polar Bear as his symbol. It was certainly an interesting pair of symbols for brothers forming a bond for the future.

Carlton Towers, Saint Petersburg, Florida

Florida Brown Pelican, photo credit: Florida Nature Photography

As those two trial years working for my father ended, I was ready to make my decision. I found myself really enjoying working for my father's company in Saint Petersburg. I wanted to be a part of his vision for the future. I developed a burning passion for growing the company, as my father and brother did, and I felt a great deal of pride and personal value handling the company's financial responsibilities. I realized that I did not need to go to graduate school to pave my own way. The Mahaffey Company *was* my path, and there was plenty more pavement to lay there.

One day, after coming home from work to our small, but well-appointed apartment (that was finally completed) I said to Marianne, "I think I'm going to really like this."

She sighed in relief. "Thank God. I don't know if I could handle another move." She smiled and leapt into my arms. Saint Petersburg was officially our home sweet home.

This commitment to make Saint Petersburg home was one of the best decisions I had ever made. I reflected on the advice that Captain Murphy gave me two years before. His wisdom granted me the time to learn for myself that my path continued in Florida, and graduate school was not what I really wanted. Only time could teach me that. I remember wondering whether I would ever see Captain Murphy again. He had made such an impact on my life, and I pondered if he ever knew how much his guidance influenced me. It turned out that years later, I would finally get my opportunity to tell him how much he meant to me.

After I had left the Navy, Captain Murphy ended up advancing to the position of a Four-Star Admiral, which was a huge honor for him. I believe he was the first person in Naval history to get his fourth star despite not attending the Naval Academy. It was not until 1977 that he retired from active service. In the early 1980s, he left retirement to become Chief of Staff for Vice President George W. Bush during Ronald Reagan's administration. It was during this time that Captain Murphy and I reconnected.

The year was 1983. It had been almost fifteen years since I had seen Captain Murphy, or rather, Admiral Murphy, as was his title now. At this time, he resided in Washington D.C. and worked in the Old Executive Office Building adjacent to the White House. My own life had changed drastically since those old Navy days. Namely, I now had my beautiful wife, Marianne, with whom I shared my life. She and I were accompanying my father and mother on a trip to Washington D.C. My father, being a fundraiser for Ronald Reagan in Florida, had been invited to a grand White House fundraiser dinner. He was kind enough to reserve a large table for me and my wife, my brother and his wife, and my two sisters.

During all those years, I had kept a continual close friendship with my fellow shipmate, Steve Bettcher. He had recently spent some time in Washington D.C. and told me, "Mark, you've got to go see Admiral Murphy while you are in town. I just saw him, and it was incredible. He is still that great Captain we always loved, and it brought back so many great memories."

I said, "Well, gee, Steve. I'd love to see him! How do I connect with him?"

"I'll get you his secretary's phone number."

"Thanks, Steve!"

About two weeks before our scheduled trip, I gave Admiral Murphy's secretary a call. I explained to her that I was an old shipmate from a carrier that the Admiral had captained. I was not sure if it was possible, but I asked her if my wife and I would be able to see Admiral Murphy while we were in town. I was ecstatic to get an appointment with him that Friday at 1:00pm. That day could not come soon enough.

In the days preceding the visit, I reflected on our days on *Bennington*. I thought about all those long watches on the bridge, the drills and shooting exercises, and the tour to Vietnam during the war. I also thought about all the fun moments we had. I laughed to myself as I thought about Captain Murphy in those orange swimming trunks speeding off to meet the Admiral. I also remembered all that he taught me—from leadership skills and strong work ethic to the importance of kindness and respect for all people. I contemplated how far he had advanced in his career, how many people he must have inspired, and how grateful I was to be a part of his life. I truly idolized him. Perhaps I had put him on a pedestal, but I was getting myself nervous to see him.

Finally, the day arrived. Marianne and I had a lovely lunch at the Jockey Club, just north of the White House, before heading to meet him. Marianne attempted to calm my nerves, but the anticipation was overwhelming. We entered the Old Executive Office Building and went through the standard security checks.

They told us, "Just go down this hallway. Admiral Murphy's office is right next to Mr. Bush's office."

Beautiful, intricate wood-paneling covered the walls. I pinched myself. Was this really happening? Following the long hallway, we finally entered into the secretary's lobby. We saw a secretary with Admiral Murphy's name on her desk. We also noticed many others waiting to see him.

"Oh, God," I whispered to Marianne. "This could be a while."

After we introduced ourselves, the secretary jumped out of her seat to tell the Admiral we were there. Upon returning to the lobby, she said to us, "The Admiral will be out in a few minutes."

Well, it was not more than a few seconds later when Admiral Murphy swung open the double doors to his office. He was as suave as ever, still reminding me of Cary Grant, with his slicked silver hair, tanned skin, and great looking suit and red tie.

"Mark!" he exclaimed. He walked over to Marianne and me and hugged us.

"Come on, come on. Come back into my office," he said. He looked at his secretary and said, "Hold the calls. I'm with an old shipmate."

He spent an hour and twenty minutes with us. The steward came in and served us tea. We just talked and talked. All nervousness faded as we reconnected. I said, "Admiral, I've got to tell you. I really appreciate you seeing Marianne and me. It really gives me the opportunity to tell you how much you meant to me. And how much you taught me when I served under you. I'm so grateful to be sitting here right now and to be able to tell you that."

Admiral Murphy responded, "Mark, thank you. But hold that right there. I'd like to tell you how much you meant to me. You and those other three guys. You made my life easy. You worked hard. You kept me attuned. It was fun serving with you guys. And you kept me out of hot water a few times. Don't you think I've ever forgotten."

Tears welled up in my eyes. His words touched my heart. I had spent all this time looking up to him. I had no idea I meant as much to him as he meant to me. We continued to talk about some memories from the Navy days and all that we had done since. Toward the end of the visit, I reservedly said, "I hope you don't mind, but I've got a favor to ask you."

"Sure. What is it?"

I said, "Well, you know we are here for the Reagan dinner on Saturday night, but my parents are also going to a private reception tonight at the White House. Is there any way you could pull some strings so that we could tag along with them? What a thrill that would be!"

He said, "Well, let me see what I can do."

"Thank you, sir," I said.

The visit ended and we said our farewells. Steve was right—it was incredible seeing Admiral Murphy again. Even if we did not make it into the reception, the trip to Washington D.C. would have been worth it just for that visit. About an hour and a half later, as Marianne and I lounged in our hotel room, I received a call from the Admiral's secretary.

"Hang on for Admiral Murphy," she said.

Admiral Murphy came on the line and said, "Good news, Mark. I got you and Marianne into the reception. They know you are coming. Just go with your parents to the White House at the prescribed time.

"Wow! That is fabulous. Thank you so much!" I cried.

After hanging up the phone, I immediately called my father to tell him the news. Upon hearing it, however, he seemed to be wincing on the phone.

"Um, well, son. Do you think you could get your brother and his wife in as well?"

I said, "God, I don't know. I thought I was already asking a lot."

"Well, he can say no," my father said. He had a point.

"All right, I'll try," I agreed.

I called the secretary back and said, "Is there any chance I could speak to Admiral Murphy again?"

She said, "Sure. Hang on. I think he can take your call."

The Admiral got on the phone and said, "Yes, Mark, what is it?"

"Well, I've got another favor to ask you." I explained, "Blame this on my dad. My brother is here with his wife. Is there any way you can somehow get them into the White House reception as well?"

"You are pushing it," he grumbled.

"I know. I apologize. If you can't do it, I understand," I said kindly.

He said, "I'll call you back."

About an hour later, he called me back. "They are in, Mark. And I'm just warning you, do not call me back," he said good-naturedly.

"Thank you so much!" I told him.

As promised, we all went and met the President at the White House. It was such a treat. Looking back, I think those other Officers were probably right. I did seem to get away with a lot more with Captain Murphy, perhaps more than anyone else would even dare to ask. Perhaps it was the confidence that Captain Murphy himself instilled in me that allowed me to make that request. He never made me feel like a subordinate. He treated me like a fellow human being and empowered me to pave my own path. I am forever grateful to him for that.

About twenty years later, I decided to look up the Admiral again. I searched his name on the internet and learned his son of the same name proceeded to be a three-star Admiral. What a rarity to have two high echelon Admirals in one family. Searching the internet further, I was desolated to see that my beloved Captain had passed away September of 2001. I immediately called Steve Bettcher, Bill Jones, and Lou Raisler to tell them the sad news. None of them had known either. If any of us had, we would have certainly gone to the funeral in honor of his monumental life and legacy.

Steve Bettcher's response to the news matched all our feelings perfectly. "It is like you are skiing, and you are missing one of the mountains," he said.

I agreed.

Mark and Marianne with Admiral Murphy at the White House, 1983

7

HOW THE BUSINESS BEGAN

History may not repeat itself, but it does rhyme.

Mark Twain

Back in the early 1970s, after I made the decision to stay in Saint Petersburg, I came to the realization that now, my personal success was aligned with the performance of my family's business. With that in mind I felt compelled to learn about its history. My grandfather, my father, and my uncle had paved the beginning of the family's road of financial achievements, and I deemed it my turn to keep it going. Once I acquired knowledge of its roots, it helped me to better understand my role and where I fit into the story. Because of my predecessors' smart decisions, long hours of dedicated work, and determination to learn from their mistakes, they pushed the company forward despite the odds. My father, over time, developed a core business philosophy and principles that we still follow today.

Most of my family's business history was shared with me by my father years ago, and I feel blessed to still remember a great deal of it today. I was also able to find many historical newspaper articles that offered clues to help me paint the picture of what my family's development in business looked like over the years. This discovery of the past was a journey in itself—a quest I recommend everyone embarking on of their own past if they have the opportunity.

I think Matthew McConaughey couldn't have said it better in the 2014 Lincoln advertisement. *"Sometimes you've got to go back to actually move forward. And I don't mean going back to reminisce or chase ghosts. I mean going back to see where you came from, where you've been, how you got here and to see where you're going."*

It is such a simple sentiment with a powerful message. For myself, looking back at how the business began broadened my perspective of the company's growth trajectory and gave me insight into the strategies employed to achieve the success we have today. It gave me contextual knowledge of where we stand today relative to our company's past, as well as an understanding of the economic influences involved along the way. I share this history with you, the reader, in hopes that you perhaps learn a little something, like I did. I also hope to inspire you to never forget where you came from and the people that put the foundations beneath your feet. Here is my family's story:

Let's take a journey back in time to July 1, 1923. On this date, my paternal grandfather, Thomas Mahaffey Sr., founded the Consolidated Finance Corporation in Indianapolis, Indiana. This was the same Thomas Mahaffey who was married to my Grandmother Kate and ran the Indiana Brewing Company in his younger years. After the brewing company closed due to the prohibition, he gradually rose to become the Vice President of the Marion National Bank, director of the South Marion State Bank, and president of the Rutenber Electric Company of Marion. After moving to Indianapolis with his wife and two sons—Fred and Tom (my father)—my grandfather started this new finance company. With an authorized $300,000 in capital, the Consolidated Finance Corporation financed car loans, as well as other household loans, to the general public and car dealerships.

I have no doubt my grandfather began the company with a great deal of research and calculated strategy. The Consolidated Finance office was first positioned on the tenth floor of the Consolidated Building on North Pennsylvania Street. The building was situated in the heart of the business district in downtown Indianapolis—a wonderful location in a bustling city. The Consolidated Building, originally called the Lemcke Annex, was a 15-story office tower boasting beautiful, elaborate stone details and brickwork on its exterior. It was built in 1909 and housed many financial offices, as well as a Vaudeville theater and street level shops.

The Consolidated Building (originally called the Lemcke Annex Building), 1920s

Not only was the building in a prime location in downtown Indianapolis, but there was also a plethora of car dealerships in the surrounding area, flooding with potential customers needing financing. Most notable was the Foxworthy Ford dealership positioned a half-mile to the north on the famed Meridian Street. This dealership was booming with success in the mid-1920s. It was not only the largest Ford dealership in Indiana, but it was also the top performing dealership in the entire United States by vehicle sales! My grandfather was very smart positioning his finance company in close proximity to this powerhouse of a dealership, as well as many others, and forming lasting business relationships with each of them.

My grandfather, as president of the company, first appointed my Uncle Fred as secretary-treasurer. My father, Thomas Mahaffey Jr., being much younger than my Uncle Fred, joined their venture about ten years later, after he graduated with a finance degree from the University of Notre Dame. In preparation for my father joining the company, my grandfather moved the office down to the eighth floor of the building— a move, I assume, that was motivated by a need for more space.

Despite the fog of the Great Depression clouding most of the United States into crisis, my grandfather was able to stay in business. I wish he were here today for me to ask him how he did it, but I can surmise that he used his past experience in banking and finance to stay afloat. My father and uncle always said they learned a great deal from him.

Sadly, my grandfather passed away in 1936 at the age of 72. My Uncle Fred advanced to president of Consolidated Finance, and my father became the secretary-treasurer. My Uncle Fred, with a great deal of experience, and my father, whom I consider a financial genius, continued heading the company and quickly gained a solid reputation in the community. Their complementing personalities worked well together. My father was the lion—aggressive, driven, and demanding. My uncle was the lamb—kind, encouraging, and a supportive leader. Together, they pushed the company forward and rode the wave out of the Great Depression into a flourishing economic era. It is interesting to note that between 1933 and 1937, America's money supply increased by forty-two percent, causing a rise in inflation. This encouraged spending and borrowing as interest rates were lowered, and credit was easier to obtain. For the Consolidated Finance Corporation, these were certainly powerful tailwinds helping to propel the business forward by the latter part of the 1930s.

In 1939, with the business doing so well, my father and uncle could afford to relocate offices from the eighth floor down to the ground floor of the Consolidated Building. This move included the lease of basement space, which contained a safety deposit and other fireproof vaults. Most importantly, it allowed for direct, street access from the Consolidated Building's main lobby. As the building housed a Vaudeville theater, the lobby was radiating with activity and life. Ornate, colorful tiles and slabs of marble covered the walls and ceilings. With the people coming in and going out for shows and shopping, it gave the Consolidated Finance office great visibility. My father, especially, was thrilled with the move because he always craved to be in the middle of the action.

Consolidated Finance Co. advertisement in The Indianapolis News, September 18, 1941

There is a story my father used to share about those early days. It takes place right after their move to the ground floor. One day, a middle-aged man walked into the main lobby of the Consolidated Building, took a sharp turn to the right, and opened the large door that led to the Consolidated Finance office. He approached a secretary who was keying words into a typewriter at the front reception desk. I imagine him first making an entrance wearing an ill-fitted suit with a fedora and cane. He was very tall and lean with jet-black hair, and he sported a stately black mustache to match. His demeanor, filled with purpose and determination, enticed the secretary to slip her eyeglasses down her nose and eye him inquisitively.

He approached the desk and smiled politely at the secretary. He confidently, yet kindly, greeted her, "Hello, madam. How are you this lovely afternoon?"

The secretary returned his smile and folded her hands into her lap to give him her full attention. She responded, "I am doing very well. How can I help you?"

"I apologize for coming in here without an appointment. My name is George Walker. I am not looking for a car loan. But, I have heard of Tom Mahaffey's great reputation and I desire to meet him, if he is available."

The secretary politely told the man, "One moment, please."

She scurried into my father's private office. "Mr. Mahaffey, there is someone here by the name of George Walker. He wants to meet you, *specifically* you."

"Send him on in," my father responded.

My father looked up as he observed George enter his office. The tall man walked straight in and sat down assertively in my father's guest chair. George spoke with resolve, "Mr. Mahaffey, I've heard about you and your reputation, and I want to come work for you. I would like to be your mentee. I will work hard, and I will work for free until I prove myself."

My father smiled in response to George's praise and show of determination. "Well, George, number one, you're hired." He slapped his hand firmly on his desk. "Number two, you are *not* going to work for free!"

George was ever so grateful. He did not have the experience, but he was willing to put in the effort. "Thank you, Mr. Mahaffey. You won't regret it."

It turned out that George Walker proved to be an extremely valuable asset to the company. My father was a tough mentor, but he taught George a great deal about finance and made a positive impact on George's life. My father trusted George with a wealth of responsibility from the beginning. George worked very hard and elevated himself with each new challenge. If something needed to be done that nobody wanted to do, or if a job was a tad uncomfortable, my father would say, "George, go handle that." George always got the job done.

There is one story in particular that my father would tell over and over. Back then, vehicle finance companies were very strict. When a client failed to make their payments on time, the company would unapologetically repossess their vehicle. Sometimes, it was done by merely knocking on the borrower's front door and saying, "Sir, you have not made your payments. We must take your car." However, it was not unusual for people to try to dodge the bullet. They would not answer the door and would hide. In that case, the company would repossess the vehicle in the shroud of night.

One day, disastrously, an employee of Consolidated Finance went out and repossessed the *wrong* car from the *wrong* house. The unsuspecting Mr. Jones was the victim of this unfortunate event. I am sure one can imagine how irate this Mr. Jones was when he woke up the next morning to find his car missing for no apparent reason. He had no loan through Consolidated Finance at all. Mr. Jones was furious and threatened to sue. Without hesitation, my father knew just what to do.

"George Walker, I've got something for you," my father invoked.

"What can I do for you, Tom?"

My father described the situation to George, adding, "I want you to go see if you can straighten it out with Mr. Jones. Do whatever you have to do, George, but please make this mess go away."

George accepted the challenge saying, "You've got it."

After three weeks of quiet and concord, Mr. Jones made a surprise visit to the Consolidated Finance office. He stated firmly to the secretary upon entering, "I want to buy a new car, and I will not do business with anybody but George Walker!"

My father was extremely impressed. George Walker was just that way. He not only straightened out the sticky situation, but also, made a life-long customer in the process. George had a kind heart and quickly became one of my father's best friends, and eventually, Vice President of the company. I always regarded him as second father figure as well. I remember him driving me to summer camp in Michigan a few times when I was in middle school. There are few people you meet in life that are truly golden souls and genuinely good people. George Walker was most certainly one of them.

My father appreciated his employees and the dealerships he worked with, and he was very loyal to them. To show his appreciation, every year in early June, he would take them up to Burt Lake, Michigan, to host what he called a *stag party*. This stag party was essentially a week-long getaway for men only, in two adjacent cottages on Burt Lake. The cottages would sleep about 10-15 men, who would cycle in and out throughout the week. They would spend their time boating, fishing, playing cards, eating, drinking and so forth. I am sure these trips were the ideal setting to build comradery and strengthen business relationships—especially amongst the network of car dealers that helped the company flourish.

Part of the family lore, there is a funny story involving one of these stag parties. One year, my father hired two men as kitchen help to prepare meals for the guests during their stay at the cottages. In the kitchen, my father stored buckets of frogs and worms, which the men would use as fishing bait. They nicknamed the frogs, "dem boys," and the worms, "dem girls." Well, due to the abundance of drinking and merry-making, one night, the lid was not secured on the bucket of frogs. The head cook, Luther, sauntered into the kitchen on that bright sunny morning to find frogs hopping all over the place! Luther was bewildered as he observed the situation. Seeing the open bucket, he yelled out, waking my sleeping father, "Mr. Tom, Mr. Tom! Dem boys are loose! Dem Boys are loose! They are all over the place!" My father laughed about that memory for years.

In 1948, my father got involved in a side gig—an apartment deal with some friends. This was the beginning of his career in real estate development. It was a large, 650-unit apartment complex called Meadowbrook Apartments. My father was one of the investors. Being the financial whiz that he was, he ended up becoming managing partner early in the process. He and a fellow partner, Tom O'Brien, gradually bought out all the other partners over the years. Tom O'Brien happened to be a very successful car dealer as well. I imagine he and my father had much in common and most likely had done business together before.

As for Consolidated Finance, in the early 1960s, finance companies were beginning to become a thing of the past. Instead of banks offering loans to finance companies, who would then route the money to borrowers, banks began to offer loans directly to the borrowers. My father and uncle must have seen the writing on the wall because they sold out Consolidated Finance Corporation to American Security Corporation in 1962. My uncle and George Walker chose to retire at this time, as they were nearing 70 years old.

My father, however, not only would never retire, but would never lose his drive for personal growth. He had a constant passion for business development. I admire his ability to recognize that the world was changing and his courage to hang out a new shingle despite his age. He was not afraid to keep what worked and move on from what did not. When Consolidated Finance was sold, it was time for my father to start a new venture. Having the experience of running Meadowbrook Apartments in hand, he formed a vision of going into the apartment development business full-time.

That winter, when my father and my mother were on their yearly vacation in sunny Florida, my father had an epiphany. He resolved that Florida would be the perfect place to start a rental apartment business. He was 52-years-old at the time, but that did not stop him from making a huge life change. He started the property search immediately. He focused his attention on the western coast of Florida. The eastern coast primarily consisted of *closed shops*, where employers were required to hire union contractors and union labor. My father did not want any part of that. He liked the freedom of *open shops*, where union labor was not required. In general, the western coast of Florida presented less constraints to the developer.

It did not take him long to find the perfect property located in Saint Petersburg, Florida. It was a vacant piece of land in the heart of downtown, just a block from the glimmering waters of Tampa Bay. The original owner of the land was prepared to build apartments, but could not secure the financing. Luckily for my father, they had construction plans already drawn and a contractor in place. My father just needed to find the financing, which was his expertise. That same year he sold Consolidated Finance, in 1962, he formally opened the business M&M Management and formed a limited partnership. Securing an FHA loan, he bought the land and the plans, and christened the development Carlton Towers.

M&M Management stood for Mahaffey and Mahaffey Management. This included my brother, Jim, who chose to move to Florida at this time as well. Jim had worked for my father at Consolidated Finance in Indianapolis, so it was an easy decision for him to follow my father in his next venture. My mother, on the other hand, was very reluctant to make such a big life change. She had spent her entire life in Indiana and had a very established social circle in Indianapolis. She must have loved my father though, because she came with him, even if it were kicking and screaming. I always respected her for trusting my father and making the move.

To ease the transition, my father rented an apartment for my mother in Indianapolis to allow her to go back and forth as she pleased. I am sure she appreciated that. It was during the summers in those early years that I went down to work during my summer break from college. I had stayed with my father while my mother was in Indianapolis. It wasn't too long before my mother came down permanently and gradually developed a social group in Saint Petersburg. Moving south ended up being a crucial and necessary decision for the whole family.

My father not only packed up his life, his belongings, and his family to move to Florida, but he also brought with him a wealth of knowledge that he had attained from his business experiences in Indianapolis. Beyond the positive business strategies he learned, he also would tell me how he benefitted the most from learning from his mistakes.

My father would say, "I did everything wrong with Meadowbrook Apartments." His first mistake he admitted was when he and Tom O'Brien bought out the apartment complex. They had started a corporation, of which they were owners. Unfortunately, he learned quickly that he was taxed twice under that entity structure. He got taxed as a corporation and taxed personally. When establishing himself in Florida, he avoided that mishap and structured his deals as partnerships.

Another mistake he learned from was the use of performance bonds. On paper, a performance bond sounds like a great safety net. It was a contractual guarantee that the contractor would perform and follow all the terms agreed upon. Unfortunately, my father learned when managing Meadowbrook Apartments that when the contractor did not perform, it was very difficult to collect any kind of insurance. The whole thing ended up being expensive and a giant headache. Moving forward, he never again had a performance bond in his career. It was his rule. If the lender happened to require it, he would find a new lender.

Now that my father's focus was on this new venture, he and Tom O'Brien sold the Meadowbrook Apartments in Indianapolis around 1965. It was bought by a firm owned by billionaire Harry Helmsley, who was a New York financier and developer, and one of the wealthiest men in the world. At that time, Harry Helmsley's firm, Helmsley-Spear, Inc., was the largest real estate management and brokerage company in the country. The company owned much of the cream of New York real estate, including the Empire State Building.

Harry Helmsley, President of Helmsley-Spear, Inc.

My father loved to tell the story of the day he closed the deal with Harry Helmsley in New York. He boasted how he and Harry Helmsley, both being financial whizzes, hit it off right away. After the sale was completed, Harry Helmsley, in his iconic thick-rimmed black glasses and signature mustache, asked my father, "What are you up to nowadays, Tom?"

My father replied, "Well, I am down in Florida, in Saint Petersburg. I finished a high rise down there called Carlton Towers, and we are looking to build a property in Winter Park next."

Harry Helmsley was familiar with the general area where Winter Park was located. He had a strong interest in real estate acquisition and prompted my father for more details.

"Well, tell me more about it," he inquired, raising his rather bushy, gray eyebrows.

My father described to Harry Helmsley the deal he was considering. It was a small property, but a big opportunity for my father's business.

Harry Helmsley said, "Well, what is holding you back from committing?"

My father answered, "I'm looking for a financial partner. My son and I don't have enough liquidity, and we need to put some money into this. We have the financing lined up, but we need cash." My father continued to explain the details of the deal.

After listening intently, Harry Helmsley looked at my father and shook his hand saying, "Tom, you have just found your financial partner."

My father was very proud of that connection. Harry Helmsley not only became fifty percent partner in the Carlton Arms of Winter Park deal, but also in the Carlton Arms of Saint Petersburg deal a few years later. Mr. Helmsley provided the upfront money for both transactions. Those two contributions certainly got the M&M Management Company off the ground. It was also for these two properties that my father began using the term *arms* in naming his apartments. The word *arms,* as a denotation for apartments, dates back to old English Inns, which used to hang the coat of arms of the local nobility above their front entrance. *Arms* signified prestige, and in America, it became adopted as a term for luxurious apartments. It was a simple, yet very effective, marketing tool.

That first partnership with Harry Helmsley inspired my father to make financial partnerships one of his core principles in his ever-evolving business philosophy. He was very deliberate when selecting his partners, always choosing established, experienced, and trust-worthy businessmen with solid reputations. These high-status individuals, often renowned throughout business, financial, and real estate circles, provided us with invaluable acumen throughout the entire process. Maintaining those relationships was imperative to growing the apartment community portfolio. My father never failed to pay ample tribute to our financial partners, who were the bulwark of Mahaffey's success as an organization.

In August of 1969, I arrived on the scene, when Carlton Arms of Saint Petersburg was just being built. Since I had come aboard, my father, brother, and I changed the name of M&M Management to The Mahaffey Company, and later again to The Mahaffey Apartment Company. Now being a father-and-two-sons business, it had the capacity to handle the development of additional properties.

Becoming part of my family's story of business success was a real honor. I am sure my father saw a bit of history repeating itself, with the next generation continuing the tradition of a father and sons' business. I see myself in my father's shoes as the younger son joining the venture a bit late in the game, as opposed to my brother. However, that did not stop us from taking charge and pushing the company toward success. At the time, I enjoyed learning about how the business began, but only now, years later looking back, do I see that the business history was still in the making.

8

COQUINA KEY

Experience is the hardest kind of teacher. It gives you the test first, and the lesson afterward.

Oscar Wilde

My journey at the Mahaffey Apartment Company may have begun as a hesitant effort to help my father and brother, but it wound up being one of the best decisions I ever made. Over 50 years later, the Mahaffey Apartment Company is going strong, and I look back at all that we accomplished and all that I learned along the way. My father was correct—I am sure I learned more in those first 90 days than I would have learned in two years of graduate school. Nothing tops the education that you receive working in the real world with real problems and real people. My father trusted me with a steep increase of responsibility, and I worked hard to meet his expectations. I pushed my own limits of what I thought I could accomplish. I made mistakes just like anyone else, and I hit a whole series of obstacles that popped up in my path. What kept me moving was keeping the goal in focus and getting help when I needed it.

As the Mahaffey Apartment Company expanded, my role became more focused. My first big responsibility was the development and management of a property we built in the early 1970s—Coquina Key Arms. It all began when our broker at the time, Bill Davis, presented us with an opportunity to build right on the shores of Tampa Bay. He had found a piece of raw, vacant land on the southern tip of Coquina Key, which is an island in south Saint Petersburg. *Key* is another word for island. Unfortunately, the island had a bit of a despondent history. Most of Coquina Key was developed with small, single-family dwellings, financed under FHA or VA insured loans. With the deflation of the 1950s' Florida boom bubble, 145 of the homes met foreclosure. Coquina Key was becoming a ghost town. It certainly gave the island a bad look, but my father had faith that it would recover. "Waterfront is waterfront," he would say.

I wholeheartedly agree with my father that there is a great deal of value in waterfront development. Waterfront living was, and still is, a key ingredient in the properties built by the Mahaffey Apartment Company. For almost all our properties, we either build adjacent to a natural water source or create man-made lakes ourselves. This waterfront element preserves the property's value over the years. Further, it is our theory that residents tend to stay longer due to the unique and superbly attractive environment that the water gives. The water holds a beauty that offers the inhabitants of its shores a feeling of spaciousness and freedom. With the new Coquina Key potential development, we thought to ourselves, *What better location than the Tampa Bay waterfront itself?*

Coquina Key Arms, Saint Petersburg, Florida

Pleasingly, we discovered the property's shoreline had been prepped and canalled, and it was ready for development. Oddly enough, the stretches of land in between the canals made the shape of the letters *TM*, which were my father's initials. Destiny, perhaps? We knew we wanted it—we just had to get the financials in order, which was my responsibility.

The original owner of the land was the Hardaway Company, which was a large, long-standing southern Georgia construction company. They built all manner of large infrastructure, such as nuclear power plants, hydro-electric dams, and bridges. They built the original Sunshine Skyway Bridge in 1954, which has since fallen as a result of a collision from a large freighter and was rebuilt in 1987. During World War II, the Hardaway Company built giant air docks, air stations, and training camps. It had certainly made its stamp on the South.

The Hardaway Company may have owned the land on Coquina Key, but they did not have plans to develop it. They had acquired it, along with several other properties, as part of a partnership. When they decided to unwind the partnership and split the holdings, the Hardaway Company walked away with the land on Coquina Key as part of the deal.

However, their focus was on other projects, and the Coquina Key land was just sitting, not even listed for sale. Bill Davis, the realtor, was good friends with the Hardaway family, as well as the Mahaffey family. Bill Davis decided to play marriage broker and put the two families together.

I will never forget our first meeting with the Hardaway Company. We scheduled its location at our community clubhouse at Carlton Arms of Saint Petersburg. Holding the meeting at one of our properties was by design, of course, as we wanted to give the Hardaway Company a glimpse at what we were proposing to build on Coquina Key.

As the clubhouse did not have a designated conference room, we sat in armchairs in the lounge area of the main room. Ben Hardaway III, president of the Hardaway Company, brought with him three very qualified and educated men—his accountant, his assistant and his attorney. He had chosen these three very bright individuals to assist him in determining the pros and cons of the deal. I commend Ben Hardaway for bringing his best men to the meeting. He was smart enough to surround himself with good people, which to me, is the definition of a good manager.

My father and my brother were also in attendance at the meeting, but it was my job to present the deal. At this time, I had only been working for the company for two years, and was only 27 years old. These men I was presenting to were not only my seniors by at least 30 years, but they also had much more extensive experience and financial expertise than I did.

My father must have had faith in me. He told me, "This development is going to be yours. You are playing in the big league now, and it is your responsibility to head this meeting." He assigned me the task of putting together a financial package and presenting it to these men. This was certainly an example of my father throwing me into the lions' den, but I knew he watched over me. I was not going to let him down.

Ben Hardaway III, President of The Hardaway Company

My plan was to propose to the Hardaway Company the idea of a partnership. If they contributed the upfront money and the raw land, we would give them fifty percent ownership. During the meeting, I explained to them the win-win potential. I remember my heart practically beating out of my chest, but I had to maintain a competent demeanor to have any hope of persuading them of my proposal.

I fanned my spreadsheets and charts onto the coffee table and explained, "Mr. Hardaway, this will be a great deal for you and your company. You have the land and the financial connections. We have the apartment development and property management expertise. Partnered with us, you will soon begin to see a great return on your investments. It will take some time to get the properties constructed, stabilized and an income stream flowing, but even in that time, there are benefits to be had. You see, the IRS would allow us, for economic justification, to assign our fifty percent depreciation loss to a Hardaway partnership interest. You can use that as a tax benefit by applying it to your other holdings."

Ben Hardaway III slowly leaned forward and looked closely at the detailed charts. His three companions followed suit. We spent the next few hours intensely discussing the details. Their attorney knew the tax laws very well, and we dove deep into the specifics. They asked a great deal of questions that I answered to the best of my ability. My father and Jim sat there quietly, giving me the role of concertmaster.

Ben Hardaway III finally leaned back in his chair. He nodded his head slowly up and down as he looked toward his attorney, assistant, and accountant, one by one. He then turned his head to me and uttered in his thick, southern drawl, "Sounds to me like I'm going to have some more spending money." I remember clearly those were the exact words he used. "I like this deal," he happily continued. "We'll work on this, put together a plan, and get the attorneys on both sides connected. Let's do this!"

And we did it. That initial presentation I gave was a great personal learning experience for me. I must credit my father and my brother for not only giving me plenty of initial guidance, but also being great role models. They taught me three important things when making a deal. First, be prepared. Second, do not sugarcoat the details and always tell the truth. And lastly, if you can find a commonality among you, you can make a deal. That wisdom has served me well throughout the years.

Soon afterwards, I had another opportunity to practice this advice. I had to prepare and deliver a big presentation to our lender, Travelers Insurance Company. Walter Carpenter, top dog at Travelers, and his assistant, Jack Bond, were in attendance at the meeting. They had first been introduced to us by a friend of my father's, named John Hancock, believe it or not. John Hancock was a mortgage broker and one of my father's best friends. Similar to my presentation to the Hardaway Company, the four of us met in the clubhouse lounge area. In attendance were Walter Carpenter, Jack Bond, my father and me. I created a series of detailed presentations outlining our company's current financials, as well as future projections.

Evidently, after my meeting with Walter Carpenter and Jack Bond, they related to John Hancock, who then related to my father, who then finally related to me, how impressed they were with the young Mark Mahaffey. They said, "Tom, we must complement the young Mahaffey on his presentations. In our line of business, we are on the receiving end of many presentations. Today, were just wowed by Mark's professionalism and knowledge of finance. He has the composure of someone well beyond his years. We predict he will prove to be a very valuable member of the Mahaffey team for years to come."

These words meant a great deal to me, as praise was a rare delicacy in the Mahaffey office. My father was not one to freely hand out words of affirmation. His philosophy was that as a family member, you had to work hard—harder than anybody else. It was expected, not congratulated. When I heard those few words of praise from the executives at Travelers Insurance Company, it gave me a big boost, and undoubtedly increased my confidence even more moving forward. That bit of encouragement gave me the motivation I needed to overcome the trials we had ahead, as developing Coquina Key Arms was no walk in the park.

Coquina Key Arms was a huge learning experience for me in more ways than one. The biggest hurdle we had to overcome was zoning. The land was zoned for single-family residences, and the City of Saint Petersburg was very reluctant to rezone to allow apartment permits. We decided to get the current residents of Coquina Key on board by promoting our development and getting a petition signed. The overall positive advocacy we received from the community was overwhelming. The City of Saint Petersburg granted our request to rezone when they saw that 600 of the 749 residents signed the petition in support of our plan. We constructed the community in two phases. Phase one, consisting of 344 units, was finished in 1972 and phase two, consisting of 354 units, was finished in 1974.

The Coquina Key Arms development ended up being such a success that we made a second deal with the Hardaway Company and built a third phase in 1979. We partnered with them to develop apartments one mile up the street on the northern side of Coquina Key, calling the complex Coquina Key Arms North. We ran the two developments, north and south, as one community, sharing one management team. The total unit count between both locations reached 1,006.

The Mahaffey-Hardaway marriage has been a solid partnership over the years based on loyalty, teamwork, and honesty. We have maintained that partnership with the Hardaway Company to this day, partnering with them on several other deals since then, including a development in New Port Richey, Florida. Ben Hardaway III has since passed on, but his son-in-law, Mason Lampton, now has the reins and has proven to be a valued partner and close friend.

Coquina Key Arms was my first big project that I was involved in all aspects from the beginning to the end. Remembering my promise to my brother, the first thing I wanted to do when designing the complex was to make a better office space for the management team. I was done with *the shoebox* that my father and brother designed at the Carlton Arms of Saint Petersburg property. At Coquina Key, I created several private offices that opened to a larger general office area that contained four desks. The receptionist, property manager and assistants worked in the larger area, which we ended up nicknaming *the bullpen*, while my father and I worked in the private offices. I positioned an exit door near my office, anticipating it being the perfect escape hatch for myself to come and go as I please without walking through the whole office space. For a time, this office layout worked well.

Unfortunately, the addition of the exit door by my office ended up being a big mistake. It was a very busy office. The laundry building was right outside that exit door, and the staff was continually walking in and out right by my office. It was such an annoyance having Grand Central Station whizzing by as I was trying to compute numbers and manage the company's finances. All I needed was some peace and quiet.

When it came time to design the clubhouse for Coquina Key North, I was determined to draw up something better and move my office to that new location, a mile up the road. I will never forget the day I brought my proposed clubhouse floor plan to my father. Perhaps there was a more diplomatic way to present it to him, but then again, perhaps the most direct way is sometimes the best.

Clutching the rolled-up blueprints of my clubhouse design, I remember tapping on my father's office door. I peered inside and observed him sitting at his desk reading over some sort of paperwork.

"Do you have a moment?" I inquired.

"Um, yes, Mark. What it is?" He asked rather annoyed at the disturbance.

"I have finished the design for the new clubhouse."

"Alright. Let's see it," he replied as he set down the paper he was reading.

I walked over to his desk and unrolled the large, thin sheet. "Well, here's the plan," I said. "We have a large double door at the front. Over here, we have a guest suite—with a kitchen, living room, and two bedrooms. I think this would be a great place for residents to rent if they have guests in town. We can make it more affordable than a hotel room. One of the bedrooms can be closed off as a separate unit if needed. And then here—," I said, pointing in the center of the building, "—we have the main party room and bar area. It opens up to the pool in the back."

My father studied the page carefully and was paying close attention. I was delaying my point, but it was time for me to bring up the office layout. "And then over here, we have the offices. There is an office lobby with two private offices adjacent." Pointing at one of the private offices, I stated firmly, "This is where I'm moving my office."

"What!?" My father was surprised. It was the first he had ever heard of it. Reflecting on our conversation, I suppose that perhaps I should have eased him into the idea, explaining my reasons for moving first. Hearing it abruptly, I believe he took it as a personal affront, which was really not my intention.

He simply and firmly said, "No. You are not moving."

Due to his abrupt rejection of my proposal, I gathered that he assumed I just wanted to get away from him. The truth was, however, that he was not my problem. The Grand Central Station outside my office door was my problem. Nonetheless, my father was not a conversationalist. He was not one to discuss emotions, especially not hurt feelings. Sadly, we drew a line in the sand that day.

"Oh, yes, I am." I replied starkly and marched out.

Time went on, and much to his dismay, I moved offices. My poor mother was in the middle of this gunfight at O.K. Corral, but I knew it would all smooth out over time. I found myself to be much more productive in the new, quiet space. However, the strain that was put on my father and my relationship tore at my heart. I loved my father, and despite our differences, I valued immensely the close relationship that we had spent years building. That bond meant more to me than my own need for space.

I decided to make a peace offering. I presented my idea one day while we were at lunch at our favorite Cuban café. We sat comfortably at our table by the café front window and ordered our usual—half a Cuban sandwich, black beans and rice, with a side of onions and extra red wine vinegar. About midway through our meal, after multiple sips of iced tea and rather quiet conversation, I offered my olive branch. "Dad, I spoke with General Telephone, our phone company, and they are able to install a direct line from your office to mine. All you have to do is pick up the phone in your office, push a button, and the phone will ring in mine. That way, we can keep in close contact anytime we need."

My father, very diplomatically, said, "Yes, that will work well." And he continued to eat his sandwich without another word of it. I knew he appreciated this offer, though, more than he expressed. The direct phone line was put in, and it proved to be a favorite convenience used by him daily. I was his right arm, and he cherished the ability to reach out at any time without hassle. I knew father must have finally forgiven me, because one day he called me and said, "Mark, call your brother, Jim, and let's plan a meeting for 10:30 tomorrow morning. Let's meet in *your* office. It's quieter there."

I almost dropped the phone! After that point, we held all our meetings in my new office. I certainly considered that a win, as the bond that my father and I had spent years crafting was not broken. I am grateful for all the moments we shared together. Coquina Key Arms ended up being my office base for over thirty years. It was not only the place where I learned the most, matured the most, and pushed the company toward years of success, but it also, most importantly, became the place where I grew the closest with my father. For that especially, I will always remember Coquina Key.

Jim, Tom, and Mark Mahaffey at Coquina Key Arms, Saint Petersburg

9

EXPANSION

Don't judge each day by the harvest you reap, but by the seeds that you plant.

Robert Louis Stevenson

Although Coquina Key Arms was our command post, so to speak, from the 1970s until we sold it in 2005, it was far from representative of the full Mahaffey empire arising. With my father, brother, and I putting our best talents together, new land acquisition and development became our primary focus. We had the know-how and the know-who to get things running and keep them going. We prided ourselves in our uniqueness from other firms in that we maintained complete involvement in the creation of a project from start to finish. We kept, and still keep, a close line of communication directly with the architects, engineers, and builders. It was an exciting time to witness the company expand and to observe the combined multifarious efforts of people who built the framework of our success.

The first decade after I arrived in Saint Petersburg still proves to be our fastest growth period to date. By the year 1980, we developed and owned over 7,000 units within 13 apartment communities in western

Florida, as well as Indianapolis. Each development had its own story to tell of the trials we had to overcome and the people we had to bring together to reach completion. I will not begin to chronicle the details and events relating to every property, but there are a few that stand out in my memory as major tailwinds on the path to progress – for both my personal growth and the company's growth as a whole. Working at the Coquina Key Arms location was a major highway in my individual path to learning the ins and outs to real estate. But when I look back at the portfolio of properties we have built over the years, I can recall a few additional, momentous landmarks that must not be forgotten.

Our longest branch of expansion to date includes the few properties we erected in Indianapolis in the early 1970s—three properties to be exact. We did not own them for a particularly long span of time, nor was I especially involved in their management; that was primarily my brother, Jim's, focus. However, they are important in the grand scheme of things because of a very valuable person that came into the picture because of them.

The notion to initiate several projects in Indianapolis was first presented to my father in the early 1970s by Joseph Sexton, a long-time acquaintance of my father who resided in Indianapolis. Joseph Sexton had his eye on a piece of property in Indianapolis that he thought would be perfect for rental apartments. Unfortunately, he did not have the track record nor the financial wherewithal to develop it on his own. Knowing of my father's expertise and success in the apartment business, Joseph reached out to him.

Initially, my father had not planned to develop any properties in Indianapolis. When he had sold the Meadowbrook Apartments years before, he thought he was done with the Indianapolis market. His focus was on Florida now. However, when an opportunity came knocking on my father's door, he welcomed it enthusiastically. He knew he could lend a hand to Joseph Sexton and find a way for both parties to profit; he just had to get the right people together.

Passionate about partnership creation, my father formed a joint venture with Joseph Sexton. He also brought into the partnership his best friend and business companion, George Walker, and also the National

Life Insurance Company of Vermont. With solid partnerships, strongly-secured financing, and the right builders in place, the community of Lake Nora Arms was born soon after. It was a fantastic deal from our point of view because Joseph Sexton and George Walker were Indianapolis locals and could be our points of communication while we lived in Florida. We were still continuously involved throughout the purchase, development, and management of Lake Nora Arms. But, given the distance, we were thankful to have local connections whom we trusted and respected.

Lake Nora Arms, Indianapolis, Indiana

It was not long before the Mahaffey Company, Joseph Sexton, and George Walker partnered again, adding another Indiana property to the portfolio—an existing 352-unit apartment complex at West Lake, Indianapolis. We also brought in as partner our general contractor, Wayne Nelson, who had built Lake Nora Arms, as well as Intereal Company, which was a subsidiary of the National Life of Tennessee Corporation. We had partnered successfully with Intereal Company in several of our developments in Florida as well, including Lake Howell

Arms in Orlando. Intereal Company was just an example of the importance of maintaining quality partner relationships over time.

Purchasing an existing property, as West Lake Arms stood, was unusual for us. What motivated our intrigue was the potential the property promised. The sprawling landscape was massive and had an ideal location along the interstate. George Walker was good friends with the seller, Paul Voight, which proved to be a valuable connection throughout the entire acquisition process. What especially piqued our interest was that Paul Voight also owned the adjacent land parcel, which housed the West Lake Beach Club, West Lake Drive-In Theatre, and West Lake Dance Terrace. The entire West Lake complex was a very sentimental place for my family. The dance terrace, with its retractable roof, was *the* spot to host big festivities and high school proms, including my parents and my own. I remember the thrill of watching the roof of the hall open up during large gatherings, making for a romantic evening of dancing under the stars. This was many years ago, however. By the time we looked at the property, West Lake had been vacant and closed down for quite some time, and we were happy to push for progress with a new purpose for the land.

West Lake Beach Club
photo credit: The Indianapolis News, July 2, 1951

After purchasing the existing apartment buildings on the adjacent lot, we added two more phases on the West Lake property over the next two years, totaling a combined 1,378 units. My father decided to offer George Walker a large percentage ownership as a gift for all his hard work throughout the years. My brother, Jim, and I agreed wholeheartedly that George deserved it. To think of all that George had contributed since that first day he stepped through those front doors of the Consolidated Finance office. His determination, hard work, and integrity had earned him a financially rewarding career, and the residual income from this last property gave him a generous cushion for the rest of his life.

West Lake Arms also proved especially profitable to the Mahaffey Company as well, as it was during this development that we added a very special person to our team. As it was an especially sizable property with a large unit count, we decided it was time to hire an on-site director and assistant to help us manage it from out-of-state. After several interviews, we chose a retired marine colonel as the director, and a young woman, Suzanne Gray, as the assistant. Suzanne, at only 23-years-old, was a recent graduate from the University of Tennessee, had studied at Oxford, and was a member of the Phi Beta Kappa Society and a Rhodes scholar. We knew this young woman was brilliant. What we didn't realize was how influential she would be in the future of the Mahaffey Apartment Company.

Fountain view at night at West Lake Arms, Indianapolis, Indiana

Soon after acquiring the position, the marine colonel proved to be the wrong person for director. As a company, we have shown a great deal of faith in our employees, giving everyone the tools and support to be successful. However, this director seemed to view the world as binary, seeing things only as black or white. He lacked the ability to understand the gray areas in between. It was difficult to communicate reasonably with him, and he was giving the residents some trouble. We decided it was time to replace the retired colonel by promoting Suzanne to the director position. It was certainly a gamble putting someone so young in that demanding role. But as a company, we had learned time and time again that people learn best performing in the role. We had faith in her, and she exceeded even our wildest expectations. Suzanne not only proved to be extremely smart, but also, she possessed the rare quality of common sense. She helped run Lake Nora Arms, West Lake Arms, and eventually a third Indianapolis property, Lake Castleton Arms.

This last property was a product of our close partnership with our contractor Wayne Nelson, who built the first two properties in Indianapolis. He had found and purchased the raw land of the future Lake Castleton Arms with the intention of building and managing an apartment property of his own. However, merely weeks before the intended construction start date, he was involved in a devastating automobile accident. Miraculously, Wayne survived the collision, but was left with various injuries that impacted his career for the rest of his life. He had to make some difficult decisions on how to carry out his plans for developing the proposed apartment community. In his distress, he called out to us for help.

He pleaded with my father, Jim, and me, "I've got a great opportunity here, but I can't do it on my own anymore. My company still has the capacity to develop the land, but we need the assistance in financing and management. Would you join me in a partnership?"

Beyond helping a good friend, the proposal sounded like a profitable deal to us as well. We had built a solid relationship with Wayne while developing the previous two properties in Indianapolis, and we trusted him.

Lake Castleton Arms, Indianapolis, Indiana

"Of course, Wayne," we assured him.

A year later, in 1979, Lake Castleton Arms was completed. Suzanne managed the three Indianapolis properties magnificently, keeping occupancy at a constant near one hundred percent. Over the next decade, for various reasons, we ended up selling all three Indianapolis properties, the last one selling in 1986. These Indianapolis deals may have been short-term investments, but the best asset we gained from the whole experience was most certainly Suzanne Gray.

Not needing Suzanne's talents in Indianapolis any further, but knowing that we had a fine gem worth preserving, we pleaded with Suzanne to move to Florida to continue to work for our properties there. We surely needed the help managing all the new properties that were being launched year after year. My father, Jim, and I made a great team, but we realized quickly it takes more than a few instruments to play a symphony. We were growing quickly, and we knew Suzanne would be a wonderful addition to our Florida team.

After receiving our offer, I am certain Suzanne was very pleased to hear she was not losing a job. However, I was the first to understand the implications of an out-of-state move. Suzanne's husband, Thom Gray, would need to find a way to move his career to Florida as well. Luckily, that was an easy one for us to solve. Thom Gray had worked for an air conditioning company in Indianapolis for years. As we were an apartment development business in sunny and steamy Florida, air conditioning units were a priority on our sites. We promised Thom first bid on each job. We were beyond grateful when Suzanne and Thom picked up their lives and moved to Saint Petersburg, Florida.

Year after year, Suzanne Gray proved to be an invaluable member of our Florida family and was incredibly instrumental in the expansion of our company. Eventually becoming Executive Vice President of the Mahaffey Apartment Company, her financial expertise and ability to see the big picture, as well as the small details, helped us achieve consistent, positive performance time and time again. In return, we have rewarded her generously for her dedicated efforts. Just as my father did with George Walker, we started including Suzanne in our deals and giving her a percentage of ownership of the developments over time. We were pleased to see our Florida team growing with the right people as the company expanded.

Around the time that Suzanne came south, I remember one day I was sitting at my desk at Coquina Key North. My father came into my office with a suggestion to add someone else to our team roster. He reminded me of his incredibly valuable assistant, named Reba Buck, who was a great help to him for all those years he worked at Consolidated Finance in Indianapolis. He called her his "Girl Friday," which was a common phase at the time for a female personal assistant.

"Mark," he said. "You need a Reba Buck."

I knew he was absolutely right. As my responsibilities increased, I had less time to devote to the small, yet very important tasks that ensure that a company runs smoothly. It is generally not an easy undertaking to find an assistant that you can trust and who will be there for your every beck and call. I considered myself very lucky to have found the right person soon after. Her name was Lola Walters. For 30 years, she was my right arm. She not only helped me with matters of the business, but would also help Marianne with taking care of our children and dogs. She was a blessing to be sure.

Our philosophy for our employees is that they work *with* us, not *for* us. This was my father's viewpoint from the beginning, and I am proud to say we have carried it though as we have grown our team. Our doctrine is simple; we take care of the people who take care of our business. I established the tradition of personally handing out bonus checks to each employee every Christmas. It was important to me to have that personal connection with each individual—to shake their hand and say, "We appreciate you." We have been blessed with a great many wonderful employees who have shown incredible dedication and hard work in making the Mahaffey dream come true. From the housekeeper to the maintenance tech to the director, we have a continual goal of treating everyone with respect. In turn, they have rewarded us with many, many years of commitment. The longevity of many of our employees working for us for 20 to 30 to 40 and more years is astounding and a testament to our real achievement beyond what is seen on the financial statements.

I must also add that the Mahaffey team extends much beyond our direct employees. It includes our partners, brokers, builders, lawyers, and insurance agents. Each person brings tremendous value to the table that is necessary for the Mahaffey company growth. Many times, when a business relationship becomes a personal friendship, the success is even sweeter. One of my favorite examples of this involves one of our first insurance agents, Tom Rusche, who is now, almost 50 years later, one of my dearest friends. This story began back in the 1970s, just after we finished our property at Coquina Key.

One morning, as I was working in my new office, a young man entered the bullpen. I heard him tell the receptionist, "Hello, my name is Tom Rusche. I am not here to rent an apartment, but I would like to speak with Mark Mahaffey."

A few moments later, the receptionist peeked into my office. "Sir, there is a man here by the name of Tom Rusche who wants to see you."

"Send him on in," I replied. The story of when George Walker first came to see my father at Consolidated Finance, played in my head. Who could this Tom Rusche be?

A tall, burly man with dusty blonde hair stepped into my office. He looked about my age, perhaps around 30 years old. He smiled at me and said, "Hello, Mark Mahaffey. I'm Tom Rusche." He reached out his hand and shook mine. "I am with State Farm Insurance. Would you be interested in seeing what we have to offer?"

Insurance? I thought to myself. Insurance seemed to be the theme of the month. Our current insurer was Allstate, and I felt like I had been on the phone with them 20 times in the past few weeks. There had been a small fire in the Coquina Key Arms clubhouse. It was nothing too severe, but there was some surface damage to repair. Allstate eventually conceded to cover the damage, but our relationship was tainted by the struggle it took to get to that agreement. Tom Rusche's timing was impeccable.

"Show me what you've got," I said, interested in his pitch.

It turned out that his rates and coverage were much better than Allstate's, and I agreed to make the switch. Tom Rusche with State Farm ended up being the Mahaffey Apartment Company's exclusive insurance agent for 17 years. In the early 1990s, State Farm Insurance Company decided they did not want to insure any commercial properties in Florida anymore. I assumed it was due to the risk of hurricanes. I called up my childhood friend Hugh McGowan for advice, knowing that he owned an insurance agency. He ended up being a phenomenal resource and helped us get the insurance we needed. Unfortunately, at the same time, we received the reality check that we had been underpaying for insurance all those years with State Farm, and our rates increased dramatically. We appreciated the coverage, however, despite the cost jump. Hugh—and eventually his son, who continued running Hugh's insurance company— truly went to bat for us for many years. It was a marvelous thing to be able to call up my friend and say, "I need help," and he was there. Because of this connection, Hugh's and my friendship has continued to grow over the years. We have become like brothers, helping one another as we journey together through life.

Tom Rusche, for health reasons, decided to go into an early retirement. He and I, nonetheless, maintained our friendship over the years through our mutual love for fishing and boats. Tom had been a first-rate insurance agent for us for all those years, and it turned out that he was an even better boat resource. We eventually bought a 35-foot Riviera Sports Fishing boat together, where we spent many days bonding over our fishing poles. Tom had owned more boats than anyone I had ever met. He was the ideal boat partner, as he was meticulous in maintaining them.

Sadly, one day, Tom ran into big troubles with his finances. He had invested with the wrong individual—someone who was running a Ponzi scheme in the dark. Tom lost quite a bit of money and dreaded the thought of ending his retirement and going back into the insurance business. As a friend, I decided to help him out. I bought out his portion of the boat and signed him on as Manager of that boat, as well as my other boat, a 22-foot Grady White. Later, I traded the Riviera for a newly designed 35-foot Bertram Sports fisherman. I have paid Tom a monthly fee for all these years to manage and care for my boats, and he is very grateful for the income and the ability to spend his retirement at his favorite place—the sea. He also does some insurance consulting on the side. I have been so happy to see that Tom has emerged from his financial struggles, and I have enjoyed the benefit of well-managed boats.

In 1980, I met my good friend, Bill Bond and his wife Mary Ann. He is another example of a friendship that is a thread woven into the Mahaffey Apartment Company tapestry of success. After developing a wonderful friendship with him and his wife, Bill ended up providing the workers' compensation insurance for the company for many years. Marianne and my friendship with Bill and Mary Ann Bond has grown over time and is now stronger than ever. We truly cherish our "bond" together, and I am so glad that our paths have crossed.

It is a beautiful thing—friends helping friends. I cannot fathom where my life or the company would be today without Hugh or Tom or Bill. They have been wonderful assets to me throughout my journey, and I hope I have been the same to them in return. We have built the ever growing and evolving Mahaffey orchestra, each person playing a part in the grand symphony of success.

Mark on the 35-foot Bertram Sport Fisherman

10

TRIAL AND ERROR

If you are working on something exciting that you really care about,
you don't have to be pushed. The vision pulls you.

Steve Jobs

As I reflect on the Mahaffey Apartment Company's past successes, I cannot overlook some of the biggest challenges we tackled over the years. Peering at history through rose-colored glasses is deceivingly gratifying, but it blinds the beholder from the opportunity to learn from their mistakes. I would discover time and time again that success is not defined by perfection; it is defined by progress—moving forward and acquiring a deeper sense of understanding along the way. Maneuvering through trials and tribulations, I grew personally as I gained more experience and more maturity as a businessman. As a company, we learned the importance of simplifying our processes as we found out what worked and what did not. Trial and error became a crucial component of our growth. By building the same type of community in the same type of physical locale, we were able to duplicate and improve on a validated formula for success.

Colonial Williamsburg Architecture

There were, however, several properties that pushed back and forced us to step up on a business level, as well as a personal level. My father, Jim, and I did not always see eye to eye, but we somehow seemed to pull through, even if not always as I expected. Sometimes, the lesson I had to learn was merely perseverance and trust—with perhaps a dose of creativity.

Lake Carlton Arms in Tampa, Florida, is one property that taught me just that. The development phase of this community spanned a preposterous fourteen years and was by no means a walk in the park. The story began in 1972, at about the same time as we were just finishing the first phase of our Coquina Key development. With several other of our Florida communities reaching completion and occupancy rates all nearing one hundred percent, the Mahaffey Company was fixated on expansion.

I remember that one morning in late summer, when my father first shared with me the prospects of a new development. I was sitting at my desk when he entered into my office and said, "Mark, I've come across a massive lot of land for sale in northwest Tampa, and I think it would be a great spot to build another development. Are you available this afternoon? I want to go check it out."

"Sounds interesting," I replied, curiously. "I'm free later, but tell me the details first."

My father said, "My broker called me this morning and said he's got 480 acres in Northwest Tampa featuring a hundred-acre lake. *Turkey Ford*—they call the property. We'd have to change that, of course, but think of the possibilities!"

"Alright. Let's go check it out. I'll call Jim to join us."

Later that afternoon, with a Tampa map in hand, my father, Jim and I hopped into my Buick Park Avenue, which I always kept cleaned and polished. My father always preferred me to drive, and I never minded— perhaps, I think, because deep down, part of me still identified as the *Pathfinder*.

Leaving Saint Petersburg, we crossed the Howard Franklin Bridge, which stretched across the Tampa Bay and lead into the heart of downtown Tampa. Crossing this long stretch of road through a visual tunnel of sapphire blue, above and below, hypnotized one into the sensation that they were flying. With the windows down on this hot, summer day, we could taste the humid, salty air as it whipped through the car. Contrasting the wind created by a moving vehicle, the bay remained calm. Its waters reflected the sun's rays into scattering bursts of light, interrupted only by the silhouettes of brown pelicans coasting and diving without a care in the world. Occasionally, I would see a dolphin's ashen fin slice through the surface of the bay as it played in its watery palace. As the dazzling sunshine flooded through the windows and into our spirits, optimism abounded as we headed north.

My father glanced over at Jim and me. "I have a good feeling about this. This would be our largest property yet."

We had two other successful apartment communities in Tampa at this time, Lake Magdalene Arms and Carlton Arms of Egypt Lake. Both had proved to be solid investments boasting one hundred percent occupancy with a waitlist of people wanting to sign on as residents. Tampa's population was growing exponentially with a majority of the newer residents comprising of college students, young couples, Cuban immigrants, and retired individuals. There was a high demand for rental apartments from this newer cohort of the population, and Tampa was seeing a boom in multi-family developments. North Tampa had yet to be developed, but with so many people migrating to the area, urbanization had to move north. We happened to be in the right place at the right time, and we were determined to meet this housing demand like rain on parched soil. This large piece of land we were off to see could potentially not only serve a great need in the northern Tampa area as the population expanded, but also could be a great long-term investment for us.

After traversing the Howard Franklin Bridge and navigating our way through and out of the downtown district of Tampa, we saw the terrain quickly change. The sights of bustling shops and restaurants dissolved into a broad slew of dairy farms and hay fields. My optimism was beginning to fade.

"This area is mighty rural," I voiced.

My father nodded. "None of this will look the same in ten years," he predicted.

He was probably right, I thought to myself. A large urban planning project was proposed for north Hillsborough County, especially northwest of Tampa. The Dale Mabry Highway, a central artery through Tampa, had been recently extended north to this unchartered territory, and plans for multiple other residential projects, as well as retail and business developments were in the works. Land was still cheap, nonetheless, and my father could smell some real investment potential.

After following the Dale Mabry Highway about ten miles north of downtown, we took Van Dyke Road, a small country road at the time, two miles to the west. Finally, we reached our destination—*Turkey Ford*.

"We really are in the middle of nowhere," Jim commented, observing the mere nothingness surrounding the property.

My father glanced back at him with an unamused stare. "I'm telling you. You just watch this area transform. The Veteran's Expressway is proposed to be built right along this site. It will directly connect downtown Tampa and the Tampa International Airport, which was just built last year, to the northern communities. Real estate development is headed this way," he said.

"Highway frontage would be incredible...assuming it gets any traffic this north," I quipped.

We stepped out of the vehicle onto the muddy terrain. *I should have brought my boots,* I thought to myself. I kept my eyes carefully on my feet, maneuvering around murky puddles and swampy pockets of dirt. This land was very wild, primitive to say the least. Stepping onto a higher, dry, secure spot, I took a moment to observe my surroundings. Despite the rugged, natural state of the land, it was beautiful. Mature, grandeur cypress trees spanned the property, towering over the perimeter of a stunning, 100-acre lake. Egrets and cranes stood confidently in the tall grass, while woodpeckers and cicadas made their presence known through their tapping and shrills. The land was peaceful, despite the cacophony of nature sounds. I assumed there must be turkeys nearby due to the namesake, but I did not spy them from my place in the periphery.

"There are the brokers," called my father, gesturing to a car pulling up. The three of us knew these two men well. Joe Cannella and Al Dolcimascolo were old time Italians who had also shown us the land at Egypt Lake and Lake Magdalene.

"Can you believe this beauty? Almost 500 acres at your disposal. You won't find land cheaper than this," Joe said in a distinctive, Floridian/Italian accent.

We walked along the southern perimeter of the property. "Seems pretty damp," I commented. "What is the flood rating?" I asked.

"It's in a flood zone, yes. But don't let that hinder you. The whole of Florida is practically in a flood zone. It's up to the developer to be creative. There's a whole lot of folks wanting to develop up here. If you don't take the challenge, someone else will, and they will profit from it."

My father nodded. "I'll offer $836,000. Not a penny more."

"I will let you know the seller's response soon," Joe Cannella said.

We hopped back into our vehicle to head home.

"Are you sure you want to do this?" I questioned my father.

Jim agreed with me, adding, "We are playing in new territory. There are still a lot of unknowns."

My father was adamant. "If we can get the land for the price we want, we can deal with the risks. We can move the dirt around to fix whatever drainage issues there might be. Think of the potential. This would be huge development. And getting the land for cheap would ensure our cost per unit would be very low. That is how money is made, sons."

Jim and I decided to pick our battles and not argue with our father when his mind was set. Later that day, we got word our offer was accepted, and Jim and I resolved to get on board and join my father's big vision for Turkey Ford. My father, in his usual fashion, organized a team of partners to fund the project, ten partners in total, including ourselves. Our builder, the Demetree Builders, headed by Bill Demetree, was brought in as one of the partners, just as my father did with Wayne Nelson in Indianapolis. The Demetree Builders had been with us since the beginning, with the construction of Winter Park. In exchange for part ownership, Bill Demetree promised to build at cost. Several Tampa realtors joined the venture as well. Everyone was excited about the opportunity with this huge lot of land. "This is the big one!" my father would say.

As new owners of Turkey Ford, our first line item on the agenda was to get approval from the county to rezone the land from rural, single-family to multi-family. Similar to our Coquina Key property, this was not an unusual step in the process. However, our optimism was cut short as we experienced an incredibly high amount of opposition from the neighbors. Development and change can be a very scary thing, especially to people who have intentionally chosen remote, country living. For one reason or another, it is not uncommon for developers to be touted as "the bad guys" or "destroyers of God's good earth." In contrast, I like to think of myself as an improver of vacant land, building communities for my fellow mankind. Unfortunately, in our naiveté, we failed to see a wave of distaste and rage rolling toward us.

As scheduled, my father, Jim, and I, all in our obliviousness, entered into the Hillsborough County courthouse to gain approval for the rezoning. Instantly, we felt something was not right. The courthouse was filled to the brim with people. I could hear whispers of disgust and horror as we walked into the lobby. *Oh no,* I thought. *What did we get ourselves into?!*

Scanning the room for some answer to the reason for the wild display of people, I quickly took notice that Mike Wallace was amongst the crowd. Now, Mike Wallace was a sort of celebrity in the 1970s. He was host of the popular newsmagazine television show *60 Minutes.* Apparently, he had been summoned by the community to do an exposé piece on Hillsborough County zoning laws, featuring *us* as a threat to rural communities! We had heard rumors about the community's protest, but did not anticipate the measures they would employ to smother our plans for development.

I whispered to Jim and my father, "That is Mike Wallace, right?"

Colored drained from their faces. "Damn," was all my father could say.

We saw Mike Wallace standing in the back of the courtroom, all dressed up, with his film crew ready to capture the event on camera.

"We aren't going to win this," I spoke to my father softly enough that no one else could hear. "It's a flood zone for God's sake. We aren't prepared with enough artillery to face this kind of negative publicity. Let's just go. We can reschedule for when we have a solid plan. I would rather act prudently verses ardently."

"Alright Mark. I'm putting this in your hands."

I should have expected my father would hand me the reins in that moment. And I was never one to turn down a challenge, so I said, "Yes, I know just what to do."

We pulled the application without even stepping into the County Commission Chambers and snuck out the side door. *60 Minutes,* seeing there was nothing to report, packed up their gear and left. *Phew!*

I knew we were walking on thin ice, however, and our development plan had to be flawless. Our adversaries claimed that our high-density project would disrupt traffic patterns and water and energy usage in the county. They accused us of wanting to build on a flood prone conservation area that was not suitable for development. They were correct on that. The land was a mess.

Jim and I promptly contacted the Southwestern Florida Water Management District. After conducting in-depth engineering studies for many months, together we came up with a drainage plan. The plan was to dig a 59-acre lake northeast of existing Turkey Ford Lake, as well as additional finger-type lakes, and use the fill to bring the surrounding land up. All drainage was self-contained on the property as to not cause issues for any surrounding properties. We proposed building 1,966 units on the 215 acres of raised land surrounding the lakes, while retaining the natural state of the cypress trees surrounding Turkey Ford Lake. Over half the property was allotted as preservation area. To help service the community, we planned to donate one acre of land and $25,000 toward the construction of a fire station on site. To prevent potential traffic issues in the area, we suggested to offer a shuttle service that would run from the property to downtown Tampa.

When it came time for our next court date over a year later, we were very well-prepared. At this time, there was a newly elected County Commission, which we hoped would be in our favor. Gloriously, *60 Minutes* was nowhere in sight, and our proposal and rezoning request were passed by the commission board, despite a negative vote from the staff. My father boasted to reporters after the approval, "This is probably the most self-sufficient piece of land ever to be engineered in Hillsborough County!"

This was nowhere near the end of this war, however. Newspapers flooded with negativity as local residents in the area were in uproar. The Turkey Ford controversy became wildly public as people voiced strong opinions on both sides. Sixteen members of the Keystone Civic Association, which was a homeowners' association for a neighboring development, filed suit against the county, seeking to nullify the commission board's approval of the Turkey Ford development. They claimed the decision was "spot zoning" and would be a threat to the surrounding community and present water supply issues. The suit requested a permanent injunction that would ensure the Turkey Ford property would never be developed.

We were distraught to hear this. That sweet taste of success had lasted shorter than the flavor of bazooka bubble gum. Were we back where we started? We had come too far to quit now. We approached the county commission board and offered, "We would like to join this suit and help you with legal representation and expenses to fight this case."

The County Attorney, Michael O'Brien, said, "Yes, please!"

Michael O'Brien was a very capable Irish lawyer, and to back him up, we brought in an unbelievable legal team. The case was first heard at the District Court level, which decided in favor of the development. The Keystone Association was relentless. They proceeded to take the case to the appeals court, which ultimately agreed with the lower court's decision and ruled in favor of the development as well. The Keystone Association still wasn't ready to capitulate and petitioned the Supreme Court of Florida. Luckily, the Supreme Court decided the plaintiff did not have standing to bring the suit, and the suit was dropped. Finally, in 1974, two years after purchasing the land, the whole rezoning controversy was behind us. The debate was stormy, but we pulled through and won! We all took in deep sighs of relief.

However, this colossal approval battle took a tremendous amount of time and expense. We were paying monthly interest on our loan for the purchase of Turkey Ford, and I felt like we were bleeding money. Beyond that, we still needed to solve the water supply and sewer issues before development.

Back at our Coquina Key office, Jim and I decided we needed to convince our father to cut our losses, sell Turkey Ford, and move on. I remember the day that Jim and I met him in his office to show him a stack of papers outlining the problems. The projections did not look good.

"This is eating a hole in our pockets," we told him.

My father glanced at the charts and financials I had outlined for merely a moment before pushing them aside. His face looked as if it was carved in stone. Expressionless. "The potential is still there," he said. He sat as an unwavering oak, a stronghold in a windstorm. I felt the stab of his dismissal of our concerns. His office was a gloomy cave of sorts. Dark wood panels cloaked the walls, checkered with dozens of framed photos, sketches of apartment communities, newspaper articles, and letters signed by prominent political figures. It was more than an office. It was a gallery of my father's proudest achievements in his life. He lived for the dream.

Jim pressed on, "Is it really worth all this?"

My father pushed back. He was stubborn and pertinacious like none other.

"If we give up, we will have put in all this effort for a loss. As with any investment, timing is crucial. Be patient." His words sounded more like a command than a reassurance. But we took heed and agreed to keep working toward the goal.

"We'll figure it out," I said.

As I was getting out of my chair to step out of the room, I spied through the window a man looking quite out of place. He held a camera and a notepad. A reporter.

My father swung around in his chair to see what I had spotted.

"Damn reporters," he muttered.

"I'll ask Ada to take care of it for you," I promised. Ada was my father's full-time assistant, and really, his right arm in most things. The reporters were unremitting. When we were ready to talk to them, we would. But now was not the time. Now was the time to put our nose to the grindstone and make a plan.

Jim and I we knew we had to get creative with the financing. Prepping the land for development, including clearing the areas for buildings and digging the additional lakes, had a high price tag. I had the idea of selling the dirt to pay for the excavators, and we were able to accomplish that pretty early on. But we still did not have enough liquidity to begin construction.

Our builder/partner, Bill Demetree, came to us and said, "We want out of this deal."

I understood his frustration. At this point, several years had gone by without a return on investment. But my father was unrelenting and stuck to his guns. He confidently told Bill, "We are going to get this done. If you don't want to be a part of it, fine."

Partnering with National Life of Vermont and selling one of our other communities, Lake Magdalene Arms, we had enough capital to buy the Demetrees out. However, construction costs and interest rates were beginning to rise precipitously. Beyond that, the multi-family boom in the early 1970s resulted in an overbuilt apartment market, and Tampa was seeing higher vacancy rates. We could not justify beginning construction of the buildings just yet. Years and years went by, and the land sat.

Meanwhile, we were not about to sit there twiddling our thumbs waiting for a miracle. Luckily, a different, new, gleaming property was served to us on a silver platter. We decided to shift gears for the time being and focus our efforts where we could be more productive.

In the late 1970s, my father had a close friendship with a real estate developer named Dan Blalock. He worked for Wyman, Green, and Blalock Real Estate Inc., which invested in residential and commercial properties located in Bradenton, a city just south of Saint Petersburg, across the Skyway Bridge. In addition to his development background, Dan Blalock was also very involved within various City of Bradenton committees and pushed for progress in Manatee County by supporting many community projects.

Dan Blalock called up my father one day and said, "Tom, I have something you might be interested in. I, along with four other guys, own a piece on land in eastern Bradenton. It's gorgeous—100 acres of waterfront property nestled where the Manatee River meets the Braden River. It was initially zoned for 900 multi-family units, but we rezoned it to allow single family homes along the shores. We are realizing this development is a much bigger project than expected, and we just don't have the time to do it. Would the Mahaffey Company be interested in looking at the property?"

My father was familiar with the location. The Manatee River is a wide waterway that flows from Manatee County into the Tampa Bay. Used by many boaters and fisherman, it is a well-traveled channel for people and animals alike. Varied sea life, including manatees, alligators, and dolphins call the waters home, while herons and pelicans claim the shore. The river's broad girth offers phenomenal views from its shores, especially where the expansive, flowing waters meet with the Braden River. The location of this property at this rendezvous of rivers peaked my father's interest.

"Give me some more details," my father requested. "How much do you want for it?"

Dan was honest. "We bought it a few years ago for $750,000, but we still owe quite a bit to the bank we loaned it from in Wisconsin. I can't take less than $1,000,000. I'm offering it to you before I go to the market. It is really a gem of a property having waterfront on two sides where the two rivers merge."

"Hmm," my father pondered. "The biggest issue is the zoning. We don't do single family development. We would have to rezone it back to allow 900 multi-family units."

Dan Blalock attempted to put my father's concerns at ease. "Tom, you really don't have to worry about that. I can help you with the zoning no problem. I am good friends with several city officials. I can't offer any price reduction or contingencies, but you'll have my guidance."

My father appreciated the sentiment. "Let me share all this with Mark and Jim, and we will give you an answer soon."

My father later related this conversation to Jim and me, and we immediately got to work sorting out the financing. At that time, we still had a close relationship with National Life of Tennessee, which had partnered with us for several other projects in Florida as well as Indianapolis. We were their exclusive multi-family developer at that time as our relationship was very strong.

My father, Jim, and I flew up to the National Life of Tennessee office in Nashville. I prepared a portfolio of presentations and pro formas with conscious effort to convince them to loan us the capital. Now that I had a decade of experience of working in real estate, I was getting even better at these presentations. I proposed to them a two-phase deal, where we would build 450 units each phase. I negotiated for them to give us $1,000,000, and in return, we would happily grant them fifty percent ownership. We assured them that our relationship with Dan Blalock would facilitate the rezoning process. My father had the brilliant idea of inviting Dan into the ownership as well, which would keep his skin in the game, so to speak. This turned out to be genius thinking because it kept Dan motivated to push the city to allow us to rezone. After purchasing the land, and spending almost a year attending trials and conversing with the city, we were finally granted approval to build 900 multi-family units.

However, like the property at Turkey Ford, the land was in a flood zone. The National Flood Insurance Program surveyed the property and stated that we could start building as long as we kept the base elevation of the buildings at eight feet. This was not a problem, but we heard rumors that the program would soon be changing their regulations to a base of twelve feet within the next year. The property had many mature, beautiful oak trees, and the proposed increased building elevation would kill many of these wonderful trees. This would prove to be more than a mere inconvenience when building the second phase.

"How about we build all 900 units in one phase?" I suggested to my father.

"What?! That is unheard of!" He snapped.

"But can it be done?" I prodded.

My father stood in silence, mind reeling.

I offered, "Let's at least explore the idea."

"Okay," he approved.

Working through the financials and speaking with our legal team, engineers, and builder, we determined that the impossible could indeed be made possible. Inflation and interest rates were sky high, but I could still make the numbers work if I could just get our lender and partner onboard.

I will never forget the day I made that phone call to National Life requesting more funds. I dreaded the call, but I understood it was the only way to make this plan work. And in the end, we would all profit immensely from it. I picked up the phone and dialed Allen Patton, my direct contact guy at National Life of Tennessee.

"Hello, Allen," I greeted. After the initial salutation and friendly small talk, I said, "Allen, all is going smoothly with our Bradenton project rezoning, but there has been a slight change of plans. Instead of building the development in two phases, we feel it will be best to tackle it all at once and build all 900 units in one phase." I described to him the flood elevation level concern, and how this would solve that potential problem.

He replied with a mere, "Hm-mm."

I went on. "We've done our homework, and we think this is the best decision. I admit putting 900 units on the market is rather ambitious, and it may take a while to reach total occupancy. But I have no doubt that this will be good money spent in the long run because we can build at today's prices before inflation rises even higher."

"Hm-mm," Allen replied again.

I decided it was time to get to the point. "Allen, do you remember that pro forma I first showed you?"

"Yes," he said.

"Take it times two, and that is what I am asking you."

I heard a sigh on the other line. "Well, I'll get back to you, Mark," Allen replied.

"That's fine. Thank you, Allen," I concluded.

Later that afternoon, Allen called me back and said, "Go ahead." I was thrilled and relieved. If it were not for our long standing, strong relationship with National Life, I am sure we would not have received the funds. Time to build!

We acquired permits from the city, and brought the Demetree Builders in as head contractor. They became partners in the deal and built at cost, as we had negotiated in previous projects. They tackled the large project by forming two construction teams, each starting at one end of the property and meeting in the middle. It was as if we were completing two projects at once. In less than eighteen months, in 1980, all 900 units were completed. What a triumph!

Carlton Arms of Bradenton, Florida

The Bradenton apartment market, similar to Tampa, was like a runaway train. With the demand for apartments so high, developers were getting greedy, building apartments in droves and charging high rents. We, however, were able to come in and charge very affordable rates. Because we had favorable financing and were able to build at low cost, we undercut the market by quite a bit. On top of finishing ahead of schedule, we had full occupancy almost immediately. Flocks of residents left nearby apartments and moved into ours. The word on the street was that our competitors were saying, *"We'll be glad when the Mahaffeys finish their project and fill it up so we can remarket."*

It was an amazing feeling to reach such a massive success within only a few years from start to finish. I had great pride in this property, as it turned out a real beauty. My father put me at the forefront of the project, but was there to guide me along the entire way. Having this achievement under my belt gave me the courage and wherewithal to return to the Turkey Ford project and get that moving again. If we could make the numbers work, it could be a real success story too.

As a saving grace, in 1986, Jim and I discovered bond financing. Fourteen years after our initial purchase of the Turkey Ford land, we were finally able to start construction. The Demetree Builders agreed to develop our 1,912 units in three phases over three years. We changed the name of the property from Turkey Ford to Lake Carlton Arms. The development is a real beauty. Two-story, red-brick apartments line the gorgeous lakes, with sprawling cypress trees and over 200 acres of preservation area. Luckily, the widespread apartment vacancy issues throughout Tampa were not a problem for us. We bought the land when the cost was low, we waited to build until the numbers made sense, and then we were able to charge rent at a below-market rate to ensure they filled up fast and stayed full. Tenants were lined up at our doors ready to sign leases.

Lake Carlton Arms, Tampa, Florida

At the time of Lake Carlton Arms' completion, National Life of Vermont still owned sixty percent of the deal. We knew it would be in our best interest to gain full rights to this prosperous development. Therefore, Jim and I planned to buy out their portion. To negotiate the new deal, Suzanne, Jim, and I hopped on a plane and flew out to Burlington, Vermont, where National Life was headquartered. Jim's son William, who had also joined the company, tagged along with us as well. All seated together on our private plane, we debated what we should offer.

Jim led the conversation. "We have to aim low," he insisted. "The market has been unsteady, and insurance companies look at things differently. There are other metrics that they focus on beyond just value. They have to look at portfolio concentration, investment horizons, risk ratings, capital recycling, etc. I think we should offer them eight million. There is a good chance they will go for it."

Jim's son William was in utter disbelief, "There is no way they will accept that. The development is a gold mine. They aren't idiots."

I chimed in, "We should be prepared that they may not take less than twelve million. But I am open to trying for the lower number."

William, sharing the same dynamic nature as his grandfather, roared, "Your plan will not work. They will be insulted and it will damage our relationship with them."

Jim, however, was as stubborn as a bull. "We are going to offer eight. I have a plan."

When we got to Vermont, the representatives at National Life requested we meet at a local motel. *Strange,* we thought to ourselves, *but maybe neutral ground is a good thing.*

When we arrived at the motel, we spotted three men from National Life waiting for us outside. After exchanging pleasantries, the group of us made our way to the motel conference room. Although the motel was not far geographically from the National Life headquarters in Montpelier, the humble surroundings were a far cry from the sprawling, wooded campus that National Life called home. Once seated at the conference table, Jim and I presented the deal in a clear, decisive manner. We offered them eight million dollars for their ownership, adding that we would also like to finance the money through them, splitting the offer into payments. The men listened carefully, giving no hint of an expression of acceptance or rejection. They asked us to give them a few moments to discuss, and we happily obliged. We each stood up in unison and quietly stepped out of the conference room into a courtyard just outside the motel. We knew the men would be calling their superiors at the headquarters. Our minds raced through the possibilities of what they may be saying. After fifteen minutes, which seemed like an eternity, they called us back inside.

The senior man stated, "We cannot accept any form of payment plan. We need all money upfront."

"Understood," we said nodding, keeping straight faces.

The man continued, "But, we *will* accept the eight million."

Keeping our poker faces intact, as they had in the beginning, we all quietly exchanged glances. Saying we wanted to seller-finance the buyout was Jim's strategy of giving them room to negotiate. "Give us a few moments to talk it over," I said, as the four of us stepped out of the room again.

Well, there was not much to discuss. Although we did not know exactly how or from where we were going to pull together the eight million, we knew we could not miss this opportunity. We stood there again in the courtyard for about five minutes, quietly pretending to debate whether we would accept the terms. Finally, we walked back to the conference room.

"Eight million it is," we said, shaking the three men's hands.

On the plane ride home, Jim beamed with pride. "Class dismissed," he said with a smirk, winking at his son. We all laughed. What a win!

Fortunately, Jim and I were able to source the funds to close the purchase via a combination of each of our personal lines of credits. With even better luck, the following year, the economic balance shifted in our favor with interest rates sinking. We refinanced the property and were able to completely pay off the funds, plus put some extra cash in our pockets.

To this day, as I write this book in 2023, Lake Carlton Arms is the single largest apartment community by unit count in the State of Florida. In an area that is now mainly urbanized—as my father predicted—it has been a wildly profitably property. We are proud to have maintained continual, full occupancy for these past 36 years. Lake Carlton Arms sits directly along the Veteran's Expressway, which was eventually built in 1994. The highway not only provides the community great visibility, but allows for much better regional access to the site. I must hand it to my father—he had the vision, and he did not give up. Despite the hurdles we had to jump over, it ended up being a real success story. I learned a lot. We learned a lot as a company—most importantly, stick to your path. Where there is a will, there is a way.

11

GROWING A FAMILY

Other things may change us, but we start and end with the family.

Anthony Brandt

The Mahaffey business was like a laborious garden, an ever changing and growing field of fruits and flowers needing continuous care and attention. For every new seed we planted, we developed an individual plan and process for nurturing it, supporting it, and tending to its needs as it matured. Pests and problems persisted, but with strong dedication, strategic management, and a strong network of fellow gardeners, the projects flourished. My father, Jim, and I had a good thing going. But what is a garden without people to share its fruits? Money and business success are certainly worthy goals, but they are just small slivers of my proudest achievements.

While the Mahaffey Apartment Company was in its early stages of expansion, Marianne and I began to grow a little garden of our own—a family. But even that did not come without its own bumps along the way. Sometimes, even with our best efforts and commitment to painting the picture of our lives with the exact colors we chose, God has a better plan. Building a family was not easy for Marianne and me. But the patience, the struggle, the pain, and the loss we experienced along the way cultivated a deep, inner strength within our souls we never knew we had or even needed.

When Marianne and I were first married in 1969, we had hoped to have children right away. However, God had another plan. Month after month, year after year, we tried and tried with no success. In desperation, Marianne visited her doctor. He suggested she try taking a fertility medication called Clomid. Religiously, she took the pills for almost a year before we finally got the exciting news that we were expecting. Anyone who has gone through the stressful and exhausting journey of infertility understands the emotional triumph felt with a positive pregnancy test. We could not have been more elated. Our family and friends were so happy for us, showering us with love and congratulations. Marianne beamed with joy. She carried not only the fruit of her and my love, but the embodiment of the union of two incredible families.

We did not think our joy could be topped until Marianne visited her doctor for her six-month appointment. It was at this appointment that we found out we were expecting not one, but two little ones. Twins! We felt incredibly blessed.

However, it seems that with every rise, there is a fall. On Thursday, July 12th, only three days after receiving the wonderful news that we were having twins, Marianne's water broke. We were not expecting the babies for another three months. Our thoughts and emotions ran high as we quickly gathered our things and rushed to the nearby Saint Anthony's Hospital in downtown Saint Petersburg. When we arrived, a friendly nurse informed us that Marianne's regular OB/GYN was not on call. Another local doctor, Dr. Don LaPlatney, would be assisting us. Worry flooded our thoughts, but we had no choice but to trust this new doctor and succumb to being led down an unknown path.

After several hours of pushing and waiting and praying, miraculously, our two little boys were brought into this world—Thomas Mahaffey III and John Kiley Mahaffey. We were bewildered with amazement at the sweet, tiny lives before us. Each itty-bitty baby could fit into the palm of my hand. I marveled at their tiny hands, their tiny feet. There was such a precious innocence in these lives that Marianne and I co-created. But they were so delicate, so frail—too young. The nurses rushed the baby boys swiftly by ambulance to the NICU at the nearby All Children's Hospital. I am confident the medical team did everything in their power to encourage those little lungs to keep breathing. Marianne and I felt helpless. All we could do was pray.

My heart ached for Marianne, who was still healing herself. She was not allowed to leave Saint Anthony's Hospital to be with Thomas and John at All Children's Hospital. I was torn between staying by Marianne's side and following the babies, but Marianne encouraged me to go. I consider the moments that I spent with those little babies as some of the most precious in my life. For 24 hours, Thomas and John held on.

Those little fighters gave it their very best, but took their last breath on Friday, the 13th of July. I am not a superstitious man, but Friday the 13th will forever stir in me, feelings of pain and sadness. Marianne and I had never experienced such a love so strong, yet so fleeting. Our hearts expanded with such adoration, only to be deeply pierced with the pain of a double loss. Two loves. Two deaths. Two hearts broken.

When they passed, emotion overtook me. I was absolutely devastated. With Marianne still bound to her hospital bed, I had to coordinate and attend the burial ceremony the following day without her. I remember standing at Calvary Catholic Cemetery, tears filling my eyes as I watched the box lower into the ground. A priest chanted prayers, blessing the little souls. My father came to support me and brought along our dear friend John Hancock. I appreciated and needed their company, as it is never something someone should experience alone. Sorrow left its mark on my heart in a painful, yet beautiful stroke. From finding out that we were having twins, to giving birth, to burying our first two children—all within a week—was a nightmare.

Marianne was beside herself with grief. Her body recovered quickly, but her heart was reluctant to move on. Dr. LaPlatney encouraged her, "Marianne, please do not despair. We don't know why these things sometimes happen. But we can only hope that God has a bigger plan that we cannot even begin to fathom. I can promise you that your body was not at fault. Please do not give up. Do not be afraid to try again."

I commend Dr. LaPlatney for his outstanding character and bedside manner. With his support and reassurance, Marianne and I made the resolve to try again for another baby the following year, continuing the Clomid treatment.

In the meantime, we were tremendously thankful to All Children's Hospital for their care and support during that trying time. Marianne and I immensely wished to give back to the hospital, not just by granting them a monetary donation, but also by offering them our time. I joined the hospital board, and Marianne worked as a volunteer in the NICU to help care for the newborn babies. It is believed that a human presence is crucial for newborn development, and I was truly touched by Marianne's strength and willingness to return to the hospital, especially so soon after our loss. Over the years, we have continued to offer our time and money, and we are proud to witness the scientific progress that has taken place. I believe that if our twins were born today, they would have had a much better chance of survival. If our small impact has been enough to save even one life, it would have all been worth it. I know in my heart it has.

Before we knew it, less than a year after the twins' birth, Marianne was pregnant again—this time with one child. Marianne and I made the decision to keep our spirits optimistic, and eagerly readied our lives and home for the new arrival. However, we could not help also being apprehensive, as deep down we feared the worst could happen again. Nonetheless, we leaned on each other and counted down the weeks to when we would meet our little one.

Finally, on December 9, 1974, I received a call while sitting at my desk at Coquina Key.

"Mark Mahaffey speaking," I said cheerfully as I picked up my office phone.

"Mark," Marianne's voice echoed in a serious timbre. "It's time!"

I sprung out of my chair like I was being shot out of a cannon. I dashed home, gathered our things and packed the car. Luckily, this time, it was much closer to the due date. We called Dr. LaPlatney, who met us promptly at Saint Anthony's Hospital. We were so impressed with Dr. LaPlatney the first time around, we requested that he handle our second birth as well. Arriving at the hospital, the nurses calmly wheeled Marianne to the delivery room. Dr. LaPlatney quickly examined her and said, "It looks like you are not quite ready. Why don't you try walking some stairs to encourage things to progress."

Obediently, Marianne and I found a staircase located in the hospital fire escape corridor. Marianne was a champion that day. Holding her belly, she wobbled up and down those stairs hoping for some movement. And it certainly did its magic, as when we returned to Dr. LaPlatney, he said, "The baby is on its way!"

Marianne was beaming with hope, like a brilliant lighthouse amidst the fog of fear. I, on the other hand, was a nervous wreck once the train began picking up pace.

Back and forth.

Back and forth.

I paced feverishly up and down those hospital hallways waiting breathlessly while Marianne was behind those closed delivery room doors. It was 1974, and I was not yet allowed in the room with her, due to the Caesarian delivery. My parents, as well as Marianne's parents, were waiting there alongside me, wishing to support us in whatever the outcome may be. I heartily appreciated their company, but my wish was solely focused on a healthy delivery for both Marianne and the baby.

Finally, Dr. LaPlatney emerged from the room.

"We have a little problem," the doctor said coolly.

My heart sank. "What is it?" I choked out my words, as they caught in my throat.

"The baby is breech. I recommend a cesarean section, but would like your permission," he replied calmly and confidently.

"Well," I replied, "You are the doctor. You are the captain of this ship. Do what you think is best."

Dr. LaPlatney smiled and said, "All right."

As the doctor closed the door behind him, I continued to pace, striding unceasingly. Instinct told me to reach a goal, I needed to move toward it. But with all control out of my hands and nowhere to go, all I could do was pace.

Back and forth.

Back and forth.

My parents and Marianne's parents sat patiently watching me. My mind whirled. I was determined not to go down a thought trail of *what-ifs*. I did not know what to think. I just had to move. I pondered aloud, "Do you suppose Joseph paced the floors of the stable where Jesus was born?"

"Oh, absolutely," Marianne's mother answered.

"That helps," I said, continuing to walk the floors.

Less than a half hour later, which felt much longer to me and, most assuredly, to all those waiting with me, Dr. LaPlatney appeared again.

He declared with a wide grin, holding out his hand to shake mine. "Mark Mahaffey, congratulations! You are father to a beautiful, healthy, baby boy."

"Oh, my goodness. Thank you!" I cried.

He led me into the recovery room, where Marianne was resting. She held the sweetest, little bundle in her arms.

"He's perfect," she said. "I already love him so much."

I beamed with pride when I first laid eyes on that precious, baby boy. All my fears were extinguished as those little eyes met my gaze. He was truly a miracle.

"Welcome to the world, little one," I whispered to him. I wanted nothing more than to be the best father I could be. I made a resolve in that moment to be truly present in this boy's life. Having grown up with a rather busy father, I was determined to do better—to not wait until adulthood to have a father/son relationship. I did not know what I was doing, but I had Marianne by my side, and that was more than enough.

"And his name?" a nurse asked, handing us several forms to fill out.

I wanted to name him Tom, after my father. But we already named one of our twins Thomas III. That would make this baby, Thomas IV, which seemed complicated and difficult to explain. Instead, we settled on naming him after me, Mark Thomas Mahaffey, Jr. But instead of calling him Mark, we would call him Tom. It ended up being the ideal solution.

To this day, my son goes by the name Tom, even formally signing his name M. Thomas Mahaffey Jr.

Tom Mahaffey

The Mahaffey family, 1986

I cannot thank Dr. LaPlatney enough for being an advocate for our family. With his assistance, Marianne and I went on to have two more children—two girls named Kiley Kathleen and Colleen Josephine. Once Marianne had a Caesarian delivery with Tom, our two other children were destined to be born the same way. Kiley was born on November 17, 1978. When Marianne became pregnant with our third, "surprise child," the baby was due mid-November of 1985. We chose November 18, so our children did not have the same birth date. Marianne had an appointment with Dr. LaPlatney a couple of days before the picked delivery date. I will never forget when she came home and told me that Dr. LaPlatney would allow for me to be in the delivery room if we both wanted.

I then anxiously and nervously asked my wife the big question, "Do you want me there?"

Marianne exclaimed, "I really would!"

When the big day arrived, one of the nurses led me by hand to the cafeteria to make sure I had some nourishment, while Marianne was being prepped. When it was time, they positioned me on a stool near Marianne's head. She was draped in white sheets and fully conscious. I was probably the only one present that everyone was fearful of passing out, hence the food beforehand.

When Dr. LaPlatney and Dr. Mulholland, our forever pediatrician, exclaimed that the baby was a girl, both Marianne and I exclaimed at once, "What?!"

We were so adamant that this baby would be a boy, as Marianne had the same symptoms during pregnancy, that she had with Tom.

I said, "Are you sure?"

The whole operating room burst into laughter. Fortunately, we had a girl's name picked out as well, Colleen Joesphine Mahaffey. Kiley's name honors my grandmother's maiden name and Marianne's sister. Colleen's name was inspired by Marianne's sister's religious name and Marianne's mother's name. All our children's names honor some part of their ancestry, as it runs deep in Irish tradition to hold fast to your past, pay homage to your loved ones, and never forget where you came from.

1974 was a big year for the Mahaffey Family. Not only was it the year my son, Tom, was born, but also, it was the year my parents established the Mahaffey Family Vacation. I have to credit my father and mother for prioritizing the family culture and tradition, and teaching my siblings and me the importance of family values and fellowship. Like the family business, maintaining unity amongst their children and their children's families took much planning and intention. When I was a child, the summer vacations we took at Burt Lake, Michigan, were the opportune times to reconnect as a family. It was the ideal excuse to drop all other obligations and slow life down to focus on building relationships with one another.

However, as we got older, and especially after my parents moved to Florida, something certainly went missing from our lives. My mother and my aunts had sold our cottage at Burt Lake in the mid-1960s, and with that sale, the making of summer memories as a family ceased. With my sisters still living in Indianapolis, and my parents, Jim and I living in Florida, the Mahaffey family was split geographically. I still maintained a close, albeit long-distant, relationship with my sister Kate. We spoke on the phone often, sharing with each other the stories of our lives—the good, the bad, and even the ugly. We saw each other on short visits, but it just wasn't the same as the summer trips that we all looked forward to each year as kids. I have to thank my mother and father for realizing this, even as it was ten years later, when they reinaugurated the yearly Mahaffey Family Vacation. Seeing their family grow before their eyes, and wanting to be a part of all our lives, must have prompted their effort to make the initiative.

The first place they chose to host the Mahaffey Family Vacation was at Basin Harbor Club, which is positioned on the shores of Lake Champlain, Vermont. This getaway was recommended to my father by our contact at National Life of Vermont. Basin Harbor Club is a multi-generational, family-owned resort that prides itself in focusing on tradition. They offer amenities for large family and business group gatherings, encouraging visitors to return year after year. In addition to several lodges on site, the resort is outfitted with dozens of individual two- and three- bedroom cottages, all within a gorgeous golf course and lakefront setting. With a boat marina, on-site restaurant, and activities galore for the adults and children alike, my parents deemed it the ideal place for the big reunion.

Now at this time, Marianne was still pregnant with Tom. With the twins' birth still raw in our hearts, Marianne and I took this second pregnancy with much care and caution. Dr. LaPlatney had recommended that Marianne not travel at all that summer, and we prudently followed his direction. We encouraged the rest of the Mahaffey clan to go on ahead to Basin Harbor without us, even though we wished we could have joined them.

I have to laugh as I recall my phone call to my brother, Jim, during the big vacation at Basin Harbor that July. Marianne, about four months pregnant, and I were relaxing at home, sad to miss out on the festivities. However, from Jim's report on the phone call, it sounded like there were a few disasters we escaped. First, one of my nephews totaled his family's station wagon. Luckily, no one was injured. And then, two of the children, I cannot remember whom, were out boating on Lake Champlain and lost their boat motor!

Despite the near catastrophes, everyone had a splendid time and promised to return the following year when Marianne and I (and Tom) would be able to join them. Not only did they keep their promise, and we returned the following year, but we continued the Mahaffey Family Vacation tradition for the next 45 years. A few times we branched out to visit different destinations—Michigan, Maine, Colorado, and California, to name a few. But, we always ended up coming back to Basin Harbor, Vermont. The timeless tradition, the five-star amenities, and the stunning beauty of the lake and resort kept us coming back year after year, even after my parents had passed.

The Mahaffey family skiing in Colorado

Finally in 2018, we decided it was time to end the 45-year streak. Sadly, my brother, Jim, and my sister Ann were in declining health. We did not want a death to be the reason for ending the Mahaffey Family Vacations. Instead, we were proactive and settled on 2018 as the final hurrah. Amazingly, over 100 family members attended. If my parents were alive at that time, I am certain they would have been astonished to see how their little family had grown—their four children and their spouses, eighteen grandchildren and their spouses, and an ever-growing number of great grandchildren. It was an unbelievable turnout, as people traveled from near and far, across the United States, to all get together at Basin Harbor, Vermont.

Mahaffey Family Vacation photo, Basin Harbor, Vermont

I am grateful for my parents for valuing our family culture enough to make these trips possible. While they were alive, they paid for each and every trip. After their passing, the family trusts paid for them. It was a tremendous blessing to have the means to unite our massive and growing family. Although the great Mahaffey Family Vacations eventually ended, the family continues on growing and growing with each generation.

Marianne and I are extremely fortunate to have three wonderful children who have grown to be mature, accomplished adults. Each has now married and grown families of their own. Our son, Tom, was lucky to meet a remarkable girl on a weekend trip to North Carolina. Her name is Shannon, and she is originally from Henderson, Kentucky. They married in January 2002 in Raleigh, North Carolina. Soon after, they blessed Marianne and I with our first granddaughter, Ansleigh. As it turned out, Shannon's father, Ben Campbell, and I graduated from Notre Dame in

1966 from the same Business school—Ben majoring in accounting and me in finance. What a small world!

My daughter, Colleen, was next to get married, in June 2010, after falling in love with her high school sweetheart, Jared Carnes. That same year, in October 2010, my daughter, Kiley, married Jeremy Tollberg in the beautiful setting of Highlands, North Carolina. What a whirlwind it was to have two weddings in one year! But, just as the family came together for the Mahaffey Family Vacations, my children's weddings were a great bringing together of loved ones. Marianne and I were ever so delighted to have these lovely people join our family. Kiley and Jeremy now have two girls, Reese and Piper. Colleen and Jared also have two children—a boy and a girl, named Colton and Mackenzie. My hope is that my children will continue to remain close as they grow and nurture their own families—and perhaps, continue with Mahaffey family vacations of their own. The Mahaffey folklore is a treasure to be passed generation to generation.

Mark and daughter, Kiley, on her wedding day

One special, fun family event that I remember back in 2012 was when Marianne and I hosted a big, family dinner at our house. This dinner was prepared by none other than culinary master and Food Network star, Emeril Lagasse. I had won the dinner at a fundraiser auction gala benefiting All Children's Hospital. I remember bidding for the opportunity to have Emeril Lagasse cook at my home.

$50,000! $60,000! $75,000! $100,000!... Sold!!!

An expensive dinner, no doubt, but per my connection to All Children's, I could not think of a better cause. Plus, a dinner with Emeril Lagasse was certainly thrilling! After winning the bid, I shouted out in jest, gesturing to the combo band in the corner of the banquet hall, "Gee, well can I at least have the combo band play for the dinner as well?" Bill Edwards, who was running the event, replied back, "Certainly!"

Well, as promised, a few months later, Emeril Lagasse was scheduled to come to our home. The dinner was originally supposed to be for eight people, but between Marianne and I, Bill Edwards and his wife, a few close friends (including Joe & Angie Jimenez), and our children and their spouses, there ended up being 18 guests for Emeril's grand dinner. In the days before the event, Marianne and I brought in several extra refrigerators to store the quantity of food, as Emeril's crew came early to set up and prep much of the meal. Marianne and I also hired a few extra hands from a local catering company to help with service. Emeril Lagasse was every bit as entertaining as he was on television, and his food was phenomenal. Mouthwatering course after course was brought to our table, and we all feasted like kings and queens—all while being charmed by the promised combo band. The dinner was a delectable event we will never forget. It is moments like that—with the whole of our family around the dinner table, mingling and bonding— where I can't help but just sit back and think to myself how proud I am to have everyone together.

The Mahaffey family with Emeril Lagasse

The ingredients that make the folklore rich and colorful will always be the experiences we share as family. Whether arduous or exultant, the time that we spend with loved ones is the cement that binds the family together. Perhaps the profound pain that Marianne and I suffered when we lost our first two children helped us gain a perspective as parents that we may have never had without that experience. Time with our children, and now our grandchildren, is precious to us. I cannot help but feel immensely grateful for all the little moments that we share together. Perhaps the gift that our twins, Tom and John, left us were spectacles. Spectacles to see the colors of life a little brighter, a little more vibrant. Spectacles to appreciate the finer details. Spectacles to filter out the gray, and see the beauty in family that spans generations. The past, however lost, will always be a part of us.

Mark and Marianne and their grandchildren

12

EARL AND FERN

Here's to the land of the long leaf pine,
The summer land where the sun doth shine,
Where the weak grow strong and the strong grow great,
Here's to "Down Home," the Old North State!

North Carolina's official state toast, written by Leonora Martin

The years when Tom, Kiley, and Colleen were still young were some of my favorites in the span of my lifetime. They gave me the gift of being a father, offering me more opportunities than ever before to be a leader. I was not only the *Pathfinder* finding my own path, but I gained the responsibility of guiding my children on their paths as well. I have found throughout much of my life, the best way to lead is by taking a step back and letting others blossom on their own. Nonetheless, it brings me great joy to think back to those days when my kids were young, and when they looked up to me as their hero. I deem some of our fondest memories—and I am sure my children would agree—were our own little family vacations, most notable of which were those to North Carolina.

Marianne and I loved the little life we had built in Saint Petersburg when our children were young. But every year, as the summer sun began to swell in this tropical southern state, we ached to escape the heat. The dense air, thick with moisture, settled heavily along the coast like a sticky syrup pooling on a plate of pancakes. The summer also marked Florida's rainy season. Every day, at mid-afternoon, wonderful and welcomed torrents of rain passed through, fizzing out the blaze and offering a cooling splash of reprieve, like an ice-cold coke on a parched throat. The cycle continued day after day from about June to September.

Without a doubt, summers in Florida were worth enduring in order to experience the absolutely pristine weather conditions offered the remainder of the year. Low humidity, sunny skies, and cool breezes swept through the state every day from fall into spring. After living in Florida for several years and experiencing the seasonal cycle, we thought the ideal situation would be to have a summer home—a retreat from the heat—somewhere we could say longer than the week-long, larger Mahaffey Family Reunion.

I thought back to all the memories I had made at Burt Lake, Michigan, as a child. We had stayed up there for months at a time, and I wanted to give my children a similar experience. Saint Petersburg is beautiful, but there is something special about escaping the hot, summer city life, and heading north to experience open spaces, cooler weather, and tree-filled forests. Burt Lake was certainly too far of a drive from Saint Petersburg, but over time, Marianne and I found the perfect replacement.

Highlands, a quaint town nestled in the Blue Ridge Mountain Range of western North Carolina, was the special place where we chose to establish our Mahaffey summer home. Perched high on the slope of a mountain, this house was built with a great amount of love and dedication. It is a place where a multitude of memories have been made with friends and family, hearts have bonded, and curious and adventurous spirits have been nurtured.

Returning to North Carolina summer after summer since the 1980s, Marianne and I and our children have developed a deep connection with North Carolina. We have made many wonderful and longstanding friendships there, which keep us coming back year after year, even after our children have grown. To this day, our home in

Highlands is a treasure that I continue to share with my friends, children and grandchildren. The journey of how Marianne and I came to find Highlands, North Carolina, is a story in itself. We did not always love North Carolina. In fact, it started off as one of our least favorite vacations we ever took.

It all began in our early years of marriage, when Marianne and I traveled to Lake Toxaway, North Carolina, with two other couples. A friend of a friend of Marianne's graciously offered for us to rent her cabin there for a ten-day holiday. We coordinated the trip with the two other couples and could not have been more excited for the end-of-summer getaway in early September. I volunteered to drive the six of us up to the Lake Toxaway cabin, as we owned a wood-paneled, Country Squire station wagon, which had a reputation as being the quintessential vehicle for road trips. Lake Toxaway was about a nine-hour drive from Saint Petersburg, but we thought, with good friends, the time would go quickly. We could not have been more wrong.

The vehicle was rather large, but with three couples, a large load of luggage, and three sets of golf clubs, it felt as if we were resident inside a stuffed turkey. To make matters worse, one of the couples had a head cold. Their coughing and sneezing made me wonder why they even chose to come. Hour after hour we drove until we hit the mountains. Maneuvering that overstuffed station wagon up and down the slopes of the mountain had its own challenges. But as a passenger, poor Marianne began to get car sick. She had been sitting in the rear bench, which happened to face backwards in the car's design. I cannot imagine the nauseating feeling watching the mountains roll like the ebb and flow of the ocean while moving backwards. Luckily a seat change helped, and eventually, we got to our cabin before dark.

The cabin was in a lovely location, just off the shores of Lake Toxaway. However, stepping through the front door, the ladies were soon appalled.

"Oh, its filthy," Marianne cried.

Without hesitation, she and the two other ladies immediately got to work cleaning the place. They spent the next several days giving the floors, the kitchen, and the bathrooms their utmost attention. However, with no air conditioning and unseasonably warm temperatures, I was determined to get out and have some fun.

"Let's rent a boat while we are here," I suggested.

The couple with the head cold grunted. "Too expensive," they said.

I eventually talked them into it, explaining that splitting the cost would make it more affordable. But the problems did not end there. Marianne and I began to notice the other two couples arguing often about little things. Apparently, they were in the midst of some sort of feud. Luckily, on the last day, the couples finally made up, and we went out to a lovely restaurant. At least the trip ended on a high note.

Through all the challenges, I learned a few things on that trip about traveling with other couples. First and foremost, if you are driving, always drive separately if it is more than two couples. Second, ten days was too long. A week at the most would have been better. Third, when traveling with couples, it is better to travel in even numbers—two or four couples total—never three. Lastly, never rent a home without air conditioning in the summer. Overall, we enjoyed ourselves, but we vowed we would never do a trip in the North Carolina mountains again.

A few years later, we met some of our closest couple friends, Carl and Lee Ann Lambrecht. Carl and I first met serving together on the Saint Petersburg Chamber of Commerce board. He was a real estate executive, owner of a very successful local real estate brokerage firm, Lambrecht and Associates. He was president of the Suncoast Association of Realtors and was very active on the Tampa Bay area's development scene. Realizing we had a lot in common, and knowing that our wives would get along famously, we began getting together socially as couples.

As our friendship grew, one day in early spring 1984, Carl and Lee Ann extended an invitation to Marianne and me to travel with them to North Carolina. Carl said, "We would love for you to join us as we travel to Highlands later this month. It is beautiful there this time of year."

"Eh…" I muttered with hesitation. "Is it anywhere near Lake Toxaway?" I did not want to repeat our last North Carolina excursion.

Carl laughed. "Yes and no," he said. "Don't worry. You will love it."

After much convincing, we finally trusted them and graciously accepted their invitation. Hiring a babysitter to stay with our two children in Saint Petersburg (as Colleen was not yet born), we headed up to Highlands that May.

This trip could not have been more different than our first experience in the Carolina mountains. Marianne and I instantly fell in love with Highlands. This charming town, situated at 4118 feet elevation, is one of the highest towns east of the Mississippi River. This height offers its visitors cooler temperatures, stunning views, and a myriad of waterfalls and hiking trails within the surrounding Nantahala National Forest. The historic downtown is an enchanting retreat with beautiful, brick-front boutiques, fine restaurants, spas, and art galleries lining the main street. It was positively lovely.

Beyond appreciating the post-card perfect setting, we had a splendid time developing a closer friendship with Carl and Lee Ann. Our visit was so enjoyable that we returned the following two years with them as well. I distinctly remember Marianne being pregnant with Colleen during our second trip. Carl and Lee Ann's infectious personalities, full of love and laughter, brought so much joy to Marianne and me. We have traveled together with the Lambrecht's many times since, but I will never forget those first few trips we spent together in the mountains.

One of my favorite memories began one day when the four of us were merrily driving out in the mountainous country. We were giddy as could be, giggling and chatting away. As we meandered through a small mountain town—I cannot remember the name—I spied a roadside shop named Earl's Pickin' Parlor. Although it fashioned a rather shabby exterior, it appeared to be a guitar and banjo dealer. I did not bother stopping the car, as I am not an aspiring musician, but I was impacted by the name. *Earl*, I thought to myself, *What a name. Certainly, it is a mighty fine name for a mountain man.*

In jest, I announced to my fellow passengers in my best southern drawl, "All y'all. From here on out, call me Earl."

We all roared with laughter. Carl joined in on the fun proclaiming, "And call me Wilbur."

We all laughed again and used these names the entire car ride. We of course included our lovely wives in the fun bestowing Marianne with the name Fern, and Lee Ann with the name Petunia—Tunia for short. Well, these silly nicknames have stuck to this day. When we are in the North Carolina mountains, we all refer to each other as our assumed country names. It is such fun!

After our delightful experiences in North Carolina with Carl and Lee Ann, Marianne and I began to toy with the idea of getting a place of our own in Highlands. After we returned home to Saint Petersburg from the third trip, I was surprised to receive a brochure in the mail for Highlands Falls Country Club. A letter was enclosed offering us a free week to stay at the club in exchange for exploring properties with their on-site broker. The brochure was laced with gorgeous photos of mountains with vibrant sunset backdrops. Beautiful stone front homes were featured surrounded by gorgeous leaves of autumn color. Something about the photos stirred in me memories of Burt Lake. The trees, the sunsets, the summer cottages—it already felt like home.

I immediately showed Marianne the brochure. "What do you think about this?" I asked. "It may be an excellent opportunity to bring our children up to Highlands. However, I'd like to stay two weeks instead of one—to really take our time to explore the area."

"Sounds wonderful," Marianne replied.

I called the phone number on the brochure and spoke with the director. I requested to stay for two weeks instead of one, adding that I would pay for the second week. He agreed. I also asked if I could bring our three children, our housekeeper/nanny, and our dog. He also agreed. We booked the trip for July, and we all eagerly awaited the big family vacation.

When July arrived, all seven of us, including our pup, hopped into our minivan and headed north. Excitement and anticipation beamed in my children's faces as the terrain changed before their eyes. The flat landscape of Florida and southern Georgia began to transform into towering mountains as we entered into the Blue Ridge Mountain range. The layered, ombre shades of blue mountain silhouettes spread across the horizon like broad strokes of watercolor, with lighter and lighter tones reaching higher to the heavens. We were in awe at the spectacular display.

Throughout the two weeks we spent at the club, we traversed the surrounding area looking at homes with the broker. Our favorite was a two-story spec home within the Highlands Falls Country Club. It had dazzling views, but an unfinished lower level. Marianne and I were not sure we wanted to get into a construction project just yet. We hemmed and hawed over what to do.

On the last evening of our vacation, Marianne and I planned to have a date night at the country club restaurant for dinner. Cliffie, our housekeeper/nanny, offered to stay with our children. After all the house hunting, Marianne and I yearned for some quiet time to reconnect as a couple. Just as we were walking out the door, we received a call from the broker.

She said, "I have found one more house for you. It's on the next street up from the other house. It's located at a higher elevation and has a much more spectacular view."

"Oh wow!" we exclaimed. "We are just about to head to dinner. Can we look at it afterwards?"

"Yes," she consented. "It is currently being rented to a family, but the residents will be happy to show you around. How about I meet you there at eight o'clock?"

"Sounds like a plan," I said.

After dinner, we curiously drove to the home. We instantly fell in love with the homey cottage. It was a two-story, four-bedroom home with an open floorplan and a two-way fireplace between the living room and master bedroom. We arrived just at sunset, which illuminated the sky in a spectacular array of pinks and oranges spanning wide and far. A small pond, tucked in the valley, mirrored the colors in brilliant exhibition.

"This is the one!" We both exclaimed.

After negotiating with the seller, we agreed on a fair price.

On the drive home, as we were descending down the slope of a mountain, Marianne looked over at me and said, "Earl, did we just agree to buy a house? How are we ever going to pay for this?

"I have no idea, Fern," I responded with a smile, though confidently knowing that we would figure it out. A few months later, in October 1986, we were officially homeowners of a summer home in Highlands.

In April, the following year, Marianne and I went up to Highlands alone to set up the house and get it ready for the family to come visit that summer. I remember a rather funny story from our first night there, although it was certainly not humorous at the time. It was a fairly chilly evening, but Marianne and I could not resist stepping out onto the floating, second-story balcony to witness the view. Feeling toasty from snuggling next to the grand fireplace, I stepped out onto the ice-coated deck in bare feet. Marianne was smart enough to wear shoes, but neither of us wore coats. The cold temperature was the last thought on our minds as we beheld the vision before us. A frost-covered landscape glimmered in shimmering sparkle as if it were perfectly dusted with icing sugar. The glowing sun was just beginning to set in the rainbow sherbet-colored sky, setting the ice-covered trees ablaze.

Closing the door behind us, to not let the heat escape the warm house, we enjoyed the view. We breathed in the sweet, earthy scent of white pine, which brought me right back to being a child at Burt Lake. "We've done an incredible thing here, Fern," I said. "I think we found the perfect house."

Marianne agreed. "I can already imagine all the evenings I am going to sit out here, drinking a glass of wine, watching the sunset. I can't wait to bring the kids up here. They are going to love it."

We spent the next few minutes soaking in the magnificent panorama, pinching ourselves that this could be truly real. We felt so incredibly blessed.

"Let's head back in, Earl," Marianne said, starting to shiver.

I agreed and attempted to slide the heavy, glass door open. To my dismay, it would not budge. Panic rose in Marianne's eyes. "Are we locked out here?" she said, horrified at the thought of freezing to death on that balcony.

As the sun began to set behind the mountaintops, extinguishing the warmth like a pinched flame, the cold air quickly developed a bitter bite. Our minds went through several gyrations quickly conjuring ideas on how to get out of this mess. I peered over the deck railing. It was quite a steep drop. Jumping down was certainly not an option. Then, looking up, I observed that the roof line was not too far away.

"I have an idea," I suggested. "How about you get up on my shoulders, and I will lift you up to the roof. The front of the house isn't as far of a drop. I think the front door is unlocked."

Marianne glanced at me, slowly shifting her eyes in a look that said, "Are you crazy?"

"Or..." I continued. "How about I shimmy down the downspout?"

"Shimmy!?" Marianne cried.

"Didn't you ever shimmy as a kid?" I wondered out loud.

"I most certainly did not. Girls don't shimmy," she said, very matter-of-factly. "That downspout does not look very secure."

"Okay. I agree with that. One more idea," I continued. "I can tie this TV cable to your waist, and then lower you down to the ground."

We both looked over the railing at the cliff below us. I admit, that was my worst idea yet. Fortunately, I did not execute that plan, as we both nixed that idea immediately. Panic overcame us. We started screaming, "Help! Help!" to no avail. There was no one within earshot. In desperation, I went back over to the sliding glass door. I jiggled the handle hoping to break free the lock somehow. With barely any pressure, the door slid open!

Marianne and I gazed at each other in shock. The door must have jammed. It was unlocked the whole time! Quickly scurrying inside, we leapt onto the couch in front of the fire and pulled a large blanket over us. We cried and laughed at the silliness of the whole episode. What a way to spend the first evening in our new house!

We owned that first summer home in North Carolina for five wonderful years. When the children were on their summer school break, from June until mid-August, we would reside in our Highlands home, creating family memories. Cliffie, our housekeeper/nanny, would join us for many of these trips. She ended up being a fixture up there on the small lake in Highlands Falls County Club, teaching our children, as well as other children, how to fish. My obligations at the Mahaffey Apartment

Company required that I commute back and forth every other week, but I did not mind the travel. It was well worth the inconvenience to be able to give my family that little slice of heaven in the mountains.

As a housewarming gift, Carl and Lee Ann, or rather, Wilbur and Tunia, had a large plaque made for us to be stationed near the front door of our summer house. The plaque read, "Earl and Fern's." I admit it may have caused some confusion for the mailman once or twice, but we proudly displayed it front and center. It not only symbolized the relaxed and carefree life that we set up in the mountains, but also the beautiful friendship that we had with Carl and Lee Ann Lambrecht.

Earl and Fern's plaque

We loved that summer home, but in 1991, we decided it was time to upgrade a bit. The idea to buy another lot first came from our realtor a few years earlier. She had suggested I consider investing in one of the lots that was for sale on our cul-de-sac. She recommended lot #5, which looked like Sherwood Forest to me. However, she promised that when the trees would be cleared for the house, the view would be fabulous. It was an unbelievable deal at $45,000, which included the club membership fees of $15,000. Intending it to be an investment piece, I didn't think twice. "I'll take it," I said.

After owning the lot for three years, our builder friend in Highlands, Vic Wood—who had built several additions for us on our summer house—mentioned that he was going into retirement. We were sad to hear, as he had been a great help to us in improving our Highlands home. Fortunately, he promised us that if we happened to need him again in the near future, he would come out of retirement for us. We were astounded! Vic Wood was a top-rate builder. Our minds reeled with the possibilities for the vacant lot. We determined that if we were ever to build a new summer home, now was the time. That night, I pulled out a pencil and paper and began sketching floorplans. We were extremely grateful when Vic Wood agreed to build us a new, larger summer home.

Over the next 14 months, Vic Wood, partnering with Merlin Crowe, built a beautiful, 5,000 square foot summer house for our family. We hired a remarkable, local architect, who was able to deliver every detail that we requested. From the expansive back deck, to eliminating the need for any columns in the great room, to installing the biggest kitchen we could have ever dreamed, nothing was out of reach. My most challenging request was my desire for windows on the front *and* rear of the lower level, which seemed virtually impossible due to the house being constructed against the mountainside. This architect, however, was a mastermind and created a cleverly-engineered well of light that brightened the entire lower space.

Every detail of the home exemplified Marianne and my tastes in home finishes. Tennessee rock cloaked the exterior of the home. Honey oak cabinets and trim added warmth and richness to the interior space. Tall, picture windows spanned the rear of the home, inviting the panoramic views of the Blue Ridge mountains into the space. The views from the expansive deck were breathtaking, taking the spectator on a visual tour of thousands of miles of Blue Ridge peaks. The sheer openness of the gorgeous, sprawling landscape stirred in me feelings of freedom, happiness, and peace. Our friend, Carol Stewart, an accomplished interior designer, helped us with the furnishings and décor in the new house.

This masterpiece was the culmination of the skills of many master tradesmen from near and far. We requested that Jim Burreski, who was one of the best cabinet makers in Saint Petersburg, design and install the cabinets and trim work in our Highlands home. He was happy to fulfill our desire, and he worked diligently to complete the project despite the distance. Unfortunately, on the morning of installation, western North Carolina received a very rare winter storm that sheeted the mountains in five inches of snow. Being from Florida, I am sure the snowy weather was a big surprise to our cabinet maker. At first, his truck was unable to get up the steep driveway, but with Merlin's help, he eventually made it. The piece of trim work that impressed me the most was the piece of cabinetry that wrapped around our interior jacuzzi tub in a unique double angle. Merlin had relayed the measurements to Jim over the phone, and I was astonished to see the piece fit like a glove. It was amazing to witness such tremendous skill and coordination between everyone involved.

In appreciation for their hard work, I promised the builders that we would throw them a big party in the new house—if they met their completion date goal of Friday, June 27, 1992. I recall on the day of the party, the builders scurried to finish the last-minute touches. I was especially nervous they were not going to make it in time when I saw that the asphalt driveway had not yet been paved by mid-day. To my shock, at 5:00 pm, just hours before the party was supposed to start, the asphalt crew showed up and finished the job just in time. Later, I found out that the paver was Merlin's son-in-law. No wonder he was able to get the paver on the job at such a late hour on a Friday evening! The party was a true celebration of completion as we congratulated over 60 workers for a job well done. As a special thank you, we gifted the builders bonus checks to show our appreciation for their efforts. They were extremely grateful, saying that they had never before received bonus checks from a customer.

Naturally, we moved the "Earl and Fern's" plaque to the new house, and to this day, it is stationed proudly on the front door. Continuing this game of nicknames for many years, we established a tradition where we have a guest book for all our guests to sign when they come to visit us in the mountains—but with one caveat. They must give themselves a country name while they are here, and sign it in the book. It has been such fun over the years to see the names people have come up with.

There is also one other special item in our Highlands summer home that always seems to catch the attention of our visitors. It is a stained-glass art piece in our kitchen window of a 1947 MG car. People ask, "Why this car?" and I oblige them with the story.

One day, Marianne and I were sitting on our Highlands summer home deck, enjoying the beautiful panorama. Out of the blue, Marianne said, "Mark, I feel so incredibly blessed. Thank you for building this wonderful home for our family."

"Oh, you're welcome. I am enjoying it as well," I replied.

"I think this has got to be my most favorite place in the world," Marianne said. "Is there anything in the world you want, but don't have?"

Her question caught me by surprise.

"I have lived a very blessed life, and I have just about everything I've ever wanted. There is one thing, however..." I said with a smile.

Marianne, quite surprised, asked, "What is it?"

"Well, a late 40s/early 50s vintage MG," I said.

"What is that?" Marianne questioned.

"Well, it is a vintage car that used to be made in England. It was a childhood dream of mine. My neighbor up at Burt Lake owned a light turquoise MG. It was a beautiful, two-seater, convertible, classic car. He could tell how much I loved the car as a small boy and used to take me on rides when we visited for the summer. I vowed that someday, somehow, I would own one of those."

Marianne nodded, and that was the end of the conversation as our attention returned to enjoying the landscape.

That same year, on Christmas morning 2006, we exchanged gifts in our usual fashion. First, the children opened theirs, then Marianne and I exchanged our gifts last. I cannot remember what I got Marianne—most likely jewelry. But I remember her walking over to me holding a folded piece of paper. "Merry Christmas, Mark," she said as she placed the paper in my hand. I made a guess that the paper described something that she had perhaps ordered that did not arrive in time, as that had happened before. I was shocked to open it up and find a photo of a bright red, classic MG with a matching red interior.

Marianne explained, "I didn't buy it yet, but I found a few MGs for you. I wasn't sure which one I should get. I had your friends as my board of advisors—our next-door neighbor, who owned an MG, as well as Steve and Dick. They all said, 'Don't buy one; just find one. It can still be a gift from you, but let him buy it.'"

I was speechless. This was the greatest gift I could imagine. I wasn't sure if I liked the red-on-red, but I appreciated her sentiment so very much.

The next day, Marianne pulled out her laptop and showed me a listing for a maroon MG with a cream-colored interior. She said, "This is the MG that I really wanted to get you."

"Oh God! That is the car!" I exclaimed. I loved it!

I got a hold of the dealer, who was located in Atlanta, Georgia. We agreed that I would fly up there later that week to look at it and hopefully, make a deal. I chartered a plane, and invited Marianne and my son, Tom, to fly up with me to Atlanta. The dealer met us at the Peach Tree Airport. His name was Tommy Frasier. He was a retired NASCAR racer and looked like the quintessential car salesman. He let us take a ride in the car, and I instantly knew I wanted it. We made a deal, but there was one issue.

I said to Tommy, "Here's the thing. I want to keep the car in Highlands, North Carolina. But I don't need it until May."

Tommy replied, "No problem! I can hold it for you until then."

"Thank you, Tommy," I said. "And frankly, it's a '47 for God's sake. I'm worried about driving that up to the mountains."

He chucked, "I'm not going to let you drive it up to the mountains. I am going to deliver it to you on a flatbed truck. This is part of the deal."

Wow, I thought, and we shook hands.

Sure enough, Tommy Frasier held the MG, and when we arrived at Highlands for our summer trip, he delivered it. It has been there ever since.

Mark taking the grandkids for a ride in the 1947 MG

The stained-glass art piece is a tribute to that car. It was a gift given to me by my good friend Tom Rusche as a thank you for some of the travels we had shared together. This is the same Tom who had been the Mahaffey Insurance agent for many years, and eventually my boat partner and close friend. He had the stained-glass art piece custom made for me by a skilled artist in Smith Mountain Lake, Virginia. It is an exact depiction of my MG with mountains in the background. With the natural light flooding through the window, the stained-glass looks absolutely stunning. Every time I look at it, I not only feel the pride of ownership of that MG, but I feel immense gratitude. Gratitude for my wonderful wife for gifting me the fabulous car, and also, gratitude for my good friend, Tom Rusche, for thinking of me and having this special piece made.

Stained-glass window of MG

Throughout all the years that Marianne and I have visited Highlands, we, as well as our children, have been very fortunate to make many new friends. Some of them have come and gone over the years, but a few have been lasting and are very meaningful to us. Sam and Barbara Gassaway and Al and Annette Odom are two couples that Marianne and I just adore. We certainly cherish our relationship with these couples as we share our life experiences with them. Al Odom and I consider ourselves as close as brothers, as we have been on many adventures around the world together fishing, as well as bird hunting. Serving on the Highlands Falls Country Club Board for two different terms, I was fortunate to meet many other wonderful people in North Carolina as well. Working with this board was a very rewarding and great learning experience for me.

It is rather interesting for me to reflect on my life's path and comprehend the great friends that I have been lucky enough to meet as a result of Marianne and I spreading our wings a bit and establishing ourselves in more places than one. Highlands, North Carolina, has become more than a destination, more than an escape. Like many of our travels over the years, it has become a place of sharing and connecting with family and friends. However, it holds an extra quality that makes it more special than anywhere else we have visited. It is home.

The Mahaffey family in Highlands, NC

Autumn view from the Highlands summer home deck

13

ELON UNIVERSITY

Those who can do, do. Those who can do more, volunteer.

Author Unknown

The summer of 1992 was a big summer. Not only did we build the house of our dreams in the mountains, but also, we began the college search for our son, Tom, who would be graduating from Shorecrest High School the following year, 1993. North Carolina had a great influence on Tom, as we had been traveling there every summer since he was twelve years old. Tom gravitated toward the idea of attending college in North Carolina, as it was the magical place where we had built so many family memories, summer after summer. Marianne and I gave Tom free rein to make the decision of where he wanted to study, but we were there alongside him throughout the entire process. We also had a high school counselor and a private counselor guiding us along the way. We toured about nine colleges, first focusing on the larger schools in North Carolina, but nothing seemed like the perfect fit. While vigilantly attending school tour after school tour, we were focused on choosing the college best suited for Tom. What I did not comprehend at the time, however, is how Tom's decision would also positively impact me for the rest of my life.

Last on our list of schools to tour was Elon University. When Tom heard that Elon was near the town of Burlington, he said, "Ugh, it sounds like it's in the sticks." Burlington may not be a large city, but it certainly is not "in the sticks." It is located in the piedmont region of North Carolina between Greensboro and Raleigh. Although it may have begun as a rural/agricultural community, the textile industry took root there in the late 19th century. The long-standing textile company, Glenn Raven, founded in 1880 in Burlington, North Carolina, is now a global, fabric manufacturing giant. Allen Gant Sr., former president of Glenn Raven, invented panty hose in the 1950s. I ended up becoming good friends with his son, Allen Gant Jr., who is currently company chairman and CEO. Walking in his father's footsteps, he introduced another monumental textile innovation with the invention of Sunbrella fabric in the 1960s. It is incredible to contemplate the legacy Allen and his family have left in the textile industry. The town of Burlington may seem small, but it has certainly made a big impact on the world.

Adjacent to the city of Burlington resides Elon University, a beautiful, historic school that has grown to become a leading, prestigious university and one of the best schools in the nation. It recently received a #1 ranking by U.S. News and World Report for its excellence in undergraduate teaching. Also, it was the only university in the nation to rank in the top 20 of all eight categories of academic programs linked to student success and positive learning outcomes. The Elon community is very tightly knit, as students are encouraged to form mentoring relationships with faculty and staff, alumni, and fellow peers. Their belief in the importance of experiential learning is exemplified by the resources and opportunities provided on campus. The grounds are gorgeous with bricked, Williamsburg-style buildings nestled amongst a rich, verdant landscape. The 652-acre campus is a designated botanical garden, which includes the 56-acre Elon University Forest and the sustainably-grown Loy Farm.

Elon University

When Marianne, Tom, and I first visited Elon University, which was only Elon College at the time, we were impressed by its historic charm and student-centered environment. Their campus tour was one of the best we had experienced. Run by students, the tour immersed us into the life at Elon as we walked the grounds, sat in on a few classes, talked to professors, and were introduced to some of the top administration staff. The focus on human connections and learning-by-doing reminded me of my father's philosophies that he passed down to me. The school was a perfect fit.

Marianne and I were smart enough, however, to not push our opinion on Tom, a young 17-year-old ready to make his own way in this world. When we got back into the car after the tour, Marianne and I sat quietly waiting for Tom to say the first word. We got about a mile down the road when Tom called out confidently from the backseat, "You know, I think I like that school." Marianne and I thought to ourselves, *Yes!*

Four years later, in 1997, Tom graduated from Elon University with a Business Management degree. After witnessing Tom's exceptional experience at Elon, my daughter Kiley also made the decision to attend Elon and ultimately graduated with a degree in Psychology/Counseling. Much to my dismay, our youngest daughter, Colleen—who was our Maverick—did not want to follow in her older siblings' footsteps. She attended DePaul University in Chicago in her freshman year and subsequently transferred to the University of Central Florida in Orlando. I was pleased that it ended up being a great experience for her, and she eventually graduated with a degree in Business Management.

It was not until 2001, the year that Kiley graduated, that Elon became a personal decision for me. It all began a few years earlier when the school elected their new president, Leo Lambert. It was this president that brought Elon from a college to university status just a year after he was elected. I was first introduced to him by the Director of Development at Elon. He had thought the new president should meet me after Marianne and I had donated some money to the school library in my mother's memory. From that very first day that I met Leo Lambert, I knew we would be good friends. I was thoroughly impressed by his great passion for the community at Elon. He was smart, a straight-shooter, and very down-to-earth.

The pivotal day for me was in 2001 when I received a phone call from Leo. He wanted to fly down to Saint Petersburg to meet Marianne and I for lunch the following week. I cordially agreed, but I assumed he wanted more than to merely break bread. When I mentioned the planned lunch to Marianne, she had the same thought I had. "I wonder what he wants?" she said.

"I suppose he is looking for a donation," I replied. "I don't know him well, but I hear he has big ideas for the school."

On the day of the big lunch, Marianne and I met Leo at the Vinoy Hotel in Saint Petersburg. We ate a lovely lunch at their on-site restaurant, but were curious the entire meal about the purpose of the meeting. When dessert arrived, Leo finally made his move, which I have noticed over the years is standard operating procedure.

"Mark," Leo said. "You may have wondered why I was so eager to have lunch with you. The truth is, I am here to ask if you would consider joining the Elon University Board of Trustees."

"Wow," I said, honored. "I appreciate your offer. Let me think about it and I will let you know."

"No problem," Leo assured.

After serious thought and consideration, I made the decision to graciously accept Leo's offer. It was rather ironic that I had just told Marianne a few days prior that I planned to step back from volunteer activities, after having been involved in various organizations for many years. However, volunteering was a large part of my life and my development in the business world. I got to know a lot of people and a lot of people got to know me. My involvement on various boards throughout my adult life has had a lot to do with who I've become over the years. Although I admitted to Marianne that I perhaps needed to back off a bit, something told me I needed to do this. I needed to be a part of Elon University.

Now, over 20 years later, I can reflect back and confidently say that accepting Leo's invitation was one of the best decisions I have ever made. Elon has been one of the greatest boards I have ever been on, not only because of its accomplishments, but from the moment I walked into my first meeting, it felt like family. The board is massive, holding over 40 members, but within my first meeting, I knew everybody. Leo is extraordinarily talented as a leader, and is one of the few individuals that I have met in my life who is not only a visionary, but can find the means to accomplish and execute the vision completely. He has brought together an unbelievable team, guiding Elon University to higher and higher standards through service, insightful collaboration, and pure heart. I truly cherish my friendship with Leo Lambert and consider it the greatest blessing from my time at Elon.

One year, I decided it was time for the Elon board to get together for a retreat. I had seen the benefit of the stag parties my father held for his employees and partners, and I have become a great believer in retreats over the years. I consider them essential to supporting the comradery amongst the team members, and encouraging them to become better acquainted. I organized two retreats over the years for the Elon board members—one at Highlands and one at Saint Petersburg. At Highlands, I arranged for everyone to stay at the Old Edward's Inn, which is a historic hotel right downtown. Marianne and I hosted a dinner at our Highlands summer home, which proved to be such a memorable event with its beautiful views, charming ambience, and even better company. When we hosted the retreat in Saint Petersburg, the board members lodged at the Vinoy Hotel, located right on the stunning Tampa Bay waterfront. We also held a dinner at our house, and I arranged for several golf and boat outings as well. It was so fulfilling witnessing everyone mingle in a casual setting and get to know one another better. This is the stuff in life that is truly important.

My time at Elon exemplifies a strong symbiotic relationship. As I have donated my time and money over the years, I have also had the unique opportunity to meet and collaborate with some amazing people. Beyond my friendship with Leo Lambert and the members of the board, I have had the privilege of meeting some rather famous, influential individuals.

Justice Sandra Day O'Connor is one lady that I will never forget meeting. She was well-known for her role as the first female Justice to ever serve on the Supreme Court of the United States. I had met her on a second trip to Montana, which was sponsored by Elon University as a thank you to some of the top donors and board members. I had been the first chairman of a campaign that raised one-hundred million dollars, and Leo was extremely grateful for my efforts. It was an honor for Marianne and me to be invited on two trips to Montana, and an even bigger honor to meet this famous lady. Justice O'Connor had a connection to Elon through her role on the law school advisory board.

This trip to Montana was to visit Ruby Springs Lodge, a fly-fishing resort located right off the gorgeous Ruby River. It is owned by Paul Moseley, son of Furman Moseley, who was an alumnus and long-time donor at Elon University. About six couples were invited on this weekend trip, including Leo Lambert and his wife, Laurie, as they were the hosts. It was at this resort that I met Justice O'Connor, who had recently retired from her Justice position at that time. Throughout the first few days, I only briefly saw her while fly-fishing or at evening dinners, but on Sunday, we were invited on a new adventure where I got to know her a little bit better.

I remember the owner, Paul Moseley, announcing to the group, "For anyone who is interested, we have an activity planned for you to do a little hunting during your stay. Up in the hills, we have a real problem with Montana gophers. They are a real nuisance and carry the bubonic plague, rabies, parasites, and often bite. There is no state limit on the number of gophers we can shoot, so the activity can be quite exhilarating—like a real-life Whack-a-Mole."

I had hunted quail and boar in the past, but never Montana gopher. I certainly was going to take advantage of this new opportunity. Marianne decided to stay back at the lodge, but I was surprised to see Justice O'Connor raise her hand to join the hunt.

That Sunday afternoon, Justice O'Connor, another couple from Elon, and I, as well as several guides, headed out to a ranch in the hills to catch some gophers. A large truck towed a 20-foot war wagon, as they called it, which had six rifle stations built into it. We had the absolute time of our lives shooting at those little varmints as they would pop out of their holes in the ground. The wind was blowing like a banshee up there, which delivered an additional challenge, but we were successful nonetheless. After the hunt, the guides pulled out a bottle of bourbon in triumph, and we all cheered to a job well done. We had such a wonderful time out there, as it was a lot of fun and a lot of laughs. I was surprised to see what a great shot Justice O'Connor was. I later learned that she grew up on Lazy B Cattle Ranch in El Paso, Texas. Raised a country girl, she would practice shooting jackrabbits and coyotes as a kid. No wonder she was so comfortable with a rifle. We also found out later that the ranch in the hills where we hunted gophers, was owned by the famous American entrepreneur and television producer, Ted Turner. Evidently, Paul Moseley had received special permission from Ted. I am very grateful for that unique experience.

Later that evening, we rejoined the rest of the group. I remember at the very tail end of the trip, right before heading back to the airport to return home, Justice O'Connor and I were playing a game of cards. I said to her, "You know, you remind me so much of my mother." I could tell I had caught her by surprise.

"Well," she replied. "I guess I will take that as a compliment."

I said, "It is the *highest* compliment. My mother was a very strong, Irish woman, and I wouldn't call her opinionated, but she had her opinions."

Justice O'Connor laughed. "Are you calling me opinionated?"

I clarified, "No, but you cannot deny you have strong opinions." We laughed at that.

"I've enjoyed playing cards with you," she finally said as it was time to go. "Maybe down the line, we'll play again."

I agreed, "I'd love that."

Although that was the last time I ever did see Justice Sandra Day O'Connor, I thank Elon for that moment. It was special to meet such a remarkable, strong woman, who has been an inspiration to many people throughout her career.

John Glenn and Colin Powell are two other famous people I have had the privilege of meeting through Elon University. John Glenn was an astronaut and United States Senator, and I was star struck to be able to say hello to him and shake his hand. For Colin Powell, a former United States Statesman and General, I had the honor of introducing him to over 2000 people before he gave a speech at Elon University. As we were exiting the stage after the speech, I lost my footing on the poorly-lit and un-railed stairway and almost descended into the abyss. As I began to fall, in a flash of a second, General Colin Powell grabbed my shirt collar and prevented the worst. I was completely embarrassed. I thanked the General and, humiliated, continued on walking. Luckily nobody in the audience seemed to notice—nobody, except Marianne, who was sitting in the front row.

"Oh my God," Marianne mouthed to me as I walked past her, in disbelief of what had just happened.

I whispered, "How'd you like that? General Powell just saved my life."

I suppose that was one way to get to know the general. I have a photo of him and me in my office from that day. What a great man. I had asked him that day at lunch if he ever thought about becoming president. He answered, "I decided that it wasn't for me. And besides, I'm happily married to my beautiful wife of many years, and she has made it very clear that we would no longer be married if I ran for president."

I laughed. "That's an honest answer," I said.

Meeting those three famous people were incredible experiences for me. However, they are only three small examples of all the ways that Elon University has impacted my life over the many years I have served on the board. Several years ago, Leo Lambert granted me an honorary doctorate degree. It is one of my proudest achievements, as it symbolizes a lifetime journey of dedicated service and collaboration.

Mark Mahaffey receiving an honorary doctorate from Elon University

More recently, I was honored with having the newly built campus restaurant named after me, which is located in the Inn at Elon. Leo and I had been pushing for an on-campus hotel for quite some time. I had taken Leo to a Notre Dame football game, where we had seen the benefit of their on-site hotel, The Morris Inn. When the Elon board approved construction of the hotel, we determined that the funds would come from a combination of private money and bonds. We decided that Elon University would entirely own this hotel, as opposed to leasing it out to a larger hotel company. As owners, we would have the freedom to use the profits to give back to the school in the form of scholarships. It was an incredible idea, we just needed to get the funding in order. The hotel was proposed $30 million to build. We hoped to get at least five million from personal board member donations.

One day, I received a call from Elon's Director of Development, Jim Piatt.

He said, "Leo and I want to come down and have lunch with you."

Oh boy, I thought to myself. It is never just to have lunch. I agreed nonetheless.

At lunch, Jim and Leo said, "Mark, you have been the leader of this project from the board's point of view. We would also like you to be the lead donor."

"I see," I said, not really surprised by the request. "What does that entail?" I asked.

"We want you to give $2 million," Leo said.

I was stunned for a moment. "That is a very large number," I finally said.

"Well," Jim suggested, "you can do it over time."

I said, "Yes, I understand. Let me think about it."

Marianne and I talked it over and agreed to make a ten-year plan to give Elon the funds. We even increased our pledge to $2.5 million, as the proposed cost for the hotel kept rising. With donation funds rolling in and construction on its way, Leo Lambert said, "Mark, we want to name something after you."

I appreciated the sentiment and suggested, "How about the bar located within the hotel restaurant?"

He replied, "How about the restaurant itself?"

I thought about it and decided I rather liked the idea. I reminisced back to my days serving as a waiter at Indian River Inn with Dick deVore. It was a very special time in my youth and development. I came up with the idea of calling the restaurant, "The Mark," which is not only my name, but is also fitting as we certainly hit "the mark" time and time again as we pushed for Elon University's growth. This first-class, 80-room hotel and top-notch restaurant are fine additions to the Elon campus. Not only does it offer visitors a place to stay and dine, but it has brought in a great deal of profit to the school, which has been dedicated to student scholarships. In the first year, it brought in over $800,000. What an impact!

On the day of the hotel's inauguration, my son and daughter, Tom and Kiley, and their children, came to support me as I gave the opening speech. I talked about my experience on the board and the exceptional people that I have met through Elon University. I also described the story of my experience at Indian River Inn as a waiter. I shared that I had the time of my life at that inn, and it taught me a great deal about myself and human nature.

Later that evening, after the speech, my son, Tom, shared with me that my granddaughter, Piper, had been in awe of seeing me give a speech in front of all those people. "Papa's famous!" she had exclaimed.

I laughed when I heard the story. "Piper, let's not get too carried away here," I told her afterwards.

Famous or not, I feel like I have grown so much over the last twenty years serving on Elon University's Board of Trustees. It has been extremely inspiring to see Elon grow into an even better establishment as its leaders work tirelessly to put the students first, enriching their lives and supporting their futures. Leo Lambert has become one of my dearest friends. We have worked together, traveled together, and laughed together, sharing with each other life's greatest gift—friendship.

The Inn at Elon

"The Mark" within The Inn at Elon

14

MY FATHER'S FOOTSTEPS

The quality of a father can be seen in the goals, dreams, and aspirations he sets not only for himself, but for his family.

Reed Markham

As I look back at my life—at my career, my family, my friendships, and all the boards I've served on—I can't help but see the strong influence of my father. From the family business to family vacations, to nurturing friendships and contributing to the community, he was my guiding light and exemplar through it all. So much of my drive to be a devoted leader to my family was inspired and demonstrated by my father. He had such a strong, Irish spirit with a passion for human connections. Partnerships in the business were just a small fragment of his capacity to build relationships with the people around him. He had a strong friendship network, but most importantly, he prioritized the bonds he held with his family.

I treasured the precious moments that my father and I had while he was alive. I was beyond grateful for the chance to work alongside him for most of my career and for the chance to learn all I could from him. It is ironic that those moments gain exponential value only after they are gone. It is only after the time has passed that I look back and reflect on what an impact my father has made on my life and cherish it.

I remember the day my father passed away, at the ripe age of 80-years-old. It stirred up every raw emotion that I had buried deep inside me. I will never forget how significant that day was in my life—for on that day, a generational shift occurred. I felt a colossal amount of new responsibility for continuing the Mahaffey story where my father left off. It was a day of immense sadness, but in that pain, I felt closer to my father than I had ever been before. I will never forget the evening of the day before Christmas Eve, 1990.

"He doesn't have much longer. It is time to prepare," the nurse gently advised my mother and I as we stood in the hallway outside my father's bedroom on that fateful day.

I nodded solemnly with understanding, as I had known for a while, he was nearing the end. Despite his razor-sharp mind and determination to never retire, my father's health had been in a gradual decline for the past few months. Tears began to swell in my mother's balmy blue eyes. But like my father, she had that tough, stubborn Irish blood. She would not let herself break down in front of her son. I carefully wrapped my arms around her petite frame, sensing her need for comfort. My mother tenderly rested her head on my shoulder.

"Go see him," I urged her. "I will get Tom."

My mother slowly looked up at me as if she carried all the weight of the world, and nodded. Pain stretched across her face. Her delicate features were enhanced by the strain of stress and lack of sleep. Her thin hands trembled with fear as she unlatched the door to my father's bedroom, knowing that any moment could be the last. It tore at my heart to see my mother suffer.

I reached out to offer her stability as she stepped toward my father. I barely recognized him slouched in the over-sized lounge chair. He appeared incredibly frail and weak, like a delicate eggshell, so contrary to the hard-charging Irishman he had always been. His usually combed, smooth white hair was in a tousled nest, and his pale complexion seemed almost transparent. He was awake, but in distant thought—perhaps pondering all that he had accomplished in his life, and what may possibly lay ahead. Clasping my fingers around my mother's soft hand and guiding her to my father, I then retreated to offer them some moments of privacy.

I meandered down the long, photo frame-embellished hallway to the adjacent living room where my son, Tom, was waiting. I observed him casually slumped in a rich, chestnut leather armchair. He was reading the newest edition of Sports Illustrated magazine. With the approaching threat of death, I could not help but cherish the life before me. Freshly 16 years old, Tom had grown into a man in what seemed like a blink of an eye. I thought of all the things that I admired in my father and hoped that I was half the man he had been.

I reflected on the influence my father had made on my life. It was monumental. He gave me the first tools necessary for success—education and opportunity. Without his ever-evolving vision of growing the family business, I cannot imagine where my life would be now. He gave me the seeds of business, and he taught me how to water them and nourish them. The bountiful garden of apartment developments we have today is a testament to the wisdom that he bestowed upon those around him. I can just hear him saying:

"Put the residents first. Prioritize low-cost living...Waterfront is the secret to increased real estate value... I would rather have a cheaper product that is maintained impeccably than the fanciest upgrade... The numbers have to work from the start. You can't just raise rents to make the budget work... Your employees don't work for you, they work with you... Have trust in your employees; give them responsibility, and watch them meet the role... Finding established, trustworthy partners is the key to getting started. Maintaining those relationships is how you keep going."

I will always remember my father as a living library of philosophies. Beyond his business acumen, he had a theory and rule for just about every aspect of his life. His unwavering and stubborn personality bound him to these rules. And despite his rather unemotional and unaffectionate nature, he was selfless in his determination to support his family, nurture his friendships, and serve his community.

These principles were his compass that guided him on his own path in life, and I have strived to do the same in mine.

I made a resolution in that moment in 1990, as I looked upon my son, to pass as much of my father's wealth of wisdom as I could to my own children. I would start by teaching them the most notable of all his principles, which was to focus and prioritize what is truly important in life—the people around you.

I thought back to earlier that same year. My father's 80th birthday was that February 23rd. Marianne and I had intended to throw a big party for him, as we had other years, but we had been invited to ski in the Alps for that very same weekend. We debated postponing the party a few days for when we would be back from the trip. However, something came over me in the midst of making plans, and I said to Marianne, "We can't go on this trip. There is something more important to do than ski in the Alps."

Tom and Jane Mahaffey

Tom Mahaffey blowing out his candles at his 80th birthday party

Family photo at Tom Mahaffey's 80th birthday party
Back row: Jim, Ann, Jane, Kate, and Mark
Front row: Tom

My father had just learned earlier that month that he had congestive heart failure that was inoperable, and we knew he did not have much longer to live. We cancelled our trip, and instead, planned a big, 80th birthday bash for my father on February 23rd, hosting it at our home in Saint Petersburg. We invited the whole Mahaffey clan and told my parents they could invite whomever they wanted as well. With my siblings help, we really did it up in style.

The party ended up being a roaring success. About 80 people were in attendance. We had oysters and a beautifully catered dinner. A professional artist drew caricatures of the guests, and one of the extended family members, who was a professional musician, Matt Roush, played the piano in our game room. Everyone had a sensational time and stayed until after midnight.

The next morning, my mother called me in gratitude. She said, "I just want to thank you for hosting that party. It was like winding the clock back 30 years for your father. He had so much fun. It was such a joy for me to see that." I could tell how deeply touched she and my father were for the opportunity to celebrate with all their family and closest friends. I pondered how Marianne and I had almost considered traveling to the Alps instead of celebrating with my father on his special day. I had clearly seen my path splitting before me with two potential roads, and I could not be gladder that I chose the road that led to my father.

Family, friends, and community were extremely important to my father. Saint Petersburg, home to my father for the final 28 years of his life, owes a great deal to his influence. He, as well as my mother, were extremely invested in the betterment of this city, generously donating their time and money to many local projects. My father, like my mentor Richard Earle Jr., ardently encouraged me to do the same. When it came to our personal contributions to the community as a family, my father and I tried to keep out of the limelight. We donated quietly without recognition or acclaim. My father would say that serving the community was a duty, not something for which to seek glory. Ironically, of all my family's accomplishments, perhaps the thing for which we will be remembered the most is for a donation we made to the local theater a few years back, in 1987.

I laugh to myself how often the situation occurs nowadays when people, upon hearing my last name, mistakenly utter, "Oh! You are in the theater business!" Many people associate the name, Mahaffey, with the Mahaffey Theater, located on the Tampa Bay waterfront in downtown Saint Petersburg. It was named in honor of the Mahaffey family (specifically my father, my mother, myself, and Marianne) for contributing significantly to its renovation capital campaign. The theater is a very noble namesake and a beautiful orchestral concert hall, which has hosted highly esteemed performers from around the world. Many are familiar with the theater, but few know of the story behind the name.

My family has been a promoter of the arts for as long as I can remember. When I was a child in Indianapolis, my mother and father would often take me to the theater to see live performances. My parents' dreams came true when the Bayfront Center Complex, which included a performing theater and a large arena, was built in 1965. It was just a few years after my father and mother had made Saint Petersburg home. It was the prime venue to view all acts of the stage. My mother, especially, was a fervent theater goer. She went to all the big shows at the Bayfront Center–Louis Armstrong, Elvis, Luciano Pavarotti, and especially her favorite, the Ringling Brothers/Barnum and Bailey Circus. The theater was the heart of the city, but by the 1980s, it was beginning to show some wear. Other notable theaters were being built in Clearwater and Tampa, and it was time for the Bayfront Center to step up to meet the competition.

1960s Vintage postcard photo of the Bayfront Center Complex

During that time, I held a chair on a city committee called the Environmental Development Commission. This committee decided it was time to look into renovating the Bayfront Center. According to protocol, they raised around $50,000 to conduct a study to determine how best to improve the space. The study concluded that the Bayfront Center Theater could handle a full renovation, stripping the building to the studs and creating a completely new design. The large adjacent arena, however, was too close to its expiration date. It needed to be torn down in the near future, which it eventually was. The Dali Museum now sits in its place. Newspapers around Tampa Bay burst with excitement. The Bayfront Theater would be renovated and be better than ever!

Renovation of the theater, 1986

As it seems with any renovation project, funding soon became an immense issue. The proposed $20 million budget kept rising, and the city needed help. At that time, Saint Petersburg was undergoing a metamorphosis. The sleepy, retirement-focused waterfront city was implementing various improvement projects across town. This included the $9.7 million renovation of the Pier. Therefore, city funding was tight.

Being involved in several city committees, I felt an obligation to help. Not only would a community theater be very special personally to my family, it would be a profitable and valuable asset to the city. I imagine my father saying, *"If you invest in your community, they will invest in you."*

The mayor at the time, Bob Ulrich, pulled me aside one day after one of the council meetings: "Mark, we need help. The pier and the theater will put Saint Petersburg back on the map. But the budget can only stretch so far. I know your company is wildly successful these days. Would your family consider making a private donation?"

I responded assuredly, "Bob, I would love nothing more than to help this cause. The Bayfront Center is very cherished among my family and friends. I agree it is imperative to the revival of downtown Saint Petersburg. Let me discuss with my father and I will let you know what we can do."

"Thank you, Mark. It would be most appreciated. When it is finished, you must honor us again with your *Goodnight, Irene* number," the mayor added in jest.

I laughed. A few years earlier I had performed at the Bayfront Theater in Marianne's Junior League Follies fundraiser skit. My act included me singing the classic 1950s hit "Goodnight, Irene" with my miniature German Shephard, Patty. The audience roared at the performance—not on account of me singing, but due to the comedic timing of Patty howling, every time I would inflect my voice, singing "Goodnight, Irene."

"Be careful what you wish for!" I teased.

"Well, I'll tell you what," The mayor continued, "We want to name the new center after your family for all you have done for the community. If you donate $1 million, I know we can make it happen."

I was surprised. "There is definitely no need for our name to be on the building, but I will discuss with my father."

The following morning, I corralled my father, mother, and Marianne into my office to discuss the donation. It was a very big decision, not only because $1 million was a lot of money—especially in 1987—but also because we were not sure we wanted our name up in lights. It is a risky thing having your name so prominent. After much thought, discussion, and looking at our company's balance sheet, we finally came to a conclusion.

I called up the mayor, "Bob, you have $1 million pledged by the Mahaffey family."

"Wow! Thank you, sir. This is a tremendous gift to the community. And can we name the center, The Mahaffey Theater?" he implored.

"Yes, go ahead. It would be an honor," I approved.

"Wonderful!" the mayor exclaimed.

The Mahaffey Theater exterior

The Mahaffey Theater interior

The following year consisted of a great deal of planning and designing, which was all sent to our family for approval. My mother especially enjoyed the design component of picking out colors and fabrics and such.

In 1988, the Mahaffey Theater was completed. To this day, the theater has regained its place as the crown jewel in Saint Petersburg. It is home to the renowned Florida Orchestra, and a treasure to behold for locals, as well as visitors to the city. It's crimson, European box-style seating is the definition of luxury as spectators are transported to multidimensional musical realms. The theater also contains a glamorous atrium housing a dramatic, three-story, glass-paneled oriel that overlooks the sweeping Tampa Bay.

If the Mahaffey Theater is all my family is remembered for, it would still be an honor. It symbolizes our devotion to Saint Petersburg, for which I completely credit my father. Without his vision and encouragement for his family to invest all their hopes and dreams into Florida living, I would not be where I am now. He always believed in Saint Petersburg, even during its transitional period. I know he would be proud to see the flourishing city it is today and applaud the developers for preserving the charm of years past. He would be deeply aware of the dedication and strategic planning of its leaders. He would commend the necessary efforts and contributions of the community members. I am honored to be part of that legacy and hope to pass this tradition on to my children.

Bringing all my drifting thoughts back to the living room of my parent's house in 1990, I walked over to my son, Tom.

"Hey, Tom. Sadly, it looks like Dadoe doesn't have too much longer," I disclosed to my son, trying to keep my composure. Dadoe was how my children referred to their grandfather.

Tom looked up from his Sport Illustrated magazine. "Oh man," was all he could muster. Setting down his magazine, he stood up. "Can I see him?" he requested calmly.

"Yes."

Tom somberly followed me down the long hallway that led to my father's bedroom. It felt as if we were stepping through a portal into an alternate universe as we entered the bedroom. The heaviness of grief that hung in the air caused me to choke a bit upon entering. Light streamed through the bedroom window glazing all objects with glowing halos. My father sat upright in his chair while my mother held his hand. He seemed at peace and smiled at Tom and me. Without speaking, he gestured with his eyes, "Come in."

I swallowed hard as I realized this could be the last time I would speak with my father. I thought back to all those years we spent together building the business. I reminisced about those summers I spent in Florida during my college years when my father and I shared that small waterfront motel room. I recalled going to the dog races with him, and the time he said, *"I know you more than you think I do."* I remembered all those early days working for him where he would throw me into the lions' den time after time—all the while coaching me, pushing me, and most importantly, teaching me to believe in myself. He was preparing me for this, for now, for when I would take over the business and take care of the family.

One of the best decisions I ever made was five years earlier, in 1985, when I encouraged my father to switch offices from Coquina Key

South to Coquina Key North, where my new office was located. The move was motivated by me not only wanting to be closer to my father, but also by the desire to have my niece, Jane, take my father's office and assume a more senior role at the company. I knew I had to be delicate in how I suggested it to my father, however. He, in all his stubbornness, was *never* told what to do. Introducing the idea gently, I had given him two options. Option one: move offices to the back clubhouse at another property, Lynn Lake Arms. Or option two: move into a larger office next to mine at Coquina Key North. My two-option strategy worked well. He wanted nothing to do with the Lynn Lake option, but welcomed moving closer to me.

"Looks like we are going to spend a lot more time together," my father had said.

"That's the idea," I had replied with a wink.

Spending those final five years with my father was something I value and cherish to this day. I consider it a blessing to have been in a position to do so, and an even bigger blessing that my father was in good enough health to go to the office right up until the very end. We became very close during those final years.

I remember one mid-morning in his final summer here on earth, he came into my office. Without a word, he slowly made it from the doorway to one of my guest chairs that were positioned across from my desk. He sat down without saying a word. I was not sure if he wanted to talk about something or merely wanted company, so I did not press him. I knew he would talk when he was ready. Finally, after perhaps five minutes or so, he looked up at me.

"You know, you are the one," my father finally articulated.

I gazed back at him and smiled in acknowledgement. "Yes, I know," I replied.

Perhaps another five minutes went by in silence, and he got out of his chair and left the room. In an instant, I realized the significance of that moment we shared. It was in that exchange that my father handed me the baton to run the company. Although I was the youngest of his four children, my father had chosen me. My brother, Jim, was still very active in managing the business, but my father wanted me to lead it from then on. I had known that was his wish for a while because he had been preparing me for a long time. *"I'll teach you more in 90 days than you will learn in two years of graduate school,"* he had said all those years ago. He was right. We developed a close relationship over the twenty-plus years we worked together. We performed well together and merged our business philosophies into one. I respected him and looked up to him as a role model. In return, he trusted me. I took that baton and ran with it. I, in turn, am now preparing my son to take the next lap.

As Tom and I stepped into my father's bedroom in his final moments, there was something special about three generations of Mahaffeys being in the same space. My father seemed to get a burst of life at our presence.

"Oh man, Tom. That is a great car," my father complemented, gesturing out the window to Tom's new jet-black, Chevy Blazer. He swiveled his large chair toward the window to get a better look.

"Thanks, Dadoe!" Tom beamed.

After a few moments of light conversation, Tom and my mother exited the bedroom to give my father and me a few moments alone. I knew that this could be it. The last conversation. My mind raced with thoughts of what to say. *"Everything is going to be okay?"* No, that wasn't right. *"Thank you for all you've done?"* No, that didn't seem like enough.

My father and I had never had an intimate, emotional relationship. I learned from a young age not to expect hugs and kisses or frilly words of affirmation. We were never the lovey-dovey, touchy-feely, "I love you" type of family. I never begrudged my parents for it. I did not even realize anything was missing in my life until I met Marianne's family. They were the complete opposite of my family. They were full of affection and love, and they filled a void I had in my life. My adult life had been immersed into an extremely loving family, and I did not need that emotional connection with my father by then. He showed his love for me by supporting my professional development, and I understood that.

Perhaps my father had always been detached emotionally, but perhaps it was due to some deep latent trauma that I would never understand. There is a story from when my father was nineteen years old; he was a passenger in a terrible automobile accident in Indianapolis.

Considering this was in the late 1920s, I imagine the vehicle being a shy step up from the Model T. There were four young men in the vehicle and devastatingly, one of my father's friends was killed. My father evaded any serious injuries and was merely left with a broken nose. I cannot begin to comprehend the pain and hurt that he and his friends must have endured. That automobile accident was timed when my father played football under Knute Rockne at Notre Dame. Considering the respect my father had for him as a life coach and mentor, I am sure Knute Rockne helped my father and his friends through this tough time. I can only imagine that this incredible loss partially contributed to my father's reluctance to express vulnerability and create emotional connections with his own family. He buried that past pain with thick layers of concrete, and used that strong unmovable base to support the rest of his life. I couldn't help but respect him for that.

But now in these last moments, I craved that intimacy with him. I wanted him to know how I felt for him and what he meant to me. I couldn't let him go without him knowing what was in my heart. As I was walking out of his bedroom, I stopped and looked back. We locked eyes, and I looked deep into his soul as he looked into mine. I then said three words that I don't believe I had ever said to my father, and he had never said to me. These three words mean everything, and somehow never seem enough. But for my father and I, they were enough.

"I love you," I finally blurted. Tears rose up in my eyes as it took all the strength and emotion in my being to utter those raw words.

"I love you too, Mark." He nearly chuckled as he said it, almost as if to say, "It's about time we express how we feel." As we shared that special moment, we acknowledged a connection that had been almost 50 years in the making.

The next morning, on Christmas Eve, I received a call from my mother saying that my father had passed away early that morning. I thanked God that in that moment, I was able to reach deep inside myself to tell my father that I loved him. A little late perhaps, but better than never.

Later that week, at the funeral, I gave my father's eulogy. I am thankful I wrote down what I wanted to say, as it was an extremely emotional experience. But I figured I would try my best to make everyone feel a little better. I kept it light and positive, sharing my fondest memories with my father, a few funny stories, and focusing on it being a celebration of life. My father had lived a complete life, full of family, friendships, and business success. In his last year of his life, my sister had asked him what he would do, if he could do anything he wanted at that time. My father's answer had been, "I've done it all." And he had.

Thank you, Dad, for your influence, leadership, advice, and love. Your presence will never be forgotten. Your footsteps left an imprint on my heart and in all of our lives.

15

THE QUEEN OF MEAN AND

HER MOST TRUSTED ADVISOR

The pessimist sees difficulty in every opportunity.
The optimist sees the opportunity in every difficulty.

Winston Churchill

About eight years after my father's death, my mother joined my father in heaven on February 17, 1998, at the age of 87. Like my father, she was an extraordinary leader of the Mahaffey family, while always maintaining an immense amount of active involvement in the community. It amazed me every day to see a woman give no credence to her age, especially in her final years—as she even bought a brand new, red Cadillac just a week before her death. She always had a plan. Years ago, she had given me a paperweight inscribed with the words, *The view never changes unless you are the lead dog.* The paperweight now rests on the end table next to my favorite chair in our summer home in Highlands, North Carolina. Looking back at my younger years, I am forever grateful to her for pushing me to join the NROTC program at Notre Dame and giving me the *Fountainhead* book, which I read again at the ages of 30 and 60. The book was very inspirational to me each time I read it, as I had different perspectives at different ages and stages in my career. My mother was always such a wise woman. Reflecting on my journey, my father may have always been my role model, but my mother always seemed to be directing in the background.

As with the death of any family patriarch, there was a long to-do list waiting for my family on the other side of my parents' passings. My brother, Jim, and I were left with the specific task of ensuring all family business financials were in proper order. Luckily, my father, being the financial wizard that he was, had done a great deal of the planning before his death. Even still, there was one large detail overlooked. As Albert Einstein was credited with saying, "Even a genius has to make every mistake once."

This error involved the trusts he and my mother had set up as gifts to his children and grandchildren. Jim and I had looked them over, but not being trust experts by any means, it soon became a project set to the side. Business was growing, new properties were being developed, and our primary focus was keeping the business stable and running smoothly now that my father was gone. Perhaps by good fortune, or perhaps by providence, we were given the opportunity to take heed of the problem before disaster struck.

One day in early spring of the early 2000s, Jim came darting into my office with as much enthusiasm as a kindergarten teacher on the first day of school. He did not usually spend much time at the Coquina Key location, so seeing him caught me by surprise. Brilliance shown in his eyes, and he seemed rather out of breath. I knew he had something big to tell me.

"Hey, Mark. I just got off a plane from Houston, and I had to come straight here to tell you. You wouldn't believe who I just met on the plane!"

"Tell me," I inquired.

"Deane Kanaly."

"Who?" I questioned.

"The *who* is not as important, as the *what* he does. He is head of a family focused trust company. His firm advises businesses, especially

214

family businesses, on succession planning, estate planning, and so forth. He could be our saving grace!" Jim exclaimed.

I laughed to myself. He acted as if he had won the lottery jackpot.

"Yes, Jim," I concurred. "I agree. I have no idea if Dad's trust structure is set up correctly, and I really don't have the time to figure it all out. It is very complicated and a huge job."

"I think having some outside expertise would be immensely beneficially. Can I set up a meeting between us and him? I think you would really like him. He's a great guy."

"Sure thing, Jim. Go ahead," I offered him my blessing.

The following week, a few men from the Kanaly Trust Company visited Jim and I at my office at Coquina Key. One of these men was David Doll, who was the lead guy for their team. We were impressed with their knowledge and experience in handling and setting up trusts, and we hired them on the spot. As quickly as a diamond expert spots an imperfection in a precious gem, these estate experts identified a subtle, yet substantial flaw immediately.

My father was familiar with a law that allowed a person to gift $10,000 to anyone tax-free. According to the law, he and my mother, as a two-person couple, could gift $20,000 tax-free. So, that was exactly what they did. They had 18 grandchildren, and so, they gifted $20,000 worth of partnership interests, which was appraised to each one of the grandchildren every year until my father's death in 1990. Then, at the advice of Jim and myself, my mother continued the gifting afterwards, but only at $10,000 to each grandchild until her death. Overall, we believed this to be very good estate planning. Neither party was taxed, and a large sum of the ownership was gradually given to the future generations over the years.

However, the advisors from the Kanaly Trust Company inspected the documents and stated, "Yes, this was great planning. However, you all made one big mistake."

"What was that?" I questioned. In the seconds before he responded, my mind spiraled with notions of what that error might be. Did we miss something?

David Doll said, "Your parents gifted *general* partnership interests rather than *limited* partnership interests. The problem with gifting general partnership interests is that you are essentially gifting voting rights to each person in terms of business decision making. For instance, as general partners, if one person owns ten percent and another person owns ninety percent, they both get equal say in business matters. You have 18 grandchildren here. That is a lot of voices. There is bound to be conflict down the road."

I was astounded. "Okay. I understand. How do we fix this?"

"Mark and Jim, you both are trustees of 13 of those trusts. You can fix this by changing them to limited partnership interests right now. They will not lose any money or assets already gifted. They will merely lose voting rights, which was most likely not intended for them to start with. However, five of those 18 grandchildren have already hit 40-years-old, and the assets are held by them directly. You must convince those five people to agree to convert their ownership to limited partnership interests."

"We can do that," we agreed.

Fortunately, after speaking with those five individuals, they readily agreed. *Phew!* That was easy. However, the challenging facet was that we also had to go back to each lender of every single deal involved and get them to approve the conversions. This took a great deal of focus and organization, but I managed to get everything signed and approved in a reasonable amount of time—except for one.

Leona Helmsley was the widow wife of the now deceased Harry Helmsley, the famous New York billionaire developer. As you might recall, Harry Helmsley was my father's first financial partner back in the 1960s for two of our properties, Carlton Arms of Saint Petersburg and Carlton Arms of Winter Park. Since Harry had passed away, the deals were now in the name of his wife, Leona Helmsley. Unfortunately, Leona was not only a very forceful businesswoman, but she also had an awful reputation for having an arrogant, belligerent personality. Leona's greed led her to prison in the 1980s for tax evasion. Those few years in prison, unfortunately, did not calm her flaring temper and willingness to flatten anyone on her path to financial success. When Harry died in 1997, Leona inherited a large portfolio of real estate, which even included the prominent Empire State Building. Despite her attitude, she continued to develop a booming hotel empire in New York City. Her employees would shake at the knees in her presence. Her uniquely abrasive personality turned her into an icon, prompting the film industry to create a movie chronicling her life, titled "The Queen of Mean." Somehow, just somehow, I had to get Leona Helmsley's signature to convert these interests!

Leona Helmsley and her dog, Trouble
photo credit: Trust Counsel

The first step I took was contacting Leona's head attorney, whom I had met on a few occasions over the years. Unfortunately, this attorney was just as scared of Leona as most others were. After much persistence, I realized I was getting nowhere with him and became quite frustrated.

A few months later, Marianne and I and some friends of ours, Gene and Ginger Grimes, went to New York City for a social weekend, unrelated to the Helmsley ordeal. We stayed at our usual hotel, the Park Lane Hotel, which happened to be owned by Leona Helmsley at the time. We chose it due to its idyllic location, right across the street from the beautifully historic Central Park.

Pulling up to the hotel on the first day of our trip, I spied an oversized, black limousine parked at the entrance. Thinking nothing of it, as the hotel attracted many celebrity guests, we walked casually through the front entrance eagerly awaiting our weekend of festivities.

"Wel-welcome to the Pa-Park Lane Hotel," the doorman greeted us with a nervous stutter, as if he were being held captive, watched and scrutinized.

"Beautiful day to be in New York!" I replied with a smile.

Upon entering the quaint, yet refined hotel lobby, the perfectly glossed ivory floors and brilliant crystal chandeliers could not disguise the draft of apprehension that wafted through the space. The staff appeared to be on edge, uptight, and anxious. At once it came to me—Leona must be here! And without a second delay, I knew this was my opportunity.

Approaching the front desk, I spotted my favorite concierge was on duty. She was an Irish lady by the name of Mary Reddy. She was a remarkable resource in New York City and could get tickets to just about any show, if you were willing to pay, of course.

"Mary," I beckoned the concierge. "May I request a private chat with you for a few minutes when you get the time?"

"Yes, sir, Mr. Mahaffey," she affirmed without hesitation. "Go ahead and relax over in the lounge area, and I'll be over there in a few moments."

I did as she directed, while the rest of my crew hustled upstairs to settle in their rooms. Sure enough, about five minutes later, Mary Reddy joined me in the lounge area and sat down on a large, wingback chair stationed across from me.

"What can I do for you, Mr. Mahaffey?" Mary inquired.

"Would you happen to know if Leona Helmsley is on the premises today?"

Mary gave a long blink that formally neither confirmed, nor denied the query. It was all I needed.

"I'm currently in a bind sorting out my father's estate after he passed away some time ago. I'm close to getting it all resolved, but Leona Helmsley is the last peg in the hole. I can't seem to get past first base with her people, including Harold, who is her head attorney. If I could somehow secure a few moments of her time while I am in town, I would be beyond grateful. Do you believe you could arrange that meeting?"

Mary sighed and frowned. "I will do what I can, Mr. Mahaffey. But, keep in mind, it will be the worst ten minutes of your entire life. She is not in great health and is more miserable than ever. I cannot promise she will agree to anything."

In despair, I rested my head into my hands. "God, I don't know what I am going to do."

Mary, exemplifying the epitome of a people pleaser, was determined to find a solution. "I'll tell you what. Let's take this from a different approach. I am good friends with John Codey, who is Leona Helmsley's most trusted advisor. He is a really great guy, a real straight shooter. Here is his phone number," she said as she pulled a pen and notepad out of her blazer breast pocket. She scrawled a phone number on a slip of paper, tore it from the pad, and handed it to me.

Leona Helmsley and John Codey
Photo credit: NY Post/ Ron Galella Collection via Getty

She added, "Wait until Tuesday, and call him after you are back home in Saint Petersburg. I will tell him to expect your call."

"Thank you so much, Mary. This is most generous of your time."

"No problem. You will like John."

With that gleam of hope and an immense amount of pressure off my mind, I made the resolve to enjoy the rest of our trip. Marianne, our friends, and I filled the weekend to the brim doing all things "New York." We attended marvelous Broadway performances, dined at the most exquisite restaurants, and shopped 'til we dropped. It was the perfect escape from all the stress I had been experiencing lately.

On the last day of our trip, after a full day of adventure, Marianne, Gene, Ginger, and I returned to the hotel still wound up and adrenaline-fueled by the New York night life. Stepping off the busy New York streets into the supremely quiet hotel lobby could not have been more therapeutic. The air smelled of lavender and linen, and a simple string quartet echoed through the air making the ambiance ever so welcoming. The staff seemed to have relaxed and composed themselves over the course of the weekend.

We sauntered over to the elevator, quietly laughing amongst ourselves, recounting all the fun we had that day. Approaching the tall, golden elevator doors, I reached out and firmly pressed the up arrow that controlled the apparatus.

Ding.

The doors slowly parted and we stepped into the marble-paneled chamber. The string quartet was a notch louder in this space, causing us all to raise our voices in laughter and chatter. The elevator began to move, but before we got to our floor, it stopped. It was apparent another passenger would be joining us, but we didn't feel the need to recess our giggles.

The tall doors began to slowly part again, unveiling the last vision I expected to witness in that moment. Low and behold, who is standing a mere few feet from the doorway was the one and only Leona Helmsley and her nurse! I was taken aback by Leona's frail condition. She was standing on her own, but was leaning heavily on her nurse, who was also holding Leona's prized pooch. Leona's piercing blue eyes manifested her deep strength of personality as it speared through her apparent physical weakness. Our conversation ceased immediately as she glared at our group. In silence, Leona and the nurse, holding the pooch, entered the elevator.

"Do not touch the dog," the nurse snarled as the doors began to close. She clasped the small, snowy-white Maltese to her chest. This well-known pet of Leona's, aptly named Trouble, offered us a similar grimace as its caretakers.

My mind was spinning. *Should I introduce myself, or say anything? She probably does not recognize me, but perhaps she would recognize my name?*

Before I could muster together two thoughts, our friend Ginger began oohing and awing over the little dog. She was still on a high from the fun-filled day and was not bothered by the cloud of negativity had that entered our space. Ginger was an animal lover beyond anyone else I ever knew. She was the type of person who would pick up a wounded squirrel and nurse it back to health if she thought it needed care. She absolutely could not resist the white, fluffy ball of fur in the nurse's arms.

In a highly animated, high-pitched voice, Ginger crooned "Oh! Aren't you a sweet little puppy? Yes, you are!" Like a moth to a flame, she reached out to pet the little dog. To her tremendous surprise, the cranky canine lashed out in a vicious *snap*! Trouble, who's attitude matched its name, nearly bit her hand off.

The irritated nurse grumbled, "I told you not to touch the dog."

Leona cracked a wicked smile in amusement at the calamity.

At this very moment, the elevator chimed, signaling the arrival to our floor. Gene, Ginger, Marianne, and I exited the elevator in relief, as if we had just hit shore after a long voyage at sea. Evidently, that was not the time to introduce myself. Crisis (narrowly) averted.

A few days later, back in Saint Petersburg, I called John Codey on Tuesday as directed. I recounted the story from the very beginning. He listened quietly until I finished.

He responded, "Mark, I will get this thing done for you, but you need to be patient—and, boy, I do mean *be patient*. I've got to get Leona Helmsley at the right time, in the right mood. It might take weeks or months. Who knows."

"Thank you, John. I'm trusting you with this."

Well, he was right. It did take months, several months. I called John a few times to check up on him, and he would say, "Be patient, Mark. I will get this done."

Finally, John Codey got the job done. How he was able to get Leona Helmsley's signature I will never know, but I am grateful. That last signature was essential to a smooth future of the Mahaffey Apartment Company. Beyond the signature, I gained a friend, if even a telephone-based friend. John Codey was as great of a guy as Mary Reddy promised.

About a year later, in August 2007, Leona Helmsley passed away from congestive heart failure at the age of 87. I read in the newspaper that John Codey gave the eulogy at her small, intimate funeral. He said, "She was wonderful and had a great sense of humor." Beneath her rough demeanor, perhaps she had a sweet side that only her closest friends and family knew. They insisted that she was misunderstood and genuinely had a very compassionate and generous heart, despite her flaring temper. They called her a "quiet philanthropist." It appeared that John

Codey was one of the few who were able to crack the ice of Leona's awful reputation and discover the real person underneath. Somehow, he had figured out the secret to Leona Helmsley, and he had worked his charm to earn her trust. I found out years later that Leona's ill-tempered Maltese dog, Trouble, had been a gift from John Codey. Believe it or not, she had left $12 million to that pup, most likely making it one of the richest canines in the world. This was just a small sliver of Leona's fortune, however, as she left the majority of her estate to charitable trusts.

After her death, it took years and years for her attorneys and real estate professionals to distribute her tremendous wealth, with the money still being distributed to this day. John Codey was extremely passionate about science and research in the medical community, and played an integral role in directing billions of dollars of charitable trust funds toward accelerated medical research.

In 2008, about nine months after Leona Helmsley's death, I received an unexpected call from a national realty firm in New York. They wanted to sell us Leona Helmsley's portion of the two properties in which Harry had partnered with us. Of the billions of dollars in assets she owned, our two developments were like two small M&Ms in a big jar. Lucky for us, due to the looming Global Financial Crisis of 2008, there were very few real estate investors in the market for new deals. The realty firm knew we were the logical (and perhaps only) buyer, and we used that as leverage to negotiate purchasing it at a somewhat reasonable price.

John Codey ended up being one of five trustees enumerated in Leona's estate documents. He was extremely cautious and conscientious in ensuring that there would be no conflict of interest. John offered great guidance through the whole process, and we ended up successfully acquiring Leona's interest in both deals. Less than a year later, we refinanced both properties with even better terms and still own both today.

Finally, the years of difficulty in sorting out the family trusts had finally been resolved with a profitable and successful ending. I am grateful to Deane Kanaly and David Doll at the Kanaly Trust Company. Without them, I do not know where the Mahaffey Apartment Company would be today. Later on, when David Doll formed his own company, Sequent Asset Management Co., we moved our account there. David and his company are still our primary advisors to this day. If it had not been for the collaboration of a few very key players, as well as a great deal of patience on my part, I am certain we would not have seen that resolution.

Unfortunately, enduring the stress involved with that deal left its mark on my health. Over the course of the end of the 2000s, I began to develop issues in my lower digestive system. At first, it was tolerable, but month after month, it became unbearable.

One day, in early 2010, I happened to be on the phone with John Codey when he said, "Mark, your voice doesn't sound the same. Are you okay?"

I responded honestly, "Well, I'm doing alright. I am just going through some digestive issues. Looks like I have diverticulitis. My doctor is recommending surgery, but I am not looking forward to that."

He firmly, "Well, I think you need to get a second opinion."

"You sound like my brother, Jim," I retorted.

John laughed. "Well, listen to this. I am good friends with the head of the Digestive Diseases Department at New York-Presbyterian Hospital. He is one of the top digestive specialists nationwide. I will contact him and tell him you will be reaching out."

He proceeded to give me this renowned doctor's contact information.

"Okay, wow! Thank you, John!" I exclaimed.

The next day, I called John's doctor friend. The doctor could not have been nicer. He directed, "Have your doctor in Saint Petersburg send me your file. I will examine it and offer you my opinion over the phone."

I was ever so grateful. "That sounds great. Thank you."

I did as he asked and had my file sent over that afternoon.

The following morning, he called me on the phone and confirmed that my doctor in Saint Petersburg is making the correct call. "You are in good hands," he reassured me.

I am grateful to John Codey—whom I had not even met face-to-face yet at that point—for his advice and connecting me with this reputable doctor. Receiving the doctor's blessing gave me the peace and confidence to go through with the surgery. Fortunately, it was a rather simple procedure, and I was back to work in three days. The surgery was successful and I have not had any of those same digestive issues since.

Later that same year, I found out that the Notre Dame football team was scheduled to play against Army Black Knights at Yankee Stadium in New York. It was going to be held on the weekend before Thanksgiving. As a hardcore Fighting Irish fan, I knew this was a game I could not miss. My father would tell stories of when he would play again Army all those years ago, when he played under Coach Knute Rockne. On top of witnessing the big game, I thought it would be a great opportunity to finally meet John Codey in person, being that I would be in New York anyway. As tradition dictated, I called up my close childhood friend Hugh McGowan, and we corralled several friends and booked the trip. Hoping that John Codey would be in town that weekend, I gave him a call.

"Hey John, it's Mark Mahaffey," I greeted my long-time telephone friend.

"Well, hello, Mark. How are you feeling these days?" John inquired.

"Never been better! I couldn't be gladder I went through with that surgery. Thank you again for connecting me with your doctor friend."

"Anytime," John replied. "Glad it all worked out."

"Well," I said, "It looks like I'll be up in New York next weekend for the Notre Dame-Army football game. As we've never met in person, I thought it would be great to meet up while I am in town. Are you available next Friday, the weekend before Thanksgiving? We can either meet for lunch or an evening cocktail. Whatever works best for you."

"Yes, that sounds wonderful. Let's rendezvous at this great hotel down the street from me. I'll meet you in the cocktail lounge at 3:00."

"Great!" I replied brightly.

He then kindly offered me the precise details of the hotel name and location, which I wish I could recall now. It was such a charming historic hotel, flaunting classic New York architecture.

Before I knew it, that Friday was already upon us. I had arrived in New York with a cocktail of emotions jumbling inside of me. My excitement for the football game was sprinkled with curiosity, eagerness, and perhaps a bit of nervousness to finally meet John Codey after so many years.

Parting from my group of football-fan friends, I quickly found my way to the historic hotel. Entering the cozy hotel parlor, I noticed a beautiful, wood-paneled cocktail lounge down the corridor to the left. In my mind's eye, I remember a long, green marble bar top stretched wall-to-wall with perhaps a dozen duets of emerald velvet lounge chairs scattered about the room. Bronze light fixtures garnished the space with dim, moody lighting. As it was 3:00 in the afternoon, well before happy hour, it was rather quiet and calm. All the lounge chairs were vacant but one.

An older gentleman sat reclined with his legs crossed reading the daily newspaper. A steaming coffee mug rest on the small table by his side. His thinning, gray hair looked wind-blown, giving him a bit of a goofy appearance. Instinctively, this prompted me to smooth my own hair. He had a deep clef chin, clear-rimmed spectacles, and bushy eyebrows that looked like they would take flight at any moment. He had a calm, relaxed demeanor, but as soon as he noticed my presence, he perked up, offering me a warm, welcoming smile. I thought, *that must be John.*

I ambled over to him as he began to stand.

"John Codey?"

"Mark Mahaffey?"

We nodded and shook hands.

"Sit down. Let's have a talk," John suggested.

There in that hotel lounge, we sat and conversed for two and a half hours. Not even touching on business topics, we spoke about life and philosophy. We laughed at old memories and shared our dreams for the future. Our friendship began to deepen as we bared our souls. We had a delightful time together, but around 5:30, it was time for us to end the meeting. I had dinner plans with Tom, Hugh, and our friends, and John had to head home to his wife. It is interesting to note that he owned a massive mansion on twelve acres on Long Island. Large lots are a rare gem near New York City, and I was glad to see that he had done so well in life. John never wore his wealth on his sleeve, however. He was very down to earth and very humble.

As we stepped out of the hotel onto the busy sidewalk, John admitted to me, "My colleague, Richard, thought you were going to come here and ask for money."

Having been in his shoes before, I understood the prediction. But this visit was purely social.

John clarified, "I told him you weren't coming to do that."

I reassured him, "Well, you are right. I didn't come here for money. I came here just to meet an old friend I've never met face-to-face."

He said, "Well, same for me. That is why I am here."

John held out his hand to shake mine and I reached out and griped his palm, looking him in the eye.

John's expression instantly shifted, as if he had just noticed something.

"Fisherman?" he inquired.

"Oh yes. Big time." I confirmed.

"I thought so," he grinned.

He walked away and that is the last time I saw John Codey. I guess I'll never know how he surmised that I enjoyed fishing.

A few years later, Marianne and I planned again to visit New York City. I attempted to call John again and schedule another meeting. I dialed his cell phone, and unfortunately, received a voice message stating, "This number is no longer active." Feeling apprehensive, I pulled out my laptop, googled *John Codey*, and found that he had passed away about a year and a half earlier. My heart sunk into my stomach. How did this happen a second time to someone I truly admired?

I thought back to when I discovered Admiral Murphy had died via Google. If I could go back in time, I would have attended both their funerals. Nonetheless, I had to settle with reading John's obituary with Marianne. He was a great man with a big heart. His biggest contribution to society is his advocacy and contributions toward medical research, which has spurred many scientific discoveries and advances. We may never know exactly how much John Codey has impacted us all. But one thing is for sure—I will never forget him.

16

TROPIC STAR LODGE

For me, Tropic Star Lodge represents the ultimate fishing destination, my idyllic corner of the planet, and I am excited just at the thought of returning. A unique formula of ingredients makes this area of land and sea magnificent, and the lodge is perfectly integrated into that recipe.

Guy Harvey

Fisherman. John Codey's shockingly accurate intuition that I was a fisherman reeled through my mind. How he saw deep into my soul that day and recognized one of my proudest identities, I will never know. Fishing has been a strong passion of mine since my youth. I blissfully think back to those summer days of fishing at Burt Lake in Michigan—the joy in the anticipation, the tension of the line, the thrill of the catch, and the release of the hook. My childhood friend Dick deVore and I had the finest time of our lives on those feeble sailboats.

It was also at Burt Lake that I first learned to fish from my father. I will never forget those first moments I had on the water with him, reeling in our lines and sharing that special feeling of victory. After moving to Saint Petersburg, my father and I continued our father/son fishing pastime. He owned a series of boats, which he kept at the dock at Carlton Arms of Saint Petersburg. We spent more times than I could count out on the Tampa Bay, beer in hand, talking about life, work, the past, and the future. It was a special time in my life, and the water has unceasingly beckoned me ever since.

Now, I reside alongside one of my heart's greatest treasures, as I own a home on the Tampa Bay waterfront. I have taken many of my friends out on my boats in the bay and the Gulf of Mexico, but it does not hold a candle to the experiences attained from traveling. There is a multitude of unique and awe-inspiring places in this world, and after traveling extensively over the years, I am able to identify clearly the places that are most special to me.

Of all the countries I have visited, the one that has made the utmost impact on my family has most assuredly been Panama. It is here where my love of fishing expanded and my skills as an angler were honed. Interestingly, the name *Panama* comes from the native Kuna Indian tribe's word for *abundance of fish*. The waters surrounding Panama are rich and diverse in sea life, but there is one spot along its jagged coastline that has a secret that has only recently been discovered by fisherman around the world.

On the southern border of the Panamanian jungle, along the coast of the Pacific Ocean, lies a cove of water called Piñas Bay. The name means "pineapple" in Spanish, and was named thus for the bay's pineapple shape. Its azure waters contain a perfect cocktail of stirred up nutrients and marine life. This bountiful brew exists due to its location at the precise point at which the cold currents from the south converge with warm currents from the north. Its rich ecosystem draws fish, big and small, to its resources, which in turn lures fisherman to this piscine treasure. Over 300 world records have been set in Piñas Bay, topping any other place in the world. The Panamanians are very proud of their ecological riches, and have banned commercial-fishing in Piñas Bay and the surrounding waters. Even recreational fishing has its limits, and clear guidelines of catch-and-release must be followed. Fisherman from across the globe happily abide to these rules in order preserve this hidden gem. Giant marlin, sailfish, grouper, billfish, and bonita are just some of the prized species that call this bay home.

The sacred waters of Piñas Bay are nestled within the exquisite Darién Province, which is one of the most untouched rainforests in the world. As mirrored in the waters below, it has a rich ecosystem living within the jungle-ladened mountains, streams and rivers, countless wetlands, and sandy beaches. It is designated as a UNESCO World Heritage site, which honors the location as having substantial cultural, historical, and scientific significance on mankind. The land is therefore protected by this organization. It's tremendous breadth and remoteness has allowed a unique evolutionary process and an extraordinary diversity of flora and fauna to exist. Two Indigenous tribes also call this dense jungle home, living simple lives fueled by self-subsistence. For the travelers who migrate here from all over the world, the diverse terrain is positively breathtaking.

Within this virginal landscape, beneath the tangled rainforest canopy, along the sandy white coast of the Piñas Bay, lies Tropic Star Lodge. This resort is located in such a remote area that there are no roads for hundreds of miles. It is only accessible by boat or charter plane. It was built in 1962 by a man named Ray Smith as a small lodge for fisherman to stay during their expedition to the Piñas Bay. Before it was built, fishermen had no other option other than to sleep and fish on their boat day after day. The resort was tastefully constructed to blend into the natural surroundings, and over the years has developed into a world-renowned fishing destination. This piece of paradise has been appropriately nicknamed *The Jurassic Park of Fishing* due to the primitive, raw jungle setting that encompasses a habitat of unreal, monster-sized fish.

Tropic Star Lodge, Panama

Dock at Tropic Star Lodge

I remember my first time experiencing Tropic Star Lodge in 1985. I had heard whispers of its wonders amongst the fishing community. But the dream only became a reality through the organization and brilliant planning by my mentor and friend in Saint Petersburg, Richard Earle Jr., and his son Richard Earle III. They had first visited Tropic Star Lodge the year before, in 1984, and touted its myriad of gigantic fish. They had caught a 750-pound blue marlin amongst others and were already excited to make plans to return.

"Oh, that sounds like a fisherman's paradise! I would love to go someday," I exclaimed.

"Well," young Richard replied, "you will get your chance soon. We are planning to return next February. We have reserved eight spots for a week of fishing. My wife and I, and my mom and dad, will take four of the spots. The other four are yours!"

I was floored. "Wow! Thank you. This will be an adventure to remember." I thought of all of my fisherman friends and debated whom I might bring. What an opportunity to get some guys together and catch our biggest fish yet!

Later that week, I attended a community luncheon at the Saint Petersburg pier. My friend Byron Shouppe, who was an avid fisherman like me, happened to be in attendance.

I will invite him! I thought to myself. *Then I only need to decide on two more guys.*

"Byron," I eagerly approached him after the luncheon had finished. "I have the perfect birthday present we can give ourselves for our 40th birthdays." We were the same age—both turning 40 in 1984.

He raised his eyebrows chuckling, "Enlighten me."

I said, "How would you like to travel to the ultimate fishing destination—Tropic Star Lodge in Panama? I've got four tickets to paradise!"

Byron Shouppe's eyes light up with astonishment and bewilderment. "Tropic Star Lodge?" he mouthed slowly, adding theatrics to his already animated expression. It had been a dream of his for quite some time to go to Panama, and he could not contain his enthusiasm.

"Woo-hoo! Oh man, count me in. Count me in!" he shouted with a fist-punching victory hurrah.

"Great!" I cried, knowing that having Byron along would ensure the trip would be a blast.

Later that evening, Marianne and I attended an evening cocktail party at the Museum of Fine Arts. That day happened to be chock full of social events. Stepping into the Marly Music room with Marianne, I was surprised to see Byron Shouppe again. He stood across the room with his wife Starin. They caught sight of us immediately and scurried across the room toward us.

"Mark, I cannot tell you how excited we are!" Starin said bright-eyed.

"We've been talking about it all afternoon," Byron chimed in. "What an adventure this will be!"

"February in Panama," Starin sang dreamily.

"Mark, we can't thank you enough for this chance of a lifetime," Byron announced overlapping Starin's song.

I was utterly confused. I had imagined this being a guys' trip. Did Byron's wife really want to travel to Panama? She just did not seem like a fisherperson to me. She was always dressed to the nines, flaunting all the trends in modern apparel. Her short, black hair was precisely cropped and styled to perfection with every hair flawlessly in place. I tried to imagine her fishing amidst the wild jungles of Panama. I just couldn't see it; but perhaps I was mistaken, and she was a fisherperson unbeknownst to me.

But poor Marianne, who was completely unaware of the entire planned excursion, was left even more confounded than I was. "What trip to Panama?" Marianne inquired later that evening when we were back at home.

I filled her in on the details. "Well, Richard Earle gave me four tickets to Panama for next February. I had initially envisioned this as a guys' fishing trip, but now that Starin thinks she is going, I guess it's more of a couples' trip. I know fishing isn't exactly your cup of tea, but would you like to go?"

Marianne reluctantly uttered, "Well, I guess it's a couples' trip now."

I must give Marianne credit for being a good sport and agreeing to go for a week down to the jungle. Tropic Star Lodge was a luxurious resort, but let's be honest, it is deep in the wild rainforest. There was not much to do there in terms of sightseeing. Fishing was the primary activity, and not one of Marianne's favorite pastimes. She agreed to go, however, to spend quality time together with me and the Shouppe's. It gave me consolation that the Earles had traveled to this resort the year before, and they spoke very highly of it. But unlike Marianne, Richard's wife was a real fisherperson. I had my doubts, but did not want to disappoint Marianne. I thought to myself, *Oh my God. I hope this goes well.*

Finally, February the following year came around, and the eight of us hopped onto a plane to Panama: Richard Earle Jr. and his wife, Richard Earle III and his wife, Byron and Starin Shouppe, and Marianne and I. We flew commercially on a Friday to Panama City, where we stayed in a small hotel near the airport for the first night. On Saturday morning, we all crammed into small propellor plane to take us deep into the Darién Jungle to Tropic Star Lodge. The small aircraft had to time its arrival near the resort precisely in order for it to land during low tide. The landing strip would often flood during high tide, and thus timing was crucial.

The plane seemed to be flying forever, farther and farther from civilization. The engine was loud, and the flight far from smooth. Looking out the window, I saw the canopy of treetops for miles and miles. I imagined my great grandfather, John Kiley, and his trek across Panama during the gold rush. I could only imagine the things he experienced, fought, and endured. Oh, the things I would ask if I had the chance to talk with him. I felt lucky to be flying above the trees, rather than trudging through them; but the flight certainly was not a luxury cruise either.

When are we going to land? I thought to myself. Marianne mouthed something to me, but amidst the roar of the plane, I could not hear a word.

At long last, gazing out the foggy window, I noticed the soft blur of green brush strokes gradually became clearer and clearer as defined individual leaves. I knew the plane must be getting close to landing. I turned my eyes to peer ahead and spotted—amidst the dense tangle of wilderness—a narrow, red clay strip of land that extended to the ocean. The pilot slowly dropped the plane, stopping it after a short deacceleration on the rough, crumbly ground. I had never been so grateful to be on land.

"That was not the smoothest flight," Marianne whispered to me.

"Glad to be on the ground," I murmured back, nodding in agreement.

Exiting the plane, we were awestruck by the beauty of the rainforest that surrounded us. Brilliant sunshine beamed through the clearing of trees that had been slashed by the runway, highlighting a thick wall of rainforest. Towering trees, larger and taller than anything I had ever seen before, were netted together in an entanglement of vines. My imagination could only go so far in pondering what kinds of creatures abounded between the large arbor pillars. I had heard stories of the dangers of the Darién Jungle—vicious jaguars, giant anacondas, deadly spiders, and mosquitos the size of hummingbirds. My concerns about bringing Marianne reached new heights as the realness of the rainforest was unveiled before my eyes. Over the buzzing cicadas and distant calls of howler monkeys, my thoughts were then startled as a cheerful voice called, "Welcome to Panama!"

I looked to the right, just ahead of the nose of the plane and saw a man walking toward us. He wore a wide-brimmed straw hat with khaki shorts and an olive-green canvas button up shirt. A logo illustrating *Tropic Star Lodge* was embroidered on his left breast pocket.

He smiled at our exhausted group and said, "My name is Manuel. I am here to take you to paradise. Follow close to me."

We grabbed our few pieces of luggage, and all set off following the man like a row of eager, yet cautious ducklings. Manuel guided us along a narrow, roughly cut trail that wove deeply into the tightly knitted jungle. Creeping silently, we were ever fearful that we were trespassing on nature's forbidden territory. After about a mile's hike, we finally saw another clearing ahead.

Spread before us, like a banquet to our eyes, was a beautiful river placidly meandering through the forest. A pair of blue and yellow macaws coasted and dove through the open air. Mullet leapt out of the rippling water in high spirits. Nestled in this natural setting was a long, narrow, yellow-painted boat, called a "panga," that was tied to the shore, bobbing in the trembling waters. This outboard-powered vessel had open seating for about 15-20 passengers and was fastened with a white canopy for shade.

"Our chariot awaits us," Manuel said as he gestured toward the designated water taxi. "This here is the Rio Pina River. It will take us directly into Piñas Bay."

Helping Marianne step carefully onto the rocking vessel, the excitement started to swell up in my body. Having the security of the guide, I knew in that moment this would be a trip to remember. I inhaled the sweet jungle air, smelling and tasting a cocktail of salty, steamy, fresh verdure. As the boat raced down the river, the strong, cool breeze embraced us like an ardent, welcome hug. On the water, I felt at home and at peace.

After about 20 minutes, the boat rounded a bend revealing a gorgeous inlet of water. A long, wooden dock extended from its sandy shores. Beyond the dock, perched high within the tree-lined hilltop, rested a large, wooden edifice with a steeply pitched rood.

"Tropic Star Lodge," I said to myself in awe.

Before we knew it, we had arrived at the lodge and checked into our rooms. We were scheduled to fish at 6:30 am the following morning, so we decided to take the evening to rest and rejuvenate after the long journey. Knowing that Marianne was prone to sea sickness, I had packed some Scopolamine transdermal patches, which were to be placed on the skin behind the ear to prevent nausea. We planned ahead by putting one transdermal patch behind Marianne's ear that night so that the medication had plenty of time to take effect before the morning. When 6:30 came around, I could not have been more excited to get out onto the water to fish. The sun was shining, our fishing vessel was waiting for us, and the sea was beckoning.

We met our friends out on the dock and boarded the fully-stocked boat with fishing gear and supplies. The captain brightly announced, "Welcome to *Costa Rica*, which is the name of our boat here.

Today, we will begin our trip by voyaging out to the reef, which will take about an hour. There, we will find a plentiful amount of bonita fish, which is ideal for bait use."

Knowing that bonita fish could be as long as 30 inches, I could only imagine the size of the fish we would be luring. I could not wait! Later I learned that many of the boats at Tropic Star Lodge are named after different places around the world.

After being on the water for about 45 minutes, I turned to Marianne to share the special moment of excitement. I was shocked to see her looking as green as the jungle we left behind us.

"Are you okay?" I asked her.

"I'm fine," she assured me patting my knee. Within minutes, she was laying down on the bench as nauseous as could be. I felt awful. *This is going to be the longest week of my married life,* I thought to myself. There was only one cure at that point—to return to dry land. I directed the captain to turn the boat around to bring Marianne back to the lodge. He did so immediately, and we dropped her at the dock and headed back out to sea.

Despite the rough beginning, it ended up being a wonderful day of fishing. We caught plenty of large fish, fulfilling my every dream of fishing in the tropics. By the third day, Marianne said she wanted to attempt riding the boat again. We had heard from some other visitors at the lodge that Marianne had most likely had too much of the transdermal patch. For someone her stature, she would only need a third of a dose. I thought it was very brave of her to want to try again. I cautiously cut the patch to about a third of the size and placed it behind her ear. Uttering several prayers to the Good Lord and the God of the Seas, we all went out on day number three.

To my great relief, the one-third patch was the key, and Marianne was spared from seasickness. She had a lovely time and went out every day of the trip from that point on. She even brought a book to read on the boat! We caught loads of large fish. Byron and Starin were in their element, and Starin surprised me with her hidden angling skills.

That trip made more of an impact on my life than I could ever imagined. Beyond it initiating a lifetime connection to that piscine paradise, returning year after year for decades to come, but also, that first trip to Panama blessed Marianne and I with an even greater gift. Nine months after our first stay at the Tropic Star Lodge, on November 18th, 1985, our third child, Colleen Mahaffey was born. What a surprise it was for Marianne and me to conceive so easily after the struggles we had with our first children. I have teased Colleen many a times that if she had been born a boy, I would have named her Panama Jack. Poor girl had to endure that story at her wedding rehearsal dinner. Panama will forever stir in me feelings of nostalgia, family, friendship, and a spirit of adventure.

It brings me great joy to think back to all the times I have visited Tropic Star Lodge—22 times to be precise. I keep an excel spreadsheet of each trip, accounting for every guest in attendance and every fish caught. Each trip is unique and special, regardless of how many fish we reel in. On our second trip to Panama, in 1987, we caught virtually nothing the entire week of our stay. However, just as our fishing vessel began to head back toward the lodge at the end of the last day, three sailfish bit onto our baits that trailed out behind us. In perfect formation and unison, they leaped into the air, exposing themselves completely out of the water. After a long week of feeling defeat, there was finally action! I am sure that is something I will never see again. My captain and mate, in their broken Spanish and English, said they had never seen anything like that before. I think in that moment God offered us a gift of hope, a little visual treat to end our trip on a high note and entice us to come back.

That same day, about an hour later, the captain was nice enough to steer the boat slowly into the bay, hoping that we would catch something beyond the three that put on the aquatic show for us. With all our attention on the water, we were shocked to see two marlin peek up at the surface. They considered our bait, decided they did not want it, and swam away flipping their dorsal fin at us. It was as if they said, *Y'all come back here.* That was the highlight of our trip. We were in such high spirits when we got back to shore. We said, "We'll be back!" And we certainly did come back, many times.

Over the years, the lodge has evolved into a first-class, luxury destination. When I visit now, I reserve the three-bedroom dwelling perched in the treetops adjacent to the main lodge building. It was the original home of the founder, Ray Smith. This home, nicknamed *The Palace*, is now rented out to visitors who are looking for more of a private dwelling. Overlooking the bay, *The Palace* patio offers sunset views over the bay that are absolutely phenomenal. The home's nickname makes me think back to my college bunk room, *The Palace—Home of Pierre Puck and the Pathfinder*. I cannot help but laugh to think how far I've come since then. But whether *The Palace* refers to a college dorm or a home in the jungle, they both symbolize to me a unique retreat from the world and a treasure in my heart containing many fond memories.

With all the time that I have spent at Tropic Star Lodge, the staff there has come to feel like family. I became good friends with the past owners, Conway D. Kittredge (who has since passed away) and his daughter, Terri, and her husband, Mike Andrews. They have since sold the lodge to the De Obladia family in 2016. Terri and Mike still call Panama home, and I still see them on occasion when I visit.

Due to the lodge's remote location, the lodge staff, captains, and crew consist of primarily native locals who grew up amongst the tribes of the Panamanian jungle. They are some of the nicest people you will ever meet, and they have always treated me and my guests like family. Since the 1990s, Senior Captain Candelo has been my most used captain, and he has never failed me. Chef Gabriel, current culinary master in the Tropic Star kitchen is one of the most creative chefs I have ever encountered. From the accommodations to the meals to the fishing charters, the Tropic Star Lodge offers an unforgettable, one-of-a-kind experience like nothing else in the world.

Tropic Star Lodge is also special to me because it is the place where I met one of my now closest friends, Mike Bonsignore. It was back in 2001 when Marianne and I and he and his wife, Sheila, happened to be lodging at Tropic Star Lodge the same week. We fished with them on multiple occasions over the course of the week and found that we got along with them famously. On the very last day of the trip, we decided to join them for breakfast at the lodge—as it was the one morning we did not have to wake up so early to fish. We learned they were from Santa Barbara, California. Mike casually mentioned at breakfast that he was now retired, but had worked for Honeywell for many years, which had allowed him and his wife to live in various parts of world. They are bilingual in English and Spanish, which came in handy when traveling in Panama. What I did not find out until later was that Mike did not only work for Honeywell for 35 years, but he was also the CEO and Chairman of the Board for the last 9 of those 35 years! I was so impressed that Mike never boasted or wore his successful, international career on his sleeve. His humility made me admire and respect him all the more. Over the years, we kept in contact and our families also became close friends. We have been on many trips back to Panama together, as well as other trips around the globe.

As for my fishing success in Panama, voyaging back to Tropic Star Lodge year after year, I have had many successful trips catching plenty of black marlin, blue marlin, dorado, and sailfish. But even more than fishing, it has become a place of sharing. Every time I travel down to that remote gem nestled in the deep jungle, I bring family and friends from all stages of my life. I first brought my son, Tom, to Panama in 1999, and he has joined me on almost every trip since. The ever hunt for a bigger fish or new record times has evolved as I have gotten older. It has metamorphosized into an eagerness for nothing more than to share my passion. I used to pray, *Please God, please let me catch a big marlin*. But now, I do not say that prayer anymore. It is not that I don't want to catch a marlin, but I would rather the people I bring down there catch one. To see them experience that same thrill that I felt the first time I caught a marlin brings me so much more pleasure than catching one myself.

Mark marlin fishing in Panama

Marlin fishing in Piñas Bay, Panama

Mike and Sheila Bonsignore and Marianne and Mark

Bringing our children to Panama, and even more recently our grandchildren, has brought Marianne and me such delight. In the summer of 2021, Tom, Kiley, and Colleen and their families finally joined us on the big fishing venture. Our grandchildren had been hearing about Tropic Star Lodge since the day they were born, as it is such a meaningful part of all our lives. The kids were so excited to finally get the opportunity to go fishing in the famous Piñas Bay. I particularly appreciated being able to spend quality time with each of my children's families as we fished for hours on the peaceful ocean.

View from "The Palace" at Tropic Star Lodge

Colton, Piper, Ansleigh, Reece, and Mackenzie in Panama, 2021

Mark and grandson, Colton, fishing in Panama

Tom, Shannon, and Ansleigh with Captain Candello and mate

Everyone enjoyed themselves immensely, but there was one moment that I will always especially cherish. One day, I was out on the boat with Colleen and her family. It was at the peak of summer season, and the scorching heat was intense. Luckily, the boat's small cabin had air conditioning, so I was resting in there with Colleen and her 10-year-old son, Colton. Out of the blue, Colleen's 8-year-old daughter, Mackenzie, came rushing into the cabin, squealing, "Papa! Papa! Fish! Fish!" Seeing her excitement touched my heart. Sharing with others that passion I have for fishing is what the trips to Panama are all about. I happily got up out of my chair, ran out with her, and we jubilantly caught a fish. That little snippet, that little memory, will stay with me forever.

Reese with her big catch

Piper reeling in her big fish

Mackenzie with her big catch

Mark and Marianne with children and grandchildren at Tropic Star Lodge, Panama, 2021

To think back to all those years ago, when Richard Earle and I first planned to go to Panama and to witness how it has become such an integral part of my family story, is unbelievable. Tropic Star Lodge is undoubtably a magical place, a legendary experience, and a story that will be told for generations to come.

17

LUCK O' THE IRISH

If God sends you down a stony path, may he give you strong shoes.

Old Irish Proverb

Panama may be my passion, but Ireland will always be my homeland. Irish blood runs deep in the Mahaffey family line. I was raised listening to Irish folklore by the firelight, chanting Irish ballads, and cheering for Irish sports teams. With light blonde hair (now, snowy white) and sky-blue eyes, my Irish heritage is ever a part of my identity. I have always taken great pride in my Irish roots, but I have never felt so connected to them as I did when I first visited Ireland in 2002.

I must preface by first stating that this was not my first trip overseas to Europe. Back in the 1970s, when Marianne and I were first married, we were fortunate to go on many trips around the world. These trips were sponsored by Carrier Air Conditioning, which used to be one of the Mahaffey Apartment Company's suppliers. For about five or six years straight, my parents and Marianne and me, and my brother and his wife, were invited, among other customers, to go on these incredible, week-long trips—all completely paid for by Carrier Air Conditioning. We went to Greece, France, Spain, as well as the Asian countries of China and

Japan. It was unbelievable that Marianne and I were able to see a good part of the world in our twenties.

A few decades later, in the 1990s, when our children were grown, we began traveling to Europe again on trips with other couples. It was then that we met our friends, Jim and Donna Nannen. This resourceful couple was well-versed in the art of trip planning and organized many of those excursions, which included France and Italy. However, for all the travels we had made to Europe, Marianne and I never had the pleasure of visiting Ireland. In 2002, we determined it was time. Now being in the 21st century, with the invention of the internet as an asset, the Nannens put their research skills to work and found the quintessential Irish dwelling to stay in Southern Ireland. Marianne and I could hardly wait!

The Linden House, as it was called, was a charming and rather large home set atop a seaside escarpment just outside the quaint coastal village of Glengarriff. This beautiful, stone-clad home provided plenty of space for the Nannens and ourselves, as well as five other couples who also joined us. My favorite feature of the home was the floor-to-ceiling gable windows that overlooked acres of lush, green meadows and gardens that toppled down to the royal blue waters of Bantry Bay. Beyond the bay towered the Caha Mountains, which resembled sleeping giants dozing in the sun. Cloaked in rich green grass, they gently rolled and bulged until they met the Celtic Sea. When the sun irradiated the sparkling waters at just the right angle, the surrounding highlands were illuminated with a vibrant, jade glow.

We were fascinated to discover that Maureen O'Hara, star of the Golden Age of Hollywood, owned the estate *Lugdine Park* just adjacent to our rental home property. We had hoped to catch a glimpse of this famous actress, but never did. Nonetheless, it was still rather exciting to imagine her just beyond the bordering landscape.

We adored the small town of Glengarriff, which was nestled between the mountains and the sea and was as charming as could be. The picturesque main street featured adorable cottage-like shops and restaurant fronts; each painted a unique buoyant color. Flowers of brilliant pinks and yellows burst out of window boxes and planters, framing the sidewalks in color.

Painting of Butlerstown House

Marianne and I absolutely fell in love with Southern Ireland. We hiked along the cliff-chiseled coast, merrily sipped whiskey in the timeless Irish pubs, and explored old villages and castles that seemed right out of a fairy tale book. I felt incredibly immersed into a history that I had always felt a connection to but had never experienced as intimately as then, walking the earth my ancestors walked.

"We must come back here," I said to Marianne as our trip was ending.

"Definitely," she concurred.

"And stay longer next time," I added.

"I would love that as well," Marianne agreed.

A few years later, in 2006, the itch to return was as strong as ever. I strategically contacted my local travel agent, Joan Bailey, and beckoned her to assist me in finding a home in Ireland to rent for about a month. I wanted it large enough that I would be able to invite some friends and family to stay with us.

"I'm on it!" Joan promised.

After extensive research, Joan was able to locate three options in Southern Ireland. My favorite was a stately, five-bedroom, five-bathroom Irish manor called *Butlerstown House*. This grand home rested upon ten enchanting acres of rippling grassy hills and gardens. Although it was over 200 years old, the home was recently renovated and promised the best in modern amenities. The listing did make a special note, however, to say there was no television. But this was excellent news for us as it was the last distraction we needed in a land with so many riches to discover. Unlike our previous rental, this home did not boast direct waterfront, but the coast was a mere mile away.

We booked *Butlerstown House* immediately, planning ahead for June 6th to July 6th the following year, 2007. It would be the longest trip that Marianne and I had ever embarked on, but we knew it would be the trip of a lifetime. Marking our calendars, we counted the days until the big trip.

Meanwhile, around this time and perhaps for the few years before, my health began to decline. I was not in any severe pain, but I had a rather vague suspicion that something was off. In the years ahead I would receive the diagnosis for diverticulitis, but this was something quite different. Some days I would feel fairly fine, but other days, I would wake up feeling exhausted before the day even began. A gnawing weakness overcame my body, and no matter my resolutions, I could not fight it. I visited several doctors in Saint Petersburg, but it was just as big of a mystery to them as it was to me.

Maybe it will just go away on its own, I encouraged myself.

I reflected on my experience with a similar conundrum of an illness I had back in the late 1980s. I had bounced from doctor to doctor, hoping for some explanation as to why I was not feeling well. My family and friends had been worried about me and even suggested I go to the world-esteemed Mayo Clinic in Rochester, Minnesota. I had suggested the idea to my primary doctor, and he scheduled an appointment for me at Mayo the following week. I could not have been more impressed by this state-of-the-art clinic. I had felt extraordinarily blessed to be in such good hands. After conducting a myriad of tests on me for three days, the doctors at Mayo Clinic concluded that a parasite was to blame for my ailments.

"Have you traveled out of the country lately?" one of the doctors had asked.

Being that this was in the late 1980s, I thought back to my trip to Panama the year before. I distinctly remembered sitting at a café table in Panama City in the early morning before heading to Tropic Star Lodge. I recalled quenching my thirst with a cold coke and crunching on the ice from my glass. I was certain the ice was to blame. The doctor predicted that the issue would either resolve on its own, or on the flip side, drastically get worse within the near future. Fortunately for me, the issue resolved on its own, and I felt back to myself within a few months.

But now, it being around 2006, almost twenty years later, that general unwell feeling was back. This time, however, it was distinctly different. I could not put my finger on exactly what was wrong. Still, my heart clung to the hope that perhaps my body would heal on its own as it did with the parasite. My friends and family, however, encouraged me to continue to get to the bottom of it.

One day, a friend of Marianne's and mine, Jane Randall Kirby, approached me with an idea I had not thought of before.

She said, "Mark, I hate to see you like this. You are not yourself. Have you looked into seeing an allergist, perhaps?"

I admitted, "Well, I've been to an allergist in the past, but not recently."

Her eyes lit up with hope, as if perhaps she had found the key to solving my problem. "Well, I highly recommend you see my allergist. She is very, very smart. She does more than the normal tests. I think it might be worth your shot."

"I appreciate your recommendation. I will give her a call," I promised.

Later that week, I was able to secure an appointment with the allergist. Upon meeting the doctor, I instantly knew Jane Randall Kirby had been correct. This doctor seemed very knowledgeable.

She explained, "Mark, I know you have already been to an allergist, so I won't bother running the normal tests. Instead, I'm going to have some lab work done to check some other things. It may take a month or so to get results, but it should give us some answers."

"I will follow your lead," I assented.

About three or four weeks later, the allergist called me into a follow-up appointment. Sitting in her office, she presented to me a long panel of blood analyses. She deciphered the results so I would understand. "All looks normal, except for these three enzymes. They are not right, but I don't really know what to make of it," she admitted. She paused, frowning. The hesitation troubled me, causing my stomach to drop. She sighed, "I highly suggest you follow up with an oncologist/hematologist."

I lost my breath for a moment. Those are two very scary words. Two words that absolutely no one wants to hear said to them.

"Really?" I said in disbelief, my brain not wanting to comprehend the speeding missile just fired at me.

She smiled. "Yes. Don't worry. This is above my field, and I want to send you to one of the best. I'm going to see if I can get you an appointment with Dr. Jeffery Paonessa."

My mind reeled. "I know Dr. Paonessa," I said. "Not very well, but I've met him socially. I have also heard that he is top of his field."

She nodded. "Yes, he is not taking any new patients, but I think I can get you in. He is very smart. He'll get to the bottom of this, I am certain."

Miraculously, the allergist was able to schedule me an appointment with Dr. Paonessa the following week. Realizing that this could be a very weighty appointment, I asked Marianne if she would accompany me. I always maintain the importance of bringing a spouse or a good friend to big appointments like this. It is not merely for moral support, but more crucially, to offer an extra set of listening ears. As doctors relay spools of information to their patients, it is beneficial to have a backup attender to facilitate absorbing it all.

Marianne was happy to be that companion for me, as she was just as curious as I was to hear the highly-esteemed doctor's opinion. Dr. Paonessa had an impeccable reputation as an oncologist. Rumor was that he had an ego to match his skill level. But that did not bother me, as I would rather put my trust in a confident doctor than the alternative.

Looking over my charts, Dr. Paonessa declared, "Mark, I am going to run some more tests. I'm ninety-five percent sure that I can figure out what is wrong with you. And if I can't, I'll send you to a clinic…MD Anderson, Shands, Mayo's…I'll find a clinic that might be able to give you an answer. But first, let me see if I can figure this out." He was just about the most confident doctor I had ever met. His assertiveness and self-assuredness may have come off as arrogance to some, but for me, it put my mind at ease. I was able to put all my fears and concerns into his hands and trust in his experience and expertise.

"Yes, sir," I said.

He proceeded to run the necessary scans and tests. For weeks, I waited patiently for the results.

In the meantime, I had plans to travel to Atlanta, Georgia, for the Final Four basketball game of that year's March Madness tournament. I had gotten the tickets as a gift from Leo Lambert, the president and my friend at Elon University. Marianne, Tom and his wife, Shannon, and some friends of ours were scheduled to stay in a hotel in Atlanta Friday through Tuesday morning. Monday evening was the big basketball game. I had never been to a Final Four basketball event before, and I certainly did not want to miss this trip, despite not feeling my best.

I called Dr. Paonessa and asked his advice. He said, "Well, I've got the tests back, but go on and have a good time in Atlanta. Come see me on Tuesday after you return from your trip. We can discuss the results then."

Having hope in the positive, I joined the clan heading north. Unfortunately, my body would not cooperate with my mental eagerness to have a good time. I felt horrible for nearly the entirety of the trip. While my group explored the city, visited the famous Atlanta Aquarium, and dined to their hearts' content, I laid in the hotel room feeling weak and exhausted.

I'm counting on you, Dr. Paonessa, I muttered to myself.

I pulled open the heavy hotel drapes, allowing light to rush into the room like a thousand caged birds set free. The sun warmed my soul, filling my core with hope and courage. I peered at the Atlanta streets below. People were busily bustling and scurrying around like little bees in a hive, all with a destination and a job to do. And here I was, held captive within my own body and this prison of a hotel room. I needed to get out.

Feeling a spark of determination, I slipped on some blue jeans and sneakers and pulled on a sweater. Riding the elevator to the main lobby, I sauntered out the front door and breathed the fresh, early spring air into my lungs. Although the breeze hit my cheeks with a cold sting, the sun peeked out from behind a cloud and whispered promises of warm days ahead, like a warm cup of tea to soothe the soul.

Then, to my surprise, I heard a rumble in the distance, like a taunting roar mocking my attempt to escape my confinement. I glanced ahead and saw rain clouds looming. The hotel doorman, whom must have noticed my gaze, remarked, "Looks like rain ahead."

"Yes, indeed," I said. I was not about to let the rain cast a deeper shadow on my day. Considering the onset of a potential washout, I asked the doorman, "Say, do you by chance know if there is a shopping mall around here?"

"Yes, the best. Lenox Square Mall, just a mile away. I will call you a cab," the man kindly offered.

"Thank you, sir," I said.

Within a few minutes, I stood outside the monstrosity of a shopping center. I generally only step inside malls once a year—at Christmastime. In general, Marianne covers all the shopping needs in our household. But, alas, my present need to get out, and stay dry, prompted my choice of adventure.

I sauntered around the mall from store to store doing nothing more than window shop for the most part. It was the ideal therapy moving my legs and getting my blood flowing after resting for so long. The mall was bright and cheery, and it thankfully lifted my spirits. After an hour of strolling down the highly ornamented corridors, I bought a steaming, hot pretzel. I sat on a bench, savoring every bite of that salty, chewy twist. I pondered my health journey thus far. I was exhausted seeing doctor after doctor, having no answer or reprieve. But I would not let despair rear its ugly head and infect my thoughts. I am the *Pathfinder*, after all. If there is a path, I will find it.

Deciding I was finished with the mall, I longed to rejoin my group. Stepping toward the door, I looked outside to see sheets of rain falling like thick waves of hammering nails. I inspected the nearby shops. *Brooks Brothers.* That'll do. I walked into the store, spied a rack of raincoats, and bought a long, gray one. I still have it hanging in my closet to this day. That raincoat is special to me because it symbolizes a turning point in my journey. That day I bought the raincoat, I made the resolve to dig deep within myself and uncover the strength I needed to make my way out of that intricate labyrinth. I did not know what results Dr. Paonessa had for me, but I would approach it like a knight in battle. Hardships may come my way, but like that raincoat to the rain, my will was my armor. And nothing could hurt me.

Reunited with my group later that evening, I felt renewed in spirit. We dined at my favorite Italian restaurant, *Pricci,* for dinner, and I even felt up to attending the big game on Monday. The trip ended as a success, and I was glad that I made the effort to participate in the events and make new memories with my family and friends.

Before I knew it, it was Tuesday afternoon, and I was back in Dr. Paonessa's office. Marianne sat by my side, holding my hand. Whatever news Dr. Paonessa had for us, we were prepared. We waited in that small, blue-painted exam room for what seemed like hours, although it was probably not very long. The anticipation vibrated in my core as if I were at the peak of a rollercoaster waiting for the impeding drop. Marianne was just as apprehensive as I was, perhaps even more so.

Finally, Dr. Paonessa entered the room.

"Mark, I am sure you are anxious to hear your results. I did find a little something."

He pulled out two large sheets of body scans, *my* body scans.

"You see, this is a PET scan, and this is a CT scan. When I overlaid them, I noticed something peculiar." He spread the large sheets on the table. All three of us peered at the image. To me, I may as well had been trying to decipher hieroglyphics.

The doctor answered my pondering thoughts. "In your right lung, here, do you see all these little white dots? There's something going on there. I'm not sure what it is. But I want you to go see a pulmonologist."

I grunted involuntarily. Another doctor referral. "Really?" I muttered. "Who do you recommend I see?"

"I have already set it up. Tomorrow, you will see Dr. Hudman Hoo."

"Okay," I complied, remembering my resolve to not veer from the path.

Dr. Paonessa continued, "The following day, I want you to see a thoracic surgeon—a heart surgeon. Dr. Joshua Rovin. Both of these doctors are very capable and are the best in their field. You will be in good hands," Dr. Paonessa assured me.

I sighed. "Let's get to the bottom of this," I said. I imagined myself in that labyrinth again. These doctors were the guides along the way, pointing which direction to go. I had no choice but to trust them and follow their advice.

The next day, Marianne and I visited Dr. Hoo. He looked over my charts and ran a few tests while I was in the office.

"Hmm," Dr. Hoo said as he intently looked over my results. "This is interesting because you live here in Florida."

I interrupted him. "Well," I said. "I haven't always lived here. My wife and I were born and raised in Indianapolis, Indiana."

He dropped the stack of papers on his desk in a thump. He looked at me straight in the eyes and said assertively, "You have histoplasmosis."

"Histoplas-what?" I echoed.

"It's a type of fungi. It's especially prevalent in the Ohio Valley. This fungus is found in pigeon and bat droppings. It's often found in dirt and can be exposed to the air and inhaled during demolition or digging projects. Perhaps you played in the dirt as a young boy? It can be in your body for a long period of time dormant, and it is not a problem. But if it becomes active, it can turn into a big, potentially fatal problem."

"Wow," was all I could think to say. I thought back to growing up in Indianapolis. I also thought back to the construction projects we did back in the 1970s in Indianapolis: Lake Nora Arms, West Lake Arms, and

Lake Castleton Arms. I had visited the sites several times. Perhaps I was exposed then. I will never know exactly.

The doctor calmed my tornado of thoughts. "Tomorrow, you will see Dr. Joshua Rovin, is that correct?"

"Yes," I replied.

"Great. You will be in good hands."

We took another turn in the maze.

Dear Lord, help me find the way out of this, I prayed.

Following orders, Marianne and I visited Dr. Rovin's office the following morning. His office was a stand-alone building that he shared with about six other doctors. One of these was the cardiologist that took care of my father before he passed.

Marianne and I sat in the office waiting room in silence, our thoughts wheeling too rapidly to be spoken. I glanced around the room. It was quite cozy for a doctor's waiting room, and I appreciated the homey décor that made me feel more comfortable. Upon the warm, chestnut colored carpet there were stationed several clusters of couches and armchairs, all set up living-room style. Fresh flowers ornamented each coffee table. The central reception desk, paneled with walnut, had potted flowers and seasonal décor (which happened to be bunnies and egg baskets as Easter was the weekend before). The walls were painted a cheery cream color with walnut-paneled wainscotting to match the reception desk. Large oil paintings of the six resident doctors hung on the walls, with no labels to identify any of them.

"I wonder which painting is of Dr. Rovin," I whispered to Marianne.

"I was just thinking the same thing," she replied, smiling.

Suddenly, the door leading to the exam room swung open. A tall, thin young man in a white doctor's coat appeared. He had tightly trimmed ginger hair, thinly rimmed glasses, and wore a smile ear to ear.

Without hesitation, he walked straight up to another couple, who were seated in the couch arrangement next to ours. This couple, looking to be about the same age as Marianne and I, leapt out of their chairs. The man immediately wrapped his arms around the doctor in a hug as enthusiastic as if it were homecoming day. Tears streamed down the man's face.

Gratitude, I thought to myself. *That doctor saved that man's life.*

Arm in arm, the couple and the doctor then retreated into the inner sanctum. I wondered who that doctor was. Perhaps he was the renowned Dr. Rovin?

About ten minutes later, the couple exited the door and left the office in smiles. The clock was moving as slow as molasses. The anticipation stirred in me, and I tired of the long wait. Finally, the door swung open again. The same doctor we saw 15 minutes earlier, emerged for the second time. He walked right up to us.

"Hello, Mark Mahaffey?"

"Yes, sir."

"I'm Dr. Joshua Rovin," he welcomed us, offering us handshakes.

I said, "Good to meet you, Doctor. I watched you greet that other couple over there."

He grinned, "Yes, he's one of my patients."

Dr. Rovin offered no more details, so I decided not to prompt him any further. He quietly led us down several back hallways into a small exam room.

"I've talked to Dr. Hoo and Dr. Paonessa," Dr. Rovin said as he closed the door behind us. "I think surgery is your best and simplest option here. All I need to do is make a tiny incision in your throat and insert a small camera to view your lung. We can take a biopsy at that time. If I see what I hope to see, then I will proceed to remove the entire upper lobe of your right lung."

I must give the doctor credit for getting directly to the point and being very clear in his intentions. He surely did not sugar coat anything, despite his cheerful and smiling demeanor.

I said, "Okay, Doctor. But, I must ask...What if you don't see what you hope?"

Dr. Rovin responded, "If we take that biopsy, and it's something other than what we hope it is, then we will close you up. We will figure out what we want to do from there and discuss it with you afterwards."

I assumed he meant cancer. He never said the word, but Marianne and I both knew what he was talking about.

"Thank you, Dr. Rovin. When do you want to do this?"

He responded, "Monday."

"This coming Monday?!" I reacted.

"Yes, we can't delay," he said.

Putting my life in the hands of this doctor, I felt the need to get to know him better.

"How old are you, if you don't mind me asking?"

"I'm 36 years old. I know what you are going to say," he teased. "I look like Doogie Howser. I get it all the time."

I laughed. He did look like Doogie Howser, star of the sitcom TV series featuring young Neil Patrick Harris as a kid genius doctor. "Well, I cannot deny you sort of resemble him," I agreed.

Nodding, Dr. Rovin's face then took on a serious expression, "Look, we have to trust one another. If you are not comfortable with this, for whatever reason, you are not offending me. I will get you into any hospital or clinic in the country."

I appreciated his boldness and humility, but I still wanted to know him better.

"Where did you go to medical school?"

"University of Virginia."

"Really?" I knew that was a good medical school.

I said, "You know, I've been on the board of Elon University for a long time, and one of my good friends, who is also a trustee, is a fellow by the name of Dr. Bill Herbert. He was the head of the OB/GYN Department at the University of Virginia Medical School. He is just retiring now, but perhaps you've met him?"

"Bill Herbert?" Dr. Rovin repeated the name slowly as if he was searching through the files in his brain. "Gosh, that name seems so familiar. Hang on a second." He pulled his personal cell phone out of his white coat pocket. "Let me call my wife. She is also a physician. She will know," he explained.

Marianne and I exchanged glances. We had never had this happen before in a doctor's office. The doctor made the phone call right there in the room. Hearing only one side of the conversation, we listened curiously.

"Hi Honey, it's me...oh, oh you are taking the kids to the movies...oh, yes, it's Spring Break...I've got a patient here who has mentioned he knows a Dr. Bill Herbert, who evidently was at University of Virginia. Do you remember him at all? Oh, really...well I'll be darned...Thanks, Honey. Have a good time. I will see you tonight."

He hung up the phone and returned it to his pocket. He looked at us and beamed. "Dr. Bill Herbert delivered one of our babies!"

"Wow! Small world." I exclaimed. I took that unexpected connection as a sign from God. I looked at Marianne and then back at the doctor. "Well," I said, "I guess this surgery needs to be done. I will trust your judgement."

Before I knew it, Monday, April 16th, 2007 came around. I remember that date exactly. My poor family was distressed, but I did my best to keep things light and positive. Thinking back, it was interesting to analyze how each person coped with the fears that we all felt. Marianne was scared, but knew she had to be the rock for all of us. Tom was pretty steady. Kiley, who has a career in counseling, almost fell apart. I teased her saying, "You are the one who is trained in all this—to handle human emotions—and you aren't doing it worth a damn." It is still a sensitive subject for her. And young Colleen—she was the bravest. I learned something about my children that day. I figured out if I were ever in a foxhole, I would want Colleen there with me. She is *Cool Hand Luke.* I know she was very concerned about her father, but she was a boulder. I didn't necessarily analyze all this as it was happening, but looking back I am able to reflect and see this.

As the nurses leisurely wheeled me on the hospital bed to the operating room, I thought back to my father's advice. It was the same advice he was given by his college football coach, Knute Rockne. *Play like you are positive on the victory.* I did not let my mind downward spiral into a series of *what-ifs*. Instead, I focused on the positive road ahead, the road that led to triumph. I focused on Ireland.

"Dr. Rovin?" I beckoned the doctor as I was wheeled into the operating room.

Dr. Rovin replied with a wide grin, "Why hello, Mark."

I asked, "Marianne and I have rented this fantastic home in Southern Ireland to stay for a month. We have a full itinerary with friends and family meeting us there."

"When is this trip?" Dr. Rovin asked, knowing what I was insinuating.

"In about a month and a half. We've rented the home from June 6th to July 6th," I said.

Dr. Rovin assured me, "I'll tell you what. If we find what we are hoping for, I'll get you to Ireland."

I said, "You've got a deal."

And that is the last thing I remember before the surgery.

Five and a half hours later, I woke up in the recovery room. Dr. Rovin, Marianne, and my three kids stood around my bed. I smiled at my family, and then turned to Dr. Rovin.

"Well?" I asked.

"It looks like you've got the luck of the Irish. You are going to Ireland," he responded confidently.

"Yes!" I was elated.

"Everything was as we hoped. I don't recommend running any marathons in the near future, but otherwise, your life can go back to normal.

"Stop right there, Doctor," I quipped with a smile. "I don't have any previous plans, nor do I have any current or future plans, to run *any* marathon. You definitely don't have to worry about that." Although I considered myself rather in shape, at 63 years old, my athletic days had been quite over for a while.

Dr. Rovin must have done a top-notch job on the surgery, as the recovery was swift. After spending three days in the hospital, I was home for a week, and then back to work the following week. Come June, Dr. Rovin gave me the a-okay to make my big voyage to my motherland—the Emerald Isle. Ireland.

18

BUTLERSTOWN HOUSE

May the road rise to meet you.
May the wind be always at your back.
May the sunshine warm your face;
The rain fall soft upon your fields.
And until we meet again,
May God hold you in the
Palm of His hand.

Traditional Irish Blessing

Leading up to our long-awaited trip, Marianne and I could not have been more ecstatic to play the role of innkeepers, sharing our love of travel with those we care most about. We thoughtfully created an itinerary and invited three groups of our closest friends and family. Each group would stay with us for one of the first three weeks we rented Butlerstown House in Ireland. Every weekend, the groups would rotate out, allowing for the next group to arrive. The fourth week was reserved for Marianne and me to enjoy on our own, as we knew we would most likely crave a bit of a reprieve from all the guests after a long month. It was the ideal plan, and the week could not come soon enough.

We were positively thrilled when everyonewe invited responded that they would be able to join us—everyone, that is, except my son, Tom, his wife, Shannon, and their daughter, Ansleigh. Devastatingly, the week before the trip, Shannon sustained a head injury falling out of a golf cart on a weekend getaway to Boca Grande. Gratefully, she eventually recovered and has endured no long-term effects. But nonetheless, we were saddened that they were not able to join us for that first family trip to Ireland. We felt awful for Shannon, but knowing that she was in the good hands of doctors and that she would be recovering soon, we decided to continue with our plans to visit Butlerstown House.

On June 6th, 2007, Marianne and I eagerly set off on our long-awaited adventure. Kiley and Colleen would be joining us in a few days for their stay the first week, but for now, it was just Marianne and me. Upon our arrival to the airport in Cork, Ireland, I strategically leased a sizable van with the foresight that it would be a necessity with all our expected visitors. Giddy as could be, I decided to get into the spirit. I ceremoniously hopped into the driver's seat and placed an Irish tweed patty cap upon my head. I turned to Marianne and grinned playfully at her.

Putting on my best Irish accent, I greeted her in jest, "Top o' de mornin' to ya! Welcome to Ireland, ah de motherland! So, I am Patrick, cousin o' Mark Mahaffey."

I was not hampered by the subsequent eye rolls and happily continued. "It's a grand day this sunny mornin'. I am sure you are knackered to be sure. But we will be to Butlerstown House in a short while."

Keeping in character, I tipped my cap, and began the short excursion to our rental home. The Butlerstown House was positioned just outside the city of Kinsale, which was about ten miles south of the Cork airport. It was a lovely drive. Vivid green meadows bounded on either side of the road offering a seemingly idyllic, pastoral setting. Dozens of sheep grazed serenely in the distance. Unruly patches of trees and vine-wreathed fences cushioned the road from the livestock pastures. It was not long before the foliage parted, making way for a stone-laid gate. A carved sign was stationed at the gate post reading, *Butlerstown House*.

Butlerstown House, Ireland

Mark and Marianne with Butlerstown House landlords, Roger and Lis Owens

"We have arrived here to our home," I announced, keeping my assumed Irish accent.

Our breath was subsequently taken away as the view beyond the gate was revealed. Before our eyes stood a grand, two-story traditional Georgian-style dwelling. The stucco exterior was painted a creamy, oatmeal color. The contrasting, ebony-hued front door was positioned precisely in the center of the massive façade, with surrounding windows in pleasing symmetry. The classical architecture offered peaceful sentiments of balance and order. Manicured gardens blanketed the estate, enhancing the home's charming, collected feel. In the distance, the Dunmanway Mountains stood like a protecting grandfather watching over the manor.

Grabbing our luggage, we sauntered slowly to the front door taking in the beauty surrounding us. As I lifted my hand to try the handle, to my surprise, the door swung open.

"Hello, welcome to Butlerstown House. I am Elisabeth. Call me Lis," greeted a smiling woman with shoulder length, white hair. I noticed her accent sounded distinctly Welsh rather than Irish. A tall, quiet man stood behind her. They reached out their hands to shake ours.

"This is my husband, Roger. We are the owners. You dears must be exhausted from your travels. Please, do come in. Make yourselves at home," she said as she quickly widened the door opening to let us through.

That moment, as we gingerly stepped through the doorway, we crossed a threshold into another world, another time. The historic ambience of the 200-year-old home could not be disguised by the recent renovations. Intricately carved plaster moldings framed the ceilings, oil paintings in gold frames decked the walls, and expansive, antique rugs added refinement to the well-worn, cherry stained floors. A lovely bifurcated staircase, which led to the second story, was a beautiful focal point in the space. *Oh, if these walls could talk, the stories they would tell,* I thought to myself. The warm, musty notes of antique cedar and oak tickled my olfactory senses.

Roger and Lis, as I would find out later, enjoyed collecting and refinishing antique furniture that they gathered during their travels around Europe. The pieces furnished the home, truly giving the residents the feeling like they had stepped back in time. The well-equipped country kitchen, with a grand, stone-accented wall, was the heart of the home. The adjoining dining room featured an impressive, long wooden table, which they christened *Butlerstown Table*. A lavish breakfast was served daily here, as well as many fine dinners. For some of the evenings during our stay, we hired Helen Conner, a superb chef recommended by Lis and Roger, who prepared beautiful, as well as scrumptious, spreads. Marianne and I also enjoyed our time in the kitchen and prepared several meals to treat our guests. Lis and Roger, of course, were always welcomed to join us.

Over the course of the month, Marianne and I experienced a fulfillment and joy beyond our wildest expectations. With each group that visited, our love of Ireland grew and grew as we shared it with others. Bringing together our greatest loves—family, friendships, and tradition—we were able to knit together our strong Irish roots with our most cherished kith and kin. Despite my surgery just seven weeks before, I was so pumped with adrenaline. I was the ever-ready battery, the first one awake and the last one to bed every night. I was ever so elated to be alive and healthy with all those health troubles behind me. I did not want to take a moment for granted.

Although the memories and emotions stirred from such a special place and time are far too various to mention, there are a few that I love to share over and over again. One memory is from the very first week we arrived, when Kiley and Colleen visited. Marianne and I and our girls had taken a day trip back to Cork, which was a big change from the small villages near Butlerstown House. The girls especially loved to walk along the bustling, historic streets, investigating all the little shops and boutiques. Strolling along, Kiley spotted a sign up ahead.

Marianne, Colleen, Kiley, and Mark in Ireland, 2007

"Look! *Kiely* Jewelers," she called out.

Considering we had named our daughter, Kiley, after my grandmother's maiden name, I could not help but wonder if there was a connection. The jewelry shop sign had spelled the name *Kiely* instead of *Kiley*, but we were still interested to check it out.

I said, "Gee, I wonder if that is family?"

Eager with interest, the four of us scurried into the jewelry shop. It was a small shop, but it had many nice pieces on display in glass cases along the walls. A small man sat behind the largest display table and was tinkering with a timepiece.

Seeing us, he set down the piece carefully, and greeted us, "Oh hello. Can I help you?"

I said, "Are you Mr. Kiely?"

He nodded, "Yes, I am."

I said, "Hello. I am Mark Mahaffey. I am curious if we are related. My grandmother's maiden name was Kiley, and I believe her family was originally from Cork. As a matter of fact, my daughter here is Kiley Mahaffey. We spell Kiley differently than you do, but perhaps we Americanized it."

The jeweler beamed, "You didn't Americanize it. We're all one family. Some people spell it differently."

I said, "Well, I guess that makes us cousins."

It was certainly amusing making that potential family connection there, especially for our daughter.

The following Sunday, our next group arrived. It included my childhood friends, Bob Desautels, and his wife, Theresa, and Hugh McGowan and his wife, Jeanmarie. My Navy friend, Steve Bettcher, and his wife, Kathy, joined us, as well as our good friends from Saint Petersburg Carl and Lee Ann Lambrecht, who had introduced us to Highlands, North Carolina. It was undoubtably a reunion of our closest friends and was such a joy to have them all under one roof in such a sentimental place as Ireland. Roger and Lis made our time even more grand by being incredibly gracious hosts, giving us insightful tours of the surrounding villages and sharing with us some unforgettable eateries.

"While you are here, you must go to O'Neill's Pub," Roger told us the very first week. "Sunday nights are special. At 9:30 in the evening, the musicians arrive along with half the town. It is a grand event and such fun. Please join us this Sunday. Lis and I will be going most certainly."

Although our group was rather tired from their travels that Sunday morning, they rested during the afternoon to save their energy for the big pub event. We were all intrigued to see how the locals of Butlerstown spent their Sunday nights.

Just before 9:30, we all piled into the large rental van. "Off we go to O'Neill's Pub. We will be sure to have a jolly time," I said to the passengers in my Irish lilt.

With Roger and Lis guiding the way, we arrived at the pub in no time. It was located in the little downtown of Butlerstown, which was so small that you might have missed it if you happened to blink. The pub was a bright, yellow-painted cottage with a bold, red-adorned entrance. A large sign hung above the door that read *O'Neill's of Butlerstown*. Parking the van in the small lot behind the pub, we all curiously entered through the old, crimson front door. We were shocked to see the place bursting with life, laughter and music. Musicians playing a fiddle, guitar and accordion birthed Irish tunes into the atmosphere as the guests crooned in unison. This old-school Irish pub was much smaller than I had expected. Peony pink walls surrounded a classic, wooden bar that lined the back wall. A few tables were scattered about the place, but most of the locals were standing. An old, cast-iron fireplace was nestled into the wall adjacent to the bar with a large painting of white horses mounted above it. An adjoining room, which was fitted with a pool table and dart board, held more space and activities for the guests. Being the only Americans in the pub, our group felt fully immersed into the Irish culture.

A woman with short, curly, ginger hair stood behind the bar. In fluid motion, she fluttered to and fro, pouring drafts and singing along with the crowd. Her face radiated with joy and purpose, and it was obvious she was the owner.

"That is Mary O'Neill," Roger gestured. "She is the owner. Her husband, Dermot, you may see from time to time, but Mary is the real life of the party. She pours the best Guinness in the area."

We did not hesitate to try the Guinness, which surely did not disappoint. We joined in the singing and had a merry time. We returned to the pub many times on that trip, as well as subsequent trips to come. We got to know Mary O'Neill, and she became another wonderful friend.

Later that week, after our group had split for the day, we decided to meet back up at O'Neill's again for drinks after dinner. Carl and Lee Ann Lambrecht and Steve and Kathy Bettcher had gone golfing for the day at Old Head Golf Links in Kinsale. This gorgeous world-class golf course was positioned on a unique headland peninsula that extended into the Atlantic Ocean. It was a beautiful experience that Marianne and I encouraged them to do. We, along with Hugh and Jean Marie McGowan, stayed back in Butlerstown having more of a leisurely day. At 9:00 pm, we arrived at O'Neill's Pub eager to hear about our friends' day of golfing. Marianne quickly spotted Carl sitting at the bar and playfully goosed him in the buttocks. Well, she was shocked when the man whom she thought was Carl spun around in his chair. It was not Carl at all, but rather, a man named Shawn! I am not sure who was more surprised—Shawn or Marianne. She was rather embarrassed, but he did not seem to mind.

Marianne and the "goosed" Shawn, 2007

Later that evening, Mary O'Neill told us, "Shawn came up to me and said, 'I surely like your friends. That woman gave me a pat on my butt. This is the best day of my life!'" Marianne blushed, but we all thought the event was such a hoot.

One time, I went to O'Neill's by myself. I was enjoying a Guinness when Mary said, "Mark, sing us a song."

I declined explaining, "I don't sing very well."

But Mary would not take no for an answer and finally persuaded me to sing Danny Boy. She pulled a thick, old songbook out from under the bar, and with a thump, placed it on the bar top. With the songbook as my guide, I sang Danny Boy with Mary as a duet. She had a beautiful, lilting voice, and it was an honor to sing with her.

Mark and Mary O'Neill singing a "Danny Boy" duet, 2007

Another time at O'Neill's, Marianne and I arrived there before the musicians. A man named Timothy was all the way at the end of the bar hunched over his Guinness. We had seen him a few times before, but he had never said a word. As she did with me, Mary had a special way of easing the nerves of her guests and coaxing them to perform. She said, "Timothy, why don't you recite one of your poems?"

Timothy grumbled, not even looking up from his glass.

Mary encouraged, "Timothy, come on now."

Mary had a special charm that you could not deny. Marianne and I were astounded to see Timothy get up and recite the most beautiful, somber poem we had ever heard. He chanted for five to six minutes, all from memory. I was not sure if he had written it, memorized it, or ad-libbed it, but it was very moving. Timothy spoke ever so eloquently. After he finished, we all clapped, and he plopped back down into his seat hovering over his Guinness again without another word. It was always a good time at O'Neill's.

The third week of our grand stay in Ireland marked the arrival of our good friends from Saint Petersburg—Byron and Starin Shouppe, Bill and Mary Ann Bond, Ron and Jane Ann Lees, and Gene and Ginger Grimes. Per tradition, we took them to the Sunday evening party at O'Neill's and toured them around the Irish countryside and villages.

Group Two at Butlerstown House, 2007

Group Three at Butlerstown House, 2007

There was one evening, in particular, that will always hold a special place in my heart. It was the evening of Thursday, June 28th, Marianne and my 38th wedding anniversary. Our stay so far had been a whirlwind of activity to be sure. Guests coming and going, Marianne and I preparing the home for each new round of visitors, and sightseeing and hiking with each group galore. Marianne is a fabulous host, and I must give her credit for making our friends feel so welcomed and cherished. I knew I wanted to do something special for her for our anniversary, I just had to think of what.

About a week before our anniversary, I asked Lis and Roger if they had any recommendations.

"Oh yes!" cried Lis. "I know just the place. *Otto's Creative Catering.* It's a picturesque, little restaurant not too far from here. The head chef, Otto Kunze, and his wife, Hilda, are from Germany and are such lovely people. Otto is truly an exquisite culinary master. I will help you book it," Lis offered.

"I would be most pleased," I said, extremely grateful for her guidance.

On June 28th, Marianne and I, along with Lis and Roger and our visiting friends from Saint Petersburg, boarded the large van. As I had kept the dinner location a surprise, Marianne had no idea what to expect. And honestly, neither did I. I put my faith in Lis and Roger as they provided navigation and I drove. After winding through pastures and prairies for about ten minutes, Lis hollered, "Turn here!"

I quickly veered the van into an almost inconspicuous driveway that was shrouded with vines and greenery. I followed the long entrance up a winding hill that meandered through acres and acres of orchards and bountiful gardens of vegetables and herbs. Cradled in the well-nourished vegetation stood a large, stone-washed cottage—part home, part restaurant. As our group entered the venue, we were guided by a server to our table. It was a long table with seating for ten. Smaller tables were scattered around the room, but they were unoccupied. I thought this was unusual considering it was dinner hour. But not thinking much of it, I seated myself in a chair next to Marianne.

I took a moment to glance around the room. It was the most unique venue at which I had ever dined. The room was a conservatory— a greenhouse of sorts—with paneled, glass walls and a ceiling that opened to the outside. Grapevines twisted and embraced one another as they mantled the glass and created a canopy that resembled intricately woven lace. Bundles of pale, chartreuse-colored Muscadet grapes hung in bunches throughout.

Wow, we all seemed to think in unison as we gazed at the unique space around us. The romantic ambiance was really something special. Before we knew it, a tall man with a gray beard, wearing a white chef coat, and a woman with colorful glasses and a black waist apron entered the room from beyond the grapevines.

"Hello," said the man. "Welcome to OCC at Dunworthy Cottage. I am Otto Kunze and this is my wife, Hilda. I hear we are celebrating something special tonight?" He raised his eyebrows, smiling, scanning our table for a hint.

Anniversary dinner at Otto's Creative Catering, 2007

"Yes," I called out. "Today is my wife's and my 38th wedding anniversary." I wrapped my arm around Marianne's shoulder as she radiated with happiness.

"Congratulations," said Hilda. "We are going to give you a unique experience tonight. We live a very self-sufficient life here on our five acres of land, and many of our meals are made with ingredients from our farm and gardens here. We will not give you any menus. Instead, we will make you a little bit of everything. Is that okay with you?"

"Of course," I replied. "That sounds very special." I hesitated, and then added, "I noticed all the other tables are empty. Where is everyone?"

Otto responded, "Our kitchen is devoted to only you tonight. This is *your* night. We are taking no other diners."

We were speechless!

As the courses came out one after another, we were overwhelmed with gratitude. So much thought, planning, and creativity went into each dish. The salads were composed of produce from their garden, the smoked charcuterie from their farm, and even the seafood was delivered daily by boat to the edge of their property. The execution of the meal was flawless. The star course in my memory was most certainly the dessert. A myriad of various flavors and colors of sorbets were served in an ornately-carved bowl that was created entirely of ice. Home grown cherries adorned the ice sculpture. Otto was much more than a gourmet chef; he was a truly talented artist. He and his wife Hilda treated us with such love and care.

Sadly, we found out that Otto and Hilda had plans to sell the restaurant and retire within the next month. We were devastated to hear this, as the restaurant was such a unique gem that we had hoped to return to someday. As we were leaving dinner that evening, I said to Hilda, "Marianne and I are beyond grateful for this heavenly meal and for you making our anniversary so memorable. We really are going to miss spending time with you, as well as eating your extraordinary food."

She responded dearly, "We appreciate your words and your company more than you know. We still plan to live in the house here on this land. If you come back, just knock on the door, and we will fix you something." It was an incredible and generous offer, but sadly that was the last time we ever did see that remarkable couple.

We have been back to Ireland a few times since, sharing our passion for travel and making many new memories with our friends and family. Tom, Shannon, and Ansleigh eventually were able to travel and joined us for the following trip a few years later in 2009. For this trip, we rented Butlerstown House again, and in addition to Tom and his family, we included another fun group of good friends—Bob and Carol Stewart,

Mack and Susan Hicks, and Leo and Laurie Lambert. We treated these group to many of the same sights that we visited on our first trip, including golfing at Old Head Golf Links, touring the beautiful countryside, dining at local restaurants (including the infamous O'Neill's Pub). We also enjoyed many meals (and comedy!) at the *Butlerstown Table,* as provided by Marianne and me, as well as professional chef, Helen Conner. It was another wonderful trip I will never forget.

Visiting Ireland again with friends in 2009

Marianne and Mark in Ireland, 2009

Several years later, we found out that Butlerstown House was up for sale. I had remarked to my brother, Jim, how saddened I would be to see it go into new hands. Although Jim and I never had a very close relationship, and he had never been to Butlerstown House, I was astounded when he said, "Why don't you and I buy it together? I know how you love it so much. Perhaps you can get Roger and Lis to stay there and run it, and rent it out."

I was shocked. I said, "Wow. That is an unbelievable gesture."

But, I took a moment to think it through. Jim's health was declining at this time. The bedrooms at Butlerstown house were all upstairs on the second level, and he certainly would not be able to use it. His offer meant the world to me, but the timing was just not right.

I finally said to him, "Thank you so much Jim. Your offer means so much to me. If it were ten years ago, I might have taken you up on it. But, now is just not the right time. I think it's been a great ride that I will always cherish."

I will never forget his gesture. Like my father, Jim was never one to shower affection, so this little act of charity meant everything to me.

Butlerstown House has since been sold to new owners, but every once and a while I wonder how Lis and Roger and Otto and Hilda are doing nowadays. I wonder whether they will ever know how much their generosity, friendship, and kindness meant to Marianne and me. Ireland was the shining light at the end of the arduous road I traveled to health and wellbeing. The Emerald Isle is a treasure, rich with resplendent landscape, enchanting villages, and the most gracious folk I have ever met. Sharing this special gift with my closest friends and family has been the mere least I could do in appreciation for the joy it has brought to my life.

Old Head Golf Links, Kinsale, Ireland

19

A FRIEND IN NEED

*The most beautiful discovery true friends make
is that they can grow separately without growing apart.*

Elisabeth Foley

I cannot think of anything more precious than a lasting friendship. I consider myself extremely lucky to have a strong network of friends who have shared this life journey with me. Hugh McGowan, Bob Desautels and Dick deVore, whom I have known since we were all children, and Steve Bettcher, whom I first met in the Navy, are all phenomenal friends whom I still keep close after all these years. To think that I have known them for 60-70 years now is incredibly amazing to me! Through thick and thin, we have stuck together, encouraged one another, and created new memories as time has progressed. The voyage has not been easy, but it is those difficult twists and turns in our paths that bring us closer together. It is in those most trying moments that we lean on each other and support each other, linking our hearts and solidifying our friendship.

As age has taken a toll on our finite bodies, health has been our biggest struggle yet. These men are closer to me than brothers. To watch them suffer through pain and illness has undoubtably been one of the hardest things I have ever experienced. Just as I felt the sting of helpless loss when my twins passed, I endured a similar feeling of powerlessness when my friends went through their own health struggles. The biggest gift I could offer was my love and care as a friend, showing presence and empathy when they needed me. In return, they have always supported me when I needed them most. Sometimes, a laugh or hug is all it takes to soothe the pain. And it is always enough when it comes from a friend.

Steve Bettcher was the first of my long-time friends to go through his health scare. We had kept in continual contact ever since I left the Navy to move to Saint Petersburg, Florida. Steve remained in the Navy for another year before he became an Admiral's aide in San Francisco for a few years. From there, he connected to the corporate world and worked for Kaiser Aluminum for many years, where he rose successfully to a high position within the company. Steve happily married his college sweetheart, Kathy, and raised two beautiful children in San Francisco. I have always admired him for paving his own success path in life, and he should be mighty proud to stand where he is today—as his life's journey was not an easy climb. Despite our physical distance, we have made much effort over the years to keep close.

Beginning in the 1970s, when we both were raising our young families, we began the tradition of hosting Steve and his family in Saint Petersburg for the Christmas holidays. We put them up in one of the apartments in Coquina Key Arms, decorating it with a Christmas tree and lights so that they would not miss out on the Christmas spirit while traveling. We spent many evenings reminiscing about the Navy and enjoying each other's company. Marianne and my children ended up becoming close to Kathy and their children as well. We began the custom of playing touch football every Christmas day as the kids got older, calling it, respectfully, the *Ho Ho Bowl*. We continued this Christmas tradition for over twenty years. It was such a fun and special time, and we still consider the Bettchers family.

The Bettcher and Mahaffey family reunion

There was one year, however, that sadly our Christmas celebration had to take a pause. It was in 1985 that Steve received the scary news that his health was in jeopardy. He was 41, the same age as I was at the time. I will never forget that awful day when Steve called me from San Francisco. It was a Friday afternoon. I was sitting at my office desk at Coquina Key Arms.

"Hello, Mark," Steve greeted me over the phone. "I just got out of my doctor's appointment, and I just had to call you." His voice resonated with grave and weary undertones.

"Is everything okay?" I asked him, worried.

"Looks like I have prostate cancer," Steve said, sounding defeated.

"What?!" I exclaimed in shock. Steve had always seemed so strong and healthy.

He explained, "I had my yearly physical at Kaiser, and something was just not right. They recommended me to a specialist, who apparently found it. I haven't told Kathy yet. I just found out this afternoon."

I was at a loss for words. I felt as if all the life had drained from me, leaving a raw and brittle shell that was ready to collapse. Emotion overtook me in a way I had never experienced. I left the office early that day and went home to Marianne. I slowly sauntered through the doorway into our home, ashen with shock and worry.

Marianne saw me come in and said, "Mark, you look like you've been hit by a train."

"I think I have," I said.

I walked somberly into our den, Marianne following behind me. I crashed into my usual place—a wide, leather armchair—as my legs were not able to hold me up any longer. I told Marianne the devastating news. I could not believe my own words coming from my mouth. Steve was so young. Life was too short.

Marianne was shattered by the news as well. She sat down on the sofa next to me. "My heart aches for Steve and his family, and also for you—as I know how much he means to you," Marianne said. "What would you like to do?"

I shrugged. "What can I do?" I asked rhetorically. I sighed and spoke from my heart. "What I would like to do is fly out there to be with him. But I understand this is a very personal and intimate thing. I don't know if I can just do that."

Marianne consoled me saying, "How about you call Kathy? Tell her how you feel and ask for her guidance on what she thinks Steve would want."

I was not so sure and said, "Well, I don't know what I'll do if Steve answers the phone instead of Kathy."

Marianne replied, "He's probably not wanting to answer the phone right now."

I said, "You're probably right."

Later, after I knew Steve had already told Kathy the news, I made the call. Marianne's prediction that Kathy would answer the phone was correct. We exchanged a few moments of shared sorrow, and then I asked for her advice. "I want to come visit Steve now and support him through this difficult time. But I am not sure if he would appreciate or be burdened by my presence. What do you think?"

Her response filled my heart with joy. She said, "I think that would just about be the most wonderful thing that could happen. I'll keep it a surprise."

The next morning, Marianne and I took a flight to San Francisco. We rented a car and pulled up to their house around 3:00 in the afternoon. Kathy answered the door beaming with excitement to see us. Steve was in a back room somewhere, but must have heard the doorbell. "Who is that?" Steve called out.

"Come out here, Steve," Kathy hollered.

We heard the slow shuffling of footsteps. The moment Steve turned the corner and saw us, he ran over to greet us. He had been so surprised and overjoyed to see us standing at his front door. He wrapped his arms around me, embracing me in a brotherly hug that must have lasted five minutes. There's a special bond that friendship holds that is ever so healing, ever so comforting.

After the initial greeting, Steve remarked, "Well, that explains why Kathy was up all night busying herself around the house, cheery as could be. She was driving me crazy!"

We all laughed, needing that bit of comic relief. Marianne and I stayed for the weekend, hoping to bring him some much-needed cheer, encouragement and support. It pleased us to hear that Steve had a top-notch prostate doctor, Dr. Thomas Stamey, at Stanford University. This doctor had many successful prostate cancer stories and had been recognized nationally for an operation he invented to remove prostate cancer. Steve's operation would be in two weeks, and we maintained such hope that all would go well. I asked Steve if he would like me to come back to San Francisco to be with him around the time of his operation. He said he would appreciate it very much.

Two weeks later, I was back in California, where I stayed five days to comfort and support Steve and his family during the surgery and recovery. This time, Marianne remained in Saint Petersburg to be with our children. Miraculously, with much prayer on our part and much skill on the part of the doctor, the surgery was a success. I remember walking into the recovery room after Steve got out of the operation. Kathy and I sat by his side as Steve laid there conscious, but tired.

Steve slowly looked over at me and smiled. I held his hand and said, "Good job, Steve."

Dr. Stamey walked into the room behind us. He took one look at me and said, "Oh, you must be the friend from Florida."

"Yes, I am," I said.

The doctor grinned and nodded at me, saying nothing and everything at the same time. His expression was one of understanding and appreciation. I knew at that moment that Steve had told the doctor about our friendship. That meant the world to me.

As the years went by, Steve regained his strength and his health back. We continued our Christmas tradition, as our families became closer than ever. Years later, we hosted his son's engagement party and wedding at our house. They now live in Colorado, where Marianne and I, as well as our children, visit them often. Our friendship is a beautiful thing, that not only spans decades, but also, generations. I am very grateful for his friendship and to have him still here today.

There is never just one bump in the road, however. Life is a cycle of hardships and renewals, and Steve was not my only friend to endure health struggles. In the early 2000s, Dick deVore, my friend from Burt Lake, Michigan, received his lion's share of suffering. His health journey was a much more arduous venture than most of us will ever experience. Sadly, he battled a great deal of pain and infirmity, and he was just inches from death's door many times. He is one of the strongest people I know. He is a fighter, strong in spirit and body, and has maintained a positive attitude through it all. I have a deep respect for this man and a high regard for his character and strength to push through challenges.

I remember back to those days serving with Dick at Indian River Inn at Burt Lake. I always looked up to him. He was a year older than I was, he had a car, and he made those summers golden. That experience I had at Indian River Inn shaped me for the rest of my life. I owe Dick for that. Although we remained in contact throughout the years, after I moved to Florida, there was about a 25-year gap where I did not see him. He had built a career as an international pilot for American Airlines, got married, and had two daughters. He unfortunately divorced his first wife, remarried, and lost his second wife to cancer. After the traumatic experience, he came down to Saint Petersburg, Florida, to attend a support group. It was at that point that we reconnected in person. It had been years since I had seen him, and despite the painful loss of his wife, our spirits were lifted seeing each other again. We recounted old memories of Burt Lake and Indian River Inn, and it was as if our friendship did not skip a beat. Later, he found happiness again in his third marriage and eventually moved back to Burt Lake to live where his roots were first planted.

It was then that Dick's strength would receive the ultimate test—blood cancer. Dick had developed a very rare type of blood cancer. The treatments were extremely intense and debilitating. It was at this time that Marianne and I were planning our first big trip to Butlerstown House in Ireland. I had hoped so much that he and his wife would join us, but there was no way he could travel. I was devastated to hear that he was going through this cancer struggle. Dick always had such a positive spirit. I remember him saying, "I have a fantastic doctor at the University of Michigan in Ann Arbor. He is top notch, and I'll get through this in no time."

I felt a stab of pain in my own heart as it ached for him. His last wife had died of cancer, and I am sure deep down, he was more afraid than ever—but he never showed it. Just as when I heard Steve had cancer, I wanted to be with Dick during this trying time. I offered to come see him, but he said, "I will tell you when the time is right."

I respected his wish and patiently waited until he was ready for me.

About a year later, Dick called me up to share with me that the chemotherapy was not as effective as the doctors had hoped. Their last resort was to perform a blood stem cell transplant. Because it would lower his blood count and immune system drastically, Dick would have to live in isolation for about a year to prevent risk of bleeding and infection. It was a risky procedure, but his doctor encouraged him, saying that it would increase his chance of survival. With strength and determination, Dick agreed, keeping his eye on the victory. The treatment process proved to be more agonizing than anything Dick had ever endured, beyond anything he experienced during chemotherapy. We prayed for him, sent him gifts and letters, and spoke over the phone, wishing so much for him to get through this.

Finally, after a long year, the treatment was over and had been successful. He was in remission. We were all beyond relieved to hear that Dick had made it. Tears streamed down my face when I heard the good news. Dick was a true fighter. I will forever be grateful for the team of doctors at the University of Michigan for helping him through this journey. I was so overjoyed for my friend, but I missed him more than ever.

At last, a year later, I received the call. "It's time," Dick said. "I am ready for visitors. I would love to see you."

Marianne and I booked a flight immediately and were at Burt Lake, Michigan, within a week. We spent five days with Dick and his wife celebrating life and friendship. Dick had fought so hard the previous few years, but his uphill battle was finally over. I cannot describe the joy I felt reconnecting with him as we sat on his deck overlooking Burt Lake. It brought back so many wonderful memories of us in our youth during that idyllic time of our lives. After returning to Saint Petersburg, I made a vow that I would make a point to see him again soon. Little did I know that our next get together would indeed be soon, and in a very special place.

A few years later, in 2010, I was pleased to win a trip to Paris, France, at a charity auction for a local school, Academy Prep Center of Saint Petersburg. Academy Prep is a not-for-profit school that offers economically disadvantaged children the opportunity for academic success. This tremendous school was generously founded by Jeff and Joan Fortune, who were past hotel executives and owners of TradeWinds Island Resort and Sandpiper Beach Resort in Saint Petersburg. When Jeff had first gotten the idea to open a school, he came to me asking if I would be interested in supporting it financially. Upon hearing the details of its monumental mission to bring education to disadvantaged children, I did not hesitate. I said to Jeff, "This is like motherhood and apple pie. How can I say no? Tell me what you need." The school has been a huge success, paving the pathway for many children to get into colleges around the country. It not only gave these students the keys to a quality education, but the chance for a better life in the future. My son, Tom, is now on the board. We are proud to be a part of such an incredible organization.

Every year, Academy Prep hosts a fundraiser auction gala, and it is here that I won the Paris experience. The auction item did not cover traveling and lodging expenses, per se, but rather offered a special tour of Paris from the eyes of locals. These locals were none other than Jeff Fortune himself and his second wife, Sherry (his first wife, Joan, had passed away years before). They owned an apartment in Paris for the past few years and had learned many of the secrets of the city.

When Marianne and I saw this chance of a lifetime, we jumped at it without hesitation. We had been to Paris once before, years and years ago, as a side excursion when visiting Nice, France on a sponsored trip by Carrier Air Conditioning. We adored our visit to *the City of Light*, but our stay was very short. We certainly did not feel like we spent enough time there to really get to know the city. A local-led tour sounded like a once in a lifetime opportunity!

With much excitement, Marianne and I, as well a few other couples who also participated in the auction, headed over to Paris, France. We had an absolutely sensational time seeing the city through new eyes. Jeff and Sherry expertly led us off the beaten path, sharing with us remarkable restaurants and showing us unique historic landmarks. They even taught us how to use the metro system. They also took us to the Museum of Monet and the Pere Lachaise Cemetery. This cemetery was featured in the Phantom of the Opera movie and holds the graves of Oscar Wilde and Jim Morrison. We were in awe at every experience.

During our stay, Jeff and Sherry introduced us to their friendly Paris apartment neighbor, John Sisk, who was originally from Jacksonville, FL. As soon as I saw him, I said, "John Sisk? I know you!" We had worked with his mortgage company back when I first moved to Florida.

"Small world!" he said.

After visiting, John Sisk offered for Marianne and me to rent his apartment whenever we wanted to return to Paris. It was very generous of him, and Marianne and I certainly planned to take him up on that offer.

Paris, France, had stolen our hearts. We felt empowered by our deeper knowledge of the city and desired to share it with our closest friends.

The next year, we rented John Sisk's apartment and took our friends from Saint Petersburg—Carl and Lee Ann Lambrecht and Ron and Jane Anne Lees—to Paris. We had such fun that Marianne and I immediately made plans to return. It was then that I had the idea to invite my dear friend, Dick deVore, to our next trip to Paris. I had been so disappointed that Dick had missed the Ireland trip, but I thought Paris would be the perfect replacement trip. Dick was of French descent, which made the destination all the more ideal. I immediately called Dick and shared my idea with him. After a few days of discussing it with his wife, he graciously accepted. We also invited Hugh and Jeanmarie McGowan on the same trip. This was going to be the trip of a lifetime!

We eagerly reserved John Sisk's apartment and returned to Paris the following year with our good friends. We were so excited to show them all the neat things we had learned about the city. I was especially thrilled to play the role of *Pathfinder* as I navigated us through Paris on the metro system.

Of all the fun we had, there is one day that will always hold a special place in my memory. It was on this day that the six of us decided to visit the beautiful Cathedral of Notre Dame. I remember marveling at the magnificent, gothic church, rich with history, which stands tall alongside the Seine River in the heart of the city. The scene was absolutely breathtaking. As we stood outside its grand, front doors, I recall gazing up at the twin towers of the western façade in awe at its grandeur. Until the completion of the Eifel tower in 1889, these two towers were the tallest structures in the entire city. It was humbling and overwhelming standing in the shadow of such a mighty, medieval monument. One of the oldest cathedrals in Paris, it conveyed an aura of timeless wisdom and strength.

Dick, moved by the pure presence and strength of God permeating this cathedral, looked to us and said, "I want to spend a few moments alone in here." We all respected his wish. As we entered the vestibule, we watched Dick reverently walk down the long aisle into main church. The exterior of the cathedral was beautiful, but it was no comparison to the rich, splendid display within its walls. A brilliant stained-glass rose window illuminated the hazy, incense-filled space, enriching our senses with a psychedelic calmness. Two rows of wooden pews ran the entire length of the church and were bordered by rows of alternating massive columns and intricately-designed chandeliers. Hundreds of visitors knelt in silent prayer and peaceful reverence.

Dick chose an empty pew about ten rows from the back. He slowly entered it and carefully dropped to his knees without making a sound. For 20 minutes, Dick knelt, praying, immersed in the sacredness of this extraordinary cathedral. There, he had his conversation with God. Dick had been so close to death, but fought his way out with God's help. I imagine it was a special moment for him to be able to thank God in such a holy place. Dick had made such an influence on my life over the years; it was a proud moment for me to be able to give him that opportunity in return.

Mark and Dick in France, 2011

The deVore's, the Mahaffey's, and the McGowan's with a guide in France, 2011

Dick, Mark, and Hugh

Hugh, Mark, and Dick with fellow veteran, folding an American flag in an American cemetery in Normandy, France

That trip to Paris was really something special for all of us. Dick and Hugh, who had not known each other well before the trip, got along famously. The six of us explored Paris, nourishing our friendships. Seeing some of my closest friends mingle and develop their own friendships brought me such happiness. They are all such dear, beautiful people, and I am blessed to be a part of their lives. I was especially delighted that Hugh was able to come on that trip, because it was not long after that he had his turn of misfortune.

I first noticed that something was wrong when Hugh and Jeanmarie came down to Saint Petersburg to visit Marianne and me a few years later. We were thrilled to see them again, but I observed Hugh was rather unsteady on his feet. I was worried for him and curiously asked if he was okay. Hugh brushed it off, saying, "Oh yeah, I'm fine."

However, as the week progressed, I could not hold back my concern. I had known him for 70 years. I knew when something was not right. "Hugh," I said, "Something is going on. You are not yourself. You are quite unstable. Let me get you a cane you can use."

Hugh was stubborn, "No, no, I don't need a cane."

I urged, "Hugh, I care about you. I don't want you to injure yourself. Are you sure there is nothing going on? Perhaps you should see a doctor."

"Maybe you are right," Hugh said, finally taking the cane.

Thankfully, he took my advice to see a doctor, because soon after, Hugh was diagnosed with a form of Parkinson's disease. Medication and therapy help him manage, but it is certainly a struggle. Like my other good friends, he is a fighter and is able to still walk without a cane. He leans on Jeanmarie, who is a rock of strength herself, as they journey down this new road together. They are an extraordinary couple, and it is awe-inspiring to watch them care for each other and support each other through this difficult time. They have a very special love that is a rare treasure.

I feel tremendously honored to have had Hugh as my friend these past 70 years, with our friendship still going strong. I can remember it like it was yesterday, playing basketball with him and Bob in the Desautels backyard when we were just teenagers. I remember the thrill of attending Notre Dame with him for the first time and all the fun parties we attended. I am grateful for all the times he was there for me, for the Mahaffey business, through the good times and bad. But it is the good times that I will remember the most—the fun we had as kids and the laughs we had as we maintained our friendship through adulthood.

The DBY high school basketball team reunited
Top row: John Wetzler, Jerry Bintz, Tom Holland
Bottom row: Mark Mahaffey, Hugh McGowan, Bob Desautels

Of all the fun we've had, my most cherished memories with Hugh will always be Notre Dame football games. For the past 40 years and continuing, Hugh and Jeanmarie and Marianne and I have traveled to Indiana to watch Notre Dame play football every fall season. As alumni ourselves, Hugh and I look forward to the big game every year. Tradition is that Hugh arranges the hotel rooms and tailgate party, and I get the game tickets and the parking spot for the party. It is a collaboration of friends that results in loads of fun and bonding in Irish pride. Bob Desautels has also joined us many times, as well Dick deVore, Leo Lambert, and many other friends we've had over the years.

The big football game of 2021 was one trip that I will never forget. That year was an extra special trip for me as Notre Dame was formally dedicating a space in the library to my family. For years, I had been on the Notre Dame Library Council, as I always credited the Theodore Hesburgh Library for making such a positive impact on my academic success at Notre Dame. My father had donated to the library years before, and following in his footsteps, I gave a five-year pledge supporting recent library improvements. In gratitude, the Library Council wanted to dedicate a space in the library to my family, calling it The Mahaffey Family Scholar's Lounge. The formal dedication of this lounge, orchestrated by my good friend at Notre Dame, Michael McLaughlin, was the weekend of the big football game. My son, Tom, and his family were planning to attend, as well as other friends and family. Per tradition, Hugh reserved seven rooms at a nearby hotel and planned the tailgate, while I got the football tickets and reserved the parking spot. It was going to be a weekend to remember!

Tragedy struck however, when three weeks before the big weekend, we were notified by the hotel that our rooms were cancelled due to lingering effects of the Covid-19 pandemic. We were distraught, as hotels near Notre Dame on football weekends were virtually impossible to reserve last minute. I was determined to find a way. I called up my good friend, Michael McLaughlin, who I now affectionately refer to as my *handler*. Fortunately, Michael works for Notre Dame's Development Department and seems to have unlimited connections.

I said, "Michael, we are in desperate need here. Our hotel has cancelled our rooms. We have nowhere to stay for the big weekend."

"I'm on it," he said. Michael is just that type of guy—he can handle anything.

Later that week, he called me back, "You won't believe where I got you seven rooms to stay."

"Where?" I said, curious.

"Morris Inn. *The* Morris Inn, right on campus," he said.

I was dumbfounded. Morris Inn, known as *the Living Room of the University*, is a first-class hotel and almost always booked on football weekends.

"Wow," I said. "I have no idea how you managed that. Thank you so much!"

I thought about Hugh and the unsteadiness that came with Parkinson's. "I have one more favor," I said.

"Anything," Michael promised.

"My friend, Hugh, is coming and will need a golf cart to get around. Can you arrange for a four-person golf cart, so his wife and son can drive him around?"

"I'm on it," he said.

"One more thing," I pushed my luck, but I knew Michael was the person to get a job done.

"Yes?" he replied.

"How about a suite at Morris Inn—so we can lounge and eat there, and we won't need to fight traffic after the game."

"Consider it done," Michael said without hesitation.

I was so excited that I called up Hugh immediately. I said, "Hugh, you're never going to believe this, but we've got seven rooms at the Morris Inn."

He said, "I've never stayed at the Morris Inn on a football weekend."

I said, "Me neither. This is going to be our chance."

When that weekend finally came around, we had the time of our lives. The golf cart proved to be invaluable to Hugh, and the suite, a real privilege.

"Go Irish!" we cheered, just as we had decades ago when we were just blossoming young men. The game ended in a big victory, which felt as much of a personal triumph as it did a team win. I looked over at Hugh, who was beaming ear to ear. The screaming and praising of fans surrounding us faded into the background as Hugh and I shared a special moment.

"Thank you, Mark," Hugh said.

I put my arm around his shoulder. "Thank *you,* Hugh" I replied. "It certainly has been a wild ride. Hasn't it?"

"It sure has."

These special moments are what I live for. Being able to travel with friends and experience new adventures with them has been such a joy and blessing in my life. Hugh, Dick, Bob, Steve, Carl, Tom, and Leo have enriched my life so much with their love, care, loyalty, and mutual adventurous spirit. My biggest wish is that they will always know how much they mean to me. Through thick and thin, young and old, we have stayed together on this path, and that's certainly a damn good thing to be proud of.

Leo, Tom, and Mark in Havana, Cuba

20

NORTH TO THE FUTURE

Alaska isn't about who you were when you headed this way. It's about who you become.

Kristen Hannah, The Great Alone

At this point in my life, as I reflect on all the places I have traveled—and there have been a great many places—the most rewarding trips are those where I have combined friends from different parts of the world and different times of my life. I have met an abundance of admirable and extraordinary people along my path, and perhaps due to us all having similar interests, worldviews, and experiences, we all have gotten along so well together and maintained our friendships over the years. Through traveling together, I have seen my friends develop friendships with each other and it has been exceedingly fulfilling.

I have introduced Bob, Hugh, Dick, and Steve—all friends from my youth—to many of my newer acquaintances I have made over the years. It is an incredible thing to sit back and watch the new friendships blossom. I cannot help but contemplate with pride, *I made that happen.* Travel and experiencing new adventures have been the best catalyst for nurturing these relationships. Panama, Ireland, Paris, and Notre Dame football games have especially been stewing pots for friendships. More recently, Alaska has claimed its stake as making a huge impact on my life and my friendships.

My first excursion to wild Alaska was in September of 2003 for a father/son fishing trip with my son, Tom. David Wilkes, whom I had first met back in the 1980s in Highlands, North Carolina, was taking his son and had invited us to join them. David and his wife, Carol, were, and still are, the proud owners of an outdoor recreation store called *Highland Hiker*. This shop specializes in nature-themed clothing and outdoor gear, as well as offering guided fly-fishing and hiking experiences. This shop is especially unique, as David and Carol also offer to their customers outdoor-oriented travel experiences to unique places around the world, such as Alaska, Chile, and New Zealand.

When Tom and I heard they were planning a camping trip to the ever mysterious and alluring Alaska to fly-fish for salmon, we could not resist. We had enjoyed fishing together in Saint Petersburg, as well as Panama, but salmon fishing in Alaska would be an entirely new adventure. The destination was a camp site positioned on the shores of Nakalilok Bay, on the southern coast of the Alaskan Peninsula. This prime fishing spot for salmon is nestled in the strikingly beautiful Aleutian Mountain Range, that extends southwestward from Alaska's main landmass, like the spiny tail of a dragon. This massive mountain range, studded with many active volcanos, tells a saga of fire and ice, spawning and slaughter, chaos and accord. Raging rivers slice deeply through the terrain, carving paths for the salmon to make their upward stream runs every year during the warmer months. Each species of salmon—king, pink, sockeye, and silver—have an allotted schedule for running that they punctually course every summer in turn. Famished bears and otters congregate to feast in the salmon-rich waters, while bald eagles soar and swoop to share in the pink banquet. It is a world governed by the unrelenting rules of nature, one of the few places left on earth dominated not by man, but by mother nature. Like Tropic Star Lodge in Panama, this camp site, along the pristine waters of Nakalilok Bay, is located in an area so remote that its only means of access is by a small, fixed-wing plane or helicopter landing in the bay at low tide. Unlike Tropic Star Lodge, this camp site is not a luxury resort with world class amenities, but rather, a collection of some simple, yet sizable, tents.

Nakalilok Bay, Alaska

Sleeping tent at Nakalilok Bay Camp, Alaska

When Tom and I first arrived at the camp in 2003, we were first awe-struck by the commanding and colossal beauty of the Alaskan terrain. Magisterial, snow-capped mountains and volcanoes stood aloft in the distance with the surrounding rocky and forest-ladened landscape, bowing in genuflect. The sloshing and rushing sounds of the fish-filled rivers echoed through the valleys and soothed our spirits. The camp site was completely off-the-grid and hundreds of miles from any civilization.

It was perched up high on a hill to keep some distance from the many bears that called the region home. Each of the tents, scattered about the lot, was assigned a purpose. The sleeping tents, which were tall enough to stand up in, had two cots, two storage boxes, and a hanging rod for clothing. The well-equipped dining tent held four dining tables and chairs, playing cards, a full kitchen, and a large, pot-bellied stove for heat. Surprisingly, the gourmet, five-star meals that were prepared in this kitchen were not your ordinary camping grub. Multi-course, well-executed feasts, all made by a creative and executive chef, were served for breakfast, lunch, and dinner. A bathroom tent and shower tent were also on site for use, which happened to boast the best mountain views of all!

Fishing in Nakalilok Bay, Alaska, 2003

Tom and Mark at Nakalilok Bay, Alaska, 2003

After settling in and allowing the tide to return and flood the bay again, one of the guides announced the first fishing excursion for silver salmon, which were making their runs that month. We were very excited to get our gear together and test out the Alaskan waters. I can remember Tom and I, wading into the bay with our fly-fishing rods—mountains to our back and the Pacific Ocean ahead—breathing in the cool, crisp northern air. A bald eagle soared above us, gracing the bay with its splendor. I began to think that there could not be a more peaceful place on earth, when all of a sudden, a team of shiny, chocolate-colored sea otters and black-and-white spotted seals came rushing into the bay. Salmon scurried in masses as the sea otters and seals fought one another over the bountiful meal. We may have had all the best in fishing gear, but these creatures distinguished themselves as the real masters. I glanced over at Tom and said, "Can you believe this?" He shook his head in amusement, grinning at the irony. Despite the competition, Tom and I reeled in about twenty silver salmon each in about two hours. It was quite a thrill!

Relishing in our victory, we climbed the hill back to camp to find the chef had prepared for us a steaming chicken pot pie that was out of this world. "We must make this a new tradition," I remarked to Tom.

"Definitely," he agreed.

As the ghost of evening began to spread through valleys, the shadows of the mountains expanding further and further, I knew my window of time to telephone my dear wife was near closing. Gathering a flashlight, bear spray, and my satellite phone, I clambered up a nearby rocky hill, hoping to obtain the best signal. Finally reaching a stable platform, I paused a moment to take in my surroundings. I was wonderstruck at the breathtaking panorama that stretched across the horizon. Perched on this ridge, I witnessed a bird's-eye view of Nakalilok Bay. The sun leisurely sunk into its sleeping place, showering rays of light only upon the highest of elevations. The jagged mountains beyond the bay stood in high contrast to the shadow-blanketed valleys. Most stunning was a towering, snow-capped, 7500-foot volcano that reflected the brilliant light like a beacon in the distance.

Feeling literally on top of the world, I pulled my phone from my pocket and dialed my love.

"Marianne? It's me, Mark. I wish you were here to see this."

"Hello, Mark," Marianne greeted. "Where are you?"

I replied, "About a mile from heaven."

I do not believe I have ever felt the presence of God so near as in the massive, vast, and glorious landscape of Alaska's wild. That father/son trip in 2003 was certainly a trip to remember. Tom and I not only caught an impressive number of silver salmon, but also had grown our relationship with one another. I am sure he would agree that sharing those experiences and building those memories together brought us closer than ever. We knew we wanted to return to Nakalilok Bay one day, and next time, bring our friends.

Eleven years later, in 2014, my 70th birthday was upon me. I pondered all the things I could do to celebrate the big milestone, and Alaska kept coming to the forefront of my mind. I had returned to Alaska once since my first time traveling with Tom, but not to Nakalilok Bay. It was in 2005 when Marianne and I were invited to stay aboard my friend

Mike Bonsignore's 90-foot luxury yacht, *Tuko,* which was docked just off Alaska's capital, Juneau. Mike, my good friend whom I had met in Panama all those years ago, and his wife, Sheila, were gracious hosts as they toured Marianne and I around the coves and channels surrounding Juneau. Aboard the *Tuko*, we ate gourmet meals that would have riveled any five-star restaurant, most of which were prepared by Sheila. We fished quite a bit that week, catching many salmon and halibut. It was a magnificent trip, and I knew that I wanted to return the favor and host Mike on a fishing trip to Nakalilok Bay one day. My 70th birthday would be the perfect lure.

I promptly called up my friend, David Wilkes, owner of *Highland Hiker,* to help me put the Alaska plan into action. My birthday wish was to include all of my best fishing buddies on this trip, as a big reunion and thank you to them for their years of friendship and support. I thought through all my friends, homing in on those whom I treasured the most. There were so many! I decided to narrow it down to those friends who were not only healthy enough to take this physically demanding trip camping in the middle of nowhere, but also those who were familiar with fly-fishing. I henceforth created a guest list quite easily: Dick deVore, Steve Bettcher, Leo Lambert, Mike Bonsignore, and of course, my son, Tom.

Dick deVore—I had to include Dick. He was one of my oldest, and dearest friends, as I had met him when I was only 15 years old. I remember it like it was yesterday—Dick and I, young high schoolers on summer break without a care in the world. Boating, fishing, serving at Dick's parents' restaurant, and partying on the dunes until the wee hours of the morning. It was a special time of my life that I still liken to the movie *Dirty Dancing*. Dick's parents were outstanding restaurateurs and treated me like a son. I learned so many life lessons from the deVores that have been the fiber of my life. I feel so lucky to have had those experiences. Dick and I have remained very close friends over these many years, and although there have been some long absences, we always—and I mean always—have this incredibly strong, permanent bond between us. He had recovered well from the blood cancer and had his health and energy back. It had been a few years since our Paris trip, and it was definitely time for another adventure.

There was also Steve Bettcher—my best friend from the Navy. Steve, who had moved from California to Colorado after retiring from Kaiser Aluminum & Al-Can, enjoyed fly-fishing from time to time. I knew he would be wild about fishing in Alaska. I reminisced about Steve Bettcher and our long history together. I thought back to the very first time I met him in the middle of the Pacific Ocean on our assigned aircraft carrier, *USS Bennington*. As Steve swung across those two boats in the bosun's chair—white knuckles holding the metal cage, waves soaking his legs—I would have never imagined that it was the start of a friendship that would last over fifty years. We became brothers in the Navy as we proudly served under Captain Daniel Murphy. We became even closer as our families got to know one another. Those *Ho Ho Bowl* football games that we would play every Christmas are such special memories in my life. I thought I was almost going to lose him back in the 1980s to prostate cancer. It almost destroyed me to contemplate losing one of my closest buddies. I could not be more thankful he conquered the battle and is still here today. He is more than a friend to me: he is family.

Leo Lambert—a recent friend compared to those of my childhood, but still a long-term friend since he first become president of Elon University in 1999. While serving on the Elon University Board of Trustees, I developed a friendship with him that has only gotten deeper as we have traveled together. Sharing an interest in travel and fishing, together we have experienced Ireland, Panama, Montana, Highlands, and many other places around the world. Having fly-fished with him in Montana, I knew he would get a big thrill fly-fishing in Nakalilok Bay as well.

Mike Bonsignore—the only friend of this group with whom I had already experienced Alaska. But now, it was my turn to invite him. He had so generously hosted Marianne and me aboard *Tuko* and taken me on so many fishing adventures around Juneau. I could not wait to share with him the experience of salmon fishing in the remote and wild Nakalilok Bay.

There was also Tom—my son, with whom I have shared many adventures in fishing. Just as my father had fished with me since I was a young boy up until he passed at the age of 80, I hoped to give Tom the same experiences that I treasured so much—but this time expanding the globe a bit more. We have gone on some wild adventures together, and there is no one that I would rather have by my side through it all.

And lastly, of course, David Wilkes—the master organizer and planner of this great Alaskan expedition. He has been my friend since 1986 when Marianne and I bought our very first summer home in Highlands, North Carolina. He has introduced me to many world-class fishing destinations around the world, including Brazil, Argentina, Chile, and Nakalilok Bay, Alaska, which prompted this very trip. I am very thankful for his expertise in finding this gem of a location.

With this list in mind, I typed out a rather long, invitational email requesting these men join me on this grand, nine-day 70th birthday trip salmon fishing in Alaska. I listed the location, dates, and itinerary hoping to entice them to come. Unsure of who would be able to carve out time in their busy lives, I prayed that at least one of these men would be free to come celebrate with me. I considered if two of them replied with a *yes*, I would be lucky. Three would be amazing. Four would be unreal—a miracle.

Unbelievably, one by one, I received confirmation that each person was indeed able to travel to Alaska with me. I was amazed! Mike almost was not able to make it. At the time, he was on the National Geographic Society Board of Trustees, and there happened to be a mandatory board meeting in Sweden on those exact dates. Mike, however, insisted that my birthday was a priority, and said he wouldn't miss it for the world. It touched my heart that all my friends wanted to celebrate with me.

These men comprised a very special group of friends of mine, but it was interesting to note that none of them had ever met each other before. As they were all friends of mine from different times in my life and all lived in various places across the United States, I had never before had the opportunity to introduce them to one another. Nonetheless, I had no doubt that they all would get along famously. I had never had a problem mixing people before and consider myself having a knack for it, so to say.

With much excitement and zeal for friendships reunited, my 70th birthday celebration began with a private flight to the small and aptly named King Salmon Airport, located at the base of the Alaskan peninsula. From there, we boarded a helicopter, which took us on a 90-mintue flight directly to the treasure cove of fishing, Nakalilok Bay. Our spirits were soaring in anticipation to reach our destination, and even the helicopter ride was an exhilarating and an unbelievable experience. At first, the view outside our windows was not very picturesque, being a rather uniform tundra with green-brown vegetation. But after ten minutes or so, the topography of the land metamorphosized into abundant rolling hills and valleys, and eventually, steep rocky ridges. I watched the pools of waters in the valleys transfigure into rivers, which we followed directly until the waters segued into the expansive and deep-blue Pacific Ocean. It was as if the water was alive, like a maddened herd of wild horses stampeding through the canyons. Reaching the ocean, the helicopter sharply turned course as it flew along the striking, rugged coastline, which bowed and crawled along the wondrous nature-carved rock ledges and inlets. It was even more spectacular than I remembered.

When our crew finally arrived at the camp site, we focused on unpacking and organizing ourselves before beginning the long-awaited salmon fishing venture. David Wilkes set up a tent with two additional friends whom he had brought along—Carlisle Overstreet and his son Jim Overstreet from Augusta, Georgia. But as for the remainder of us, I had to strategically set ourselves up in the other two-man tents. I assigned Steve and Mike to a tent, Leo and Dick to another, and Tom and myself to the last one. Steve and Mike had much in common both having a past in the corporate world and both having called California home for a portion of their lives. Leo and Dick also seemed like the perfect pair, as they both had an interest in education. Leo, of course, was president of Elon University, and Dick, beyond his career as an international airline pilot, was founder of Inland Lakes Educational Foundation. This non-profit corporation earns funds for scholarships for children up in northern Michigan. I predicted these two men would get along excellently, considering their passion for education and supporting America's youth. It turned out that I couldn't have been more right, as these men all became great friends.

After settling in and enjoying a scrumptious lunch prepared by the resident camp chef, the nine of us donned our waders, rigged our equipment, and followed our guides down the many steep steps to the bay. As we slowly walked into the chilly waters, it was as if we were dipping our boots into cold chocolate milk. To say the water was murky was an understatement. Evidently, there had been a torrential rain storm a few days before our arrival, which had churned up sediment, rendering the salmon blind to our bait. The drizzly, wet weather conditions also did not offer any help to our efforts. Needless to say, the trip was not a huge success on the fishing front, but we were able to catch a few winners throughout our nine-day stay. These few fish boosted our morale and kept our drive for even the smallest victories strong. I hoped so much to show my friends the view of the nearby, gorgeous 7500-foot volcano, but the clouds and rain kept it hidden in a milky veil.

Volcano visible above the clouds, Alaska

Nakalilok Bay, Alaska

Regardless of the variable weather and lack of biting salmon, my friends and I had a fantastic time bonding and sharing new experiences. With trips like this, I have found that the majority of the fun is based on the comradery, not the number of fish caught. We played card games, wined and dined to our hearts delight, hiked the steep trails, and spent many hours in the bay and surrounding rivers talking and sharing.

Despite the fun, we found out very quickly that Alaskan trails were no walk in the park—especially in inclement weather. On day three of the trip, Tom, Leo and I, as well as our guide, were walking on a foot trail at the edge of a forcefully flowing river. The trail, worn by the woodland's resident bears, was very narrow and close to the river embankment. We had to watch our steps carefully as we hiked across the muddy path. I was the last man in our single file trek. Without warning, the ground slipped from underneath me, and within a split second, I fell from the embankment into the wild river.

Large bear footprints along the bay

Nakalilok Bay, Alaska

Instinct took over at that point as I grabbed frantically onto the earth and roots that lined the river's edge. The icy water clawed at my skin, trying to tear me from land and sink me into its current. Almost losing my grasp, I screamed desperately for dear life. "Help!" My fellow hikers quickly spun around and rushed to my aid. Using all their strength, they tried to pull me back onto land, as if they were playing tug-of-war with the violent waters. Finally, I made it out alive and unharmed, albeit very cold and wet. I cannot imagine what would have happened if I had been hiking alone. Luckily, we could all laugh about it and sigh in relief that the rescue was a success.

Later that evening, while lounging in the dining tent after dinner, Mike Bonsignore stood up from his chair and gave a moving speech wishing me a Happy Birthday from the group. He presented to me a magnificent nine-weight Tibor reel and Sage rod, engraved with my name. I was deeply touched by this meaningful gift from my friends. With rod and reel in hand, I stood up and thanked the group for the gift and their friendship, sharing how much each individual meant to me. I recounted the stories of how I met each of them and expressed my special feelings toward them. I saved the best for last when I came to my son, Tom. I said, with my hand on his shoulder, "This is my best friend!" There was not a dry eye in the tent, including my own, as tears were streaming down my face.

On the last day, the weather finally cleared up. The sun beamed down on us, blessing us with its warmth and radiance. It was mesmerizing how that extra light changed the entire panorama. It was the most beautiful sight we had ever seen. Where clouds hung earlier, now stood the clear display of the rugged ridges of snow-capped mountains, including the rarely seen volcano that I had hoped so much to show my friends. Rainbows filled the sky, arching down to the seemingly endless Pacific Ocean beyond the bay. We all agreed that it was the perfect ending to a very exceptional trip.

Celebrating Mark's 70ᵗʰ birthday in Nakalilok Bay, Alaska, 2014

Mark fishing in Alaska, 2014

Overall, I could not think of a better way to spend my 70th birthday. To be with my closest friends, doing what I love most— traveling, fishing, and sharing. My friends told me afterwards that it was truly the "trip of a lifetime." I honestly felt that this group would, indeed, be the *All Stars*, and I was right. It still brings tears to my eyes that they made time in their active lives to share in this adventure with me. I thank

God for giving me the opportunity to become friends with each one of these men.

I have been fortunate that trip was not the last time I traveled to Alaska or with each of those men. Mike Bonsignore has invited me on several trips around the world since, including Cuba and Hawaii. Both were fabulous fishing trips and experiences I will never forget. In 2018 and 2021, I returned to Alaska again with David Wilkes bringing a new set of friends each time, including some of my good friends that I had met over the years in Highlands, North Carolina. Each trip was unique, but the camp still remains one of the most beautiful places on earth. The raw, pure Alaskan beauty stuns me every time. However, nothing matched the emotion shared on my 70th birthday trip, and plans are in the works to recreate some of those memories for my upcoming 80th birthday. The adventure will continue, embodying the spirit of optimism and promise in Alaska's state motto, *North to the Future.*

Mark and a silver salmon, 2021

Tom at Nakalilok Bay, Alaska, 2021

Nakalilok Bay, Alaska

Fishing with friends in Alaska, 2021

My friends and I have been down a lot of paths together—journeys that have taken us around the world, through illness and recovery, through business ventures, raising families, and just plain growing old together. Many people you will meet in your life will come and go with the tides. They are there for a stage of life, but not in the next. There are some friends however, that are there through it all. It takes effort on all our parts to remain close, especially as we have made our homes in various places across the United States. Traveling has been the essential means to holding on to our friendship and having fun at the same time.

My friend, Dick deVore's father once said, "If you are lucky, and I mean really lucky, when you look back on your life, you will have five or six friends that you can call true friends—friends that you can really count on."

I feel genuinely lucky to say that I am blessed with those friendships—Bob Desautels, Hugh McGowan, Steve Bettcher, Carl Lambrecht, Tom Rusche, Leo Lambert, Mike Bonsignore, and my son, Tom, to name a few. Thank you for being there for me through it all!

21

MAC – WHERE WE ARE NOW

Individually, we are one drop; but together, we are an ocean.

Ryunosoke Satoro

The privilege to be able to travel the globe with my closest friends and family has been one of the greatest blessings of my life. Sharing those experiences with those I love has been a gift, and one that keeps on giving. Not only do relationships grow deeper through shared travel, but I also continue to grow individually, exploring the world and experiencing new places and cultures. I learn something new on every single trip that I take, as I not only push the boundaries of my environment, but I also expand my horizons of understanding and hopefully, gain a little bit of wisdom along the way.

As is with most things in my life, the ability to travel has only been made possible by the cohesive effort of many people. As a youth, I thank my parents for my experiences at Burt Lake and my travels around the world as a Navy man. I thank Carl and Lee Ann Lambrecht for introducing me to Highlands, North Carolina. I would have never been to Tropic Star Lodge in Panama without being first invited by Richard Earle. Ireland was made possible, not only by the teamwork of friends who helped coordinate the trips, but also, by the doctors who contributed to the restoration of my health.

Beyond the people who made each trip possible, I also have to thank the tremendous team at the Mahaffey Apartment Company (MAC), who have been able to gradually, over the years, take the reins of the business to allow me the opportunities to travel. Without Jim and my father's co-sharing in company responsibilities, Suzanne Gray's years of dedication, and more recently, the third generation's acceptance of the baton, traveling would not be possible. The third generation of the Mahaffey Apartment Company consists of four individuals: (1) my son, Tom Mahaffey, (2) Jim's son William Mahaffey, (3) my sister Kate's son Dan Esterline, and (4) my sister Ann's daughter, Jane Link Ferguson. Embodying the concept of specialization and exchange, each of these individuals has an expertise that they contribute to the team—Tom in management, William in development, Dan in construction, and Jane in marketing and design.

Passing the baton to the third generation was a significant transition from Jim and my perspective that we did not take lightly. We had hoped for it, prepared for it, and planned for it, but it was still a monumental decision to hand over the keys to a kingdom that we had been building for decades. Treating this transition with the care it required, the changeover was an extremely gradual process over a period of many years. Throughout my years of management, from my Navy days to working at the apartment company, I have learned a thing or two about encouraging new leaders. I considered my method of training the Junior Officers of the Deck on *USS Bennington*. Giving people the opportunity to learn by performing in a leadership role proved to be the key to many successful promotions in rank. It was by this method that the third generation learned the ropes, so to speak, of the Mahaffey family business.

Looking back, it was around the year 2005 that the slow process of transitioning the company to the third generation began to take shape. This was a pivotal year, in which multiple big changes in the company transpired, prompting me to realize it was time for me to start stepping back. 2005 was the year that the Mahaffey Apartment Company sold

Coquina Key Arms, which had been my office location since 1972. Reluctant at first to bring such sweeping disruption to the company all at once, I had negotiated within the sales contract the option to maintain the office at the Coquina Key property for up to one year post-sale, leasing the space from the new owners. However, Jim, who still worked in the Winter Park office with his son William, wisely encouraged me to consider moving from the office soon after sale. He reasoned, "You are not going to want to be at the office there every day as the new owners take over."

There was sound logic in his words, and I heeded his advice, fastidiously starting the search for a new office location. I ended up settling on the Northern Trust Building in downtown Saint Petersburg, and we fully relocated our operation within one month of the property being sold. This move was not only for me, however. With the company having grown considerably since the office was established at Coquina Key, I determined it was high time we had a corporate office. Instead of our top employees being scattered at different properties, we all corraled into one space—excluding Jim and his son William, who remained in Winter Park for the time being. Tom, Suzanne, Jane, and our other longtime employees, Rob Wolfson and Mark Safko, as well as myself, all moved into the new Saint Petersburg corporate office. My *girl Friday*, Lola Walters, who was still my right arm after 30 years, also came along. It was a much better arrangement, as it was much easier to collaborate as a team in one space.

Three years later, we upgraded to an even larger office space across the street, located within the Signature Building, where it remains to this day. We chose the third floor of the Signature Building, as it had a unit that seemed to perfectly fit our needs. My brother, Jim, suggested that we also purchase the adjacent unit, reasoning that even though it was more space than we required at the time, it would be better to have the space secured in the event we may need it in the future. A renowned, local architect designed the space into a functional, yet very attractive, office area. Large individual offices, with floor to ceiling windows, over-looking the Tampa Bay waterfront and downtown Saint Petersburg, command the space. Several large conference rooms and interior breakrooms with small kitchens also exist throughout. Taking my brother's advice, I asked the architect to turn the extra space into an "annex" of offices, which we leased out to other companies for the time being. Following the architect's design, Dan Esterline's construction company finished the interior of the office space with precision and skill. I was very impressed with his team's hard work and attention to detail.

In the meantime, as we were settling into our new office spaces, the Mahaffey Apartment Company was also in the process of building a new development, Carlton Arms of Winter Haven. It was a 1,000-unit property that Dan Esterline's construction company built over two phases. While constructing the second phase, however, we ran into a large problem. At that time, in the United States, there was a massive drywall shortage. Within the previous few years, ten hurricanes had hit the Gulf Coast, including the catastrophic Hurricane Katrina, and a great deal of construction material was required to rebuild the communities.

Desperate to complete the second phase of apartments, we sourced drywall from manufacturers overseas—more specifically, China. Although the price tag was hefty, at nearly double the price we were used to paying, we calculated the long-term benefit. We prioritized finishing the project on time in order to begin leasing the apartments and initiating the income stream as soon as possible. It was a bitter pill to swallow, but a necessary one. If only we knew how bitter it would ultimately turn out to be.

When the Chinese drywall was delivered, Dan's team worked tirelessly to install the product in time. We finished the second phase later that year, and with our competitive pricing and positive reputation, we were able to bring it to full occupancy almost immediately. Unfortunately, three years later, in 2010, information began to circulate that drywall originating from certain quarries in China had been found to release a noxious off-gassing of volatile chemicals and sulfurous gases that could potentially cause respiratory problems. A ghastly, sulfur odor was the only indicator. We prayed that the drywall we installed was from one of the safe quarries, but only time would tell.

Disastrously, our worst fears were realized when a resident called our office after noticing an overwhelming sulfur smell in their unit.

Maintaining the safety of our residents as our top priority; we immediately hired professionals to examine the suspected drywall. Alas, these experts discovered that we had indeed purchased an entire lot of tainted Chinese drywall. Our only solution was to vacate the entire second phase of the development, which consisted of 440 units—all of which were occupied at the time—and completely remove the drywall. Due to the risk of fire from the potential toxic fumes corroding copper wiring, we also had to replace all the electrical wiring and appliances. Carpeting and trim work also had to be removed due to the effects of the off-gassing. In short, all of the units had to be gutted and stripped down to the studs. Further, not only were we required to destroy all of the drywall sheets, but also, a certified environmental specialist had to mark each sheet, date it, and take a photo. There were thousands of sheets! The estimated cost for the job was $11 million. This was a big, BIG problem.

To add fuel to the fire, this was in 2010, and the economy was also in the midst of what would become known as the Great Financial Crisis. It was certainly not an ideal time to be faced with such a tragedy. We could have easily just handed the keys over to our lender, Freddie Mac, defaulted on the loan, and gave up on the property. However, in all our company's history, we had never defaulted on a loan or turned a property over to a lender. We had worked for too long and far too hard to lose the Mahaffey Apartment Company's untarnished reputation. We knew what needed to be done and merely had to figure out how to secure the funds to complete the rebuild.

Given the ongoing credit market turmoil of that time, Freddie Mac, as well as our other lender, Wells Fargo, refused to loan us the money. Jim's health was already in decline at this point, so I worked closely with Tom, William, Dan, and Suzanne to come up with a solution. We decided, in desperation, if we could not obtain the money through loans, we needed to find another route.

As *The Pathfinder* on a mission, I flew out to Washington DC with Suzanne and William to meet with the representatives at Freddie Mac. We met with one of the US Senators, as well as a US Congressman, and pleaded with them to grant us a loan modification, considering our dire situation. We explained to them our Chinese drywall crisis, which required $11 million and several years to solve. Luckily, the men listened carefully to our concerns. After several months of negotiation, Freddie Mac agreed to forbear our total debt service for both phases of Carlton Arms of Winter Haven for 26 months. We also went to the tax assessor and obtained concessions for the phase two property taxes for two years. These savings gave us the breathing room to refinish the 440 units without any additional lending. With the subcontractors also agreeing to complete the job at cost, we finally had the ability to reverse the whole Chinese drywall problem.

Within twelve laborious months, we painstakingly removed every piece of contaminated Chinese drywall and refinished every unit of the second phase. Carlton Arms of Winter Haven was miraculously back in working order and ready to rent. On top of this success, we saved $1 million on the reconstruction, completing the project for only $10 million. Boasting brand new apartments for an affordable price, we were back to full occupancy within months. We were eventually able to refinance the property and pay Freddie Mac back entirely over time. The Chinese drywall catastrophe could have potentially prompted the downfall of the Mahaffey Apartment Company. Instead, it proved to be another example of how teamwork, dedication, and creative thinking are always the prime ingredients that see us through.

Carlton Arms of Winter Haven, Florida

The Carlton of Fort Myers, Florida

Mark Mahaffey

Jim Mahaffey

The silver lining of the potential disaster was that it gave Jim and me the opportunity to see the third generation in action. It was exactly as we had hoped and prepared for—Tom, William, Dan, and Jane stepped up, took responsibility for the company, and demonstrated great skill in managing the crisis. Working well with Suzanne, they proved to possess great synergy together, while maintaining Mahaffey principles and striving to always put the residents first. I can confidently declare that these four individuals have done a fantastic job continuing the integrity of the Mahaffey Apartment Company.

The third generation
of the Mahaffey Apartment Company
Dan Esterline, Tom Mahaffey,
Jane Link Ferguson, William Mahaffey

With the rise of the third generation, as well as the changing of the times and the economy, we decided the days of the red brick, colonial-style apartments were over. Carlton Arms of Winter Haven was the last of what we now affectionately call our *legacy product*. With new federal regulations requiring strict handicap-friendly layouts, we changed the apartment construction style to a more modern, craftsman-style structure that is more cost-effective to build. We have developed three more communities with this new product: The Carlton at Bartram Park in Jacksonville, The Carlton of West Melbourne, and The Carlton of Fort Myers, with several more locations in the works as of this writing. Each property, in Mahaffey tradition, reached full occupancy very soon after construction completion. Although we have modernized the design to meet the current regulatory requirements and market demands, my father's philosophies still shine through each new addition to the portfolio. We continue to deliver a high-quality product at a reasonable rental rate, while keeping customer service and resident satisfaction at the forefront of what we do every day. Each property features waterfront living, large, open floor plans, an abundance of green space, and resort-style amenities.

Meanwhile, our team at the Mahaffey office also saw one big change—a bittersweet one at that. Sadly, in 2011, my trusted assistant, Lola Walters, suffered from a brain aneurysm and died shortly afterwards at the age of 65. My daughter, Colleen, jumped in to help for a few months, but as the Maverick in our family, she had bigger and better things to do than wait on her old dad. As a saving grace, the following year, Patty Cole entered the picture. She had worked under my friend, Carl Lambrecht, for many years, but now that he was retiring, he highly recommended her to me. I couldn't have been more appreciative for the suggestion. Patty Cole has been an invaluable addition to our Mahaffey corporate office ever since—not only as my assistant, but also as a great help to everyone in the office, as well as my family at home. She is the ever-busy bee, keeping the office running smoothly and helping anyone in need. From secretary work and financial record keeping, to planning office parties and taking care of my family dogs—Patty does it all.

In 2018, Suzanne Gray announced that she would be retiring the following year. For 43 years, she had been a dedicated and invaluable asset to the Mahaffey Apartment Company. It was certainly sad to see her go, but we were so thankful for all her years of service and wished her all the best in her retirement. Jane Link Ferguson also began to phase into retirement around this time, but still remains on our board and handles community affairs and participation. We are grateful for her many years of working with the family company since the 1980s—first for her role as executive director of Lynn Lake Arms and later Coquina Key Arms. Also, for her contributions to marketing, design, and maintaining our company's high reputation.

Knowing that a myriad of new changes in the company management structure would lay ahead, we hired a consultant, Mike McGrann, with Telos Group, who specializes in family business relationships and generational transitions. At his advice, we decided to split Suzanne's role into two separate positions, as she had certainly acquired a lot of responsibilities over the course of her 43 years of service. We ultimately hired Austin Everett, as Chief Financial Officer, and Stephanie Booker, as Chief Operating Officer, to fill these roles. Later on, we also hired a controller, Andrew Sharp. These three new people have proved to be wonderful additions to the team, working well together to push the Mahaffey Apartment Company to a continued success.

In January 2020, Jim and I split our ownership of the company equally between Tom, William, and Dan, formalizing the transition of responsibility of not only keeping this ship afloat, but surging forward. Two months later, Jim passed away at the age of 83. He had been struggling with his health for quite some time and had put in many years of hard work and committed dedication to the company. With his death, I reflected on the path we had walked together. My father, Jim, and I, the original three-man team, somehow were able to use our differences as our assets to work together to get the deals done. Like my father, Jim's rigid personality was challenging at times, but we always seemed to get though the hardships leaning on each other. Jim was not an emotional man, but he had his highs and lows. His symbol was the polar bear—a hunter, with qualities of strength, tenacity, and leadership. He showed his love and care in different ways than most. Although Jim had a tough-guy façade, he had a heart of gold. The handwritten letter he wrote urging me to come work in Florida back when I was in the Navy meant the world to me. Being eight years my senior, he taught me much about real estate finance and business during my growth phase. Jim's offer to buy Butlerstown House with me, although it never came to fruition, deeply touched my heart. His passing was extremely difficult, but one thing is for sure—I will truly miss the Polar Bear who was not only my one and only brother, but also my partner and my friend.

"The brothers' command"

After Jim's death, we made the necessary changes in the company that we had been planning for a few years. We decided to close the Winter Park office where Jim and the accounting team had been working. William, as well as our senior accountant, moved to Saint Petersburg to work in the corporate office. Although it has been many years since I made the decision to phase out of the ownership and active management of the company, I still enjoy maintaining involvement and watching the new team at work. It is an amazing thing to witness.

I believe my father would be mighty proud if he were to see the company today. The company looks very different, but that was part of his philosophy from the beginning. Trial and error was always a key ingredient to the early Mahaffey success story, and it continues to play a huge role in our persistent growth. Despite the changes, we have held strong to our founding principles. We prioritize developing and managing communities that are economically sound, while still keeping rent reasonable. Our goal has been and always will be to maintain our communities with high standards and to have full occupancy with low turnover. I know we have done a good job when I hear from past residents about their fond, memorable experiences of living in one of our communities. It is sincerely gratifying when a past resident calls me up to see if I can get their child, or nowadays their grandchild, an apartment. Our residents are our best source of advertising, as they share with others about the gem of a community we provide.

As it takes all the gears in a watch to make it run, it takes a whole team of people to keep our apartments going strong. My father's philosophy, inspired by his football coach Knute Rockne, was simple: focus on the victory, and with the right players in place, you will get there. Maintain your partners. Maintain your properties. Maintain your friendships. That is the endurance needed to keep going.

The Mahaffey Apartment Company is more than a development business. It is a collaboration of friends and family of present and past, with the ever focus on serving our community and bettering the world around us. It has certainly been a long journey. As I've meandered on my life's path, I have found that the route to personal success is never straight, it is never alone, and it is never ending. Success is not defined by its destination but by the growth and collaboration along the away. I don't know where I would be today without the people who have built my foundation and continue to build the scaffolding as I climb. It has been a wild ride, but I wouldn't change a thing.

EPILOGUE

One night I dreamed
I was walking along the beach with the Lord.
Many scenes from my life flashed across the sky.
In each scene, I noticed footprints in the sand.
Sometimes there were two sets of footprints,
other times there were one set of footprints.

This bothered me because I noticed
that during the low periods of my life,
when I was suffering from anguish, sorrow or defeat,
I could see only one set of footprints.

So, I said to the Lord, "You promised me, Lord,
that if I followed you, you would walk with me always.
But I have noticed that during the most trying periods of my life,
there have only been one set of footprints in the sand.
Why, when I needed you most, you have not been there for me?"

The Lord replied, "The times when you have seen
only one set of footprints, is when I carried you.

Mary Stevenson, Footprints in the Sand

The first time I heard the poem, *Footprints in the Sand*, it struck a chord in my heart. Throughout my life, through the most difficult times and the most joyous, I never felt alone. As I reflect on my life's mission to find the right path, God always seemed to put the right person at the right time there, when I needed them the most. There were several moments in my life when I came to crossroads, and the trajectory of my path could have gone several different ways. I am proud of the decisions I've made, but I never made them on my own. I always had a team of people guiding me, supporting me, and helping me along the way. My friends and family of past and present all shaped me into who I am today. And in turn, I hope I have influenced their lives for the better as well. With God's grace, we have carried each other through the most difficult times of our lives and cheered each other in the best. I may be *The Pathfinder*, but I've had many guiding stars along the way. I am very grateful to all those people and experiences.

It is rather interesting to reminisce and ponder the most impactful moments of my life and what I learned from them. From playing basketball as a youth with my best buddies, I learned the importance of teamwork and comradery. From working with Dick at Indian River Inn, I learned about myself and human nature, and how to build rapport with people. In the Navy, aboard *Bennington*, I learned the crucial skills of team collaboration and leading by serving. When I began working for the family business in Saint Petersburg, I learned what an incredible example my father was, and I soaked up all I could from him. As the business grew, I discovered that my father's philosophies were indeed true wisdom. As I have matured over the years, I have developed many philosophies and learned many truths on my own. As with many things, you can only learn through experience. But perhaps the most important thing I have learned is to hold close to your family and friends—they are what really matter. John Dewey, American philosopher, could not have said it better when he said, "We do not learn from experience...we learn from reflecting on experience."

Although I am nearing my 80th year of life and can look back at a full life, I do not get the sensation that I am nearing the end of my path. I know I have many more adventures that lay ahead, and I am just as eager to carve my way just as I did when I was a young man. The focus, however, does change as I get older. I am less fixated on my own success story, and more focused on the people I love in my life—Marianne, my children, grandchildren, and friendships. They are the highlights of my path and the reason to keep pushing forward.

Mark and Marianne at a Notre Dame Football game

Marianne and Mark Mahaffey

The love I feel toward my family is my fuel. I couldn't be prouder of my children, who have grown beautiful families of their own. It brings me such joy to see them continue many of the Mahaffey traditions through their own family vacations, building of friendships, giving to the community, as well as continuing the Mahaffey Apartment Company with family honor.

It has been especially rewarding to build my own relationships with my grandchildren—Ansleigh, Reese, Piper, Colton, and Mackenzie. Seeing them grow up before my eyes and supporting them in finding their own paths in life has been extremely fulfilling. Traveling together to North Carolina, Colorado, Panama, and other places, has been a real opportunity to build a special bond with them that I never got to experience as deeply with my own grandparents. I am also thankful to have them all live locally in Saint Petersburg, which has allowed me to share in their life journey and grow a deep love between us.

There is a particular story, with one of my grandchildren, that has especially touched my heart. One day, when my granddaughter, Ansleigh, was about two-years-old, we were walking back to our car after eating dinner at a restaurant. She was toddling along with her sweet, little hand, holding onto mine. That special moment must have meant as much to her as it meant to me, as she looked up at me with those big hazel brown eyes. In her precious toddler voice, she said, "Papa, I love you." My heart melted in that moment. I smiled at her, and I suppose my sense of humor kicked in, because I replied, "Ansleigh, you have just gotten your college education paid for." It is moments like this, that I live for.

I have been very lucky in life, and I continue to count my blessings every day. With my brother, Jim, passing in 2020, and my sister Ann passing soon afterwards in 2022, it is merely Kate and I left of the Mahaffey siblings. Kate and I continue to maintain as close of a relationship as we can, although her memory has begun to fail her in her old age. I am very happy and proud that her son, Dan Esterline, has moved her out of an assisted living for the memory-impaired in Indianapolis and has brought her down to Florida to live with family. Kate is in a much better place in the comfort of her son's home. Alzheimer's disease seems to be a genetic condition, as my sister Ann suffered from it as well. So far, I feel extremely blessed to have held fast to my own memories as best I can, but I must be honest in that I cannot speak for the future. I pray that dementia disorders will be conquered in my children's lifetime, so they will not suffer the same fate. However, no matter where life leads us, I deem it important to keep strong optimism through the hard times, as the road will always continue to have its bumps and rough patches along the way.

My beautiful wife, Marianne, is currently going through her own health struggle. A few weeks before Christmas 2022, we received the terrifying news that she has pancreatic cancer. I will never forget the day we found out. It was on December 14, just hours before the Mahaffey Office Christmas party. We were devastated to hear the news, but the doctors promised that we were lucky in that we caught it at its very early stages. Marianne was quickly scheduled for surgery, which was successful, and now, is undergoing six months of chemotherapy. Seeing Marianne going through this journey has proved to me even more what an incredibly strong woman she is. Her resilience to defeat and her strength to push forward with positivity has been so inspiring. That strength is fueled by hope, faith, and trust.

My friends have asked me, "Mark, how are you doing through all this?"

I have replied, "I'm doing okay." Am I perfectly okay? No. Part of me is very scared, and wants so badly to take all this pain and suffering from the woman I love. But, at the same time, what keeps me "okay" is seeing how positive she is. When we lost the twins, Marianne was unbelievably strong. I'm sure she was just tearing up inside. But she kept saying, "We're going to get through this." And we did, gaining determination and hope for a better future, despite the hardship. It is interesting when you get to be my age, mortality begins to face you head on, whether it's yourself or your friends or your family. But that's just a part of life. Just as with the loss of our twins and the health scares of my friends, the struggle and the hurt brought us closer together. As we find in each other the stamina to hope, our love grows and becomes all the more vigorous.

As I look to the future, I see a beautiful continuation of the Mahaffey folklore. I offer one last piece of advice to my children and grandchildren—hold onto each other, cherish the small moments, be proud of your roots, knowing that you will be the foundation of future generations, and most importantly, invest in time with your loved ones and friends—for this is what life is all about.

THE STORY BEHIND THE COVER ART

As many of my good friends and family know, over the years, I have taken up the hobby of collecting artwork—more specifically, paintings. My homes in Saint Petersburg and Highlands, as well as the Mahaffey Apartment Company corporate office, are elegantly decked with dozens of exquisite art pieces that I have collected over the years, both locally and through travel. I enjoy the visual beauty of the paintings and the representation of the tremendous skill and patience of the artist. But most of all, I love the story that each painting has to tell. If anyone were to walk along with me down the art-studded hallways and listen to the stories behind each painting, they would hear a version of my life story through art—the places I have traveled, the people I have met, and the adventures I have sought.

I have had the privilege of meeting many of the talented artists, who are too often the hidden marvels behind the masterpieces. These artists have their own intricate and soulful stories beyond the viewer's perspective, which deepens the complexity of the meaning behind each work. There is one artist, in particular, that has a story so impactful, that I am inspired every time I look upon his work. His name is Marcus Thomas.

I can remember the first time I saw Marcus Thomas' artwork. It was in the early 2010s, when Marianne and I were visiting Highlands, North Carolina. While exploring a local outdoor art festival, we were stopped in our tracks by the marvelous, realistic paintings in one of the white display tents. Even more incredible than the artwork itself, was the opportunity to see the artist in action. This painter was no ordinary artist, however. Here was a man, paralyzed from the neck down, bound to a wheelchair, and painting with a brush between his teeth!

We learned from his wife, Anne, that Marcus had suffered from a skiing accident back in 1986, when he was only in his 20s. He had been confined to a wheelchair ever since. Although his life's vision of a career in athletics and outdoor recreation was shattered, his spirit of determination and ambition were not hindered. His wife was the first to recommend he start painting, to which he has devoted his efforts ever since. His range of motion is limited to expressions in his face and a slight shrug of his shoulders. It is with those minute movements that he controls the paintbrush. His wife is a great help to him in setting up his canvas, easel, and supplies, as well as putting the seemingly magic paintbrush in his mouth.

Marianne and I were amazed by the skill and talent displayed in Marcus Thomas' artwork, which consists primarily of nature and wildlife scenes. The details in each square inch of the paintings were mind-blowing, as every feather or strand of fur was impeccably defined. That first day we met him, Marianne and I bought a print that exhibited finches in flight. Since then, we have seen Marcus Thomas many times, at festivals in both Highlands, as well as Saint Petersburg. Over the years, we have purchased many more beautiful paintings from him—perhaps 15 or so—most of which are originals. Some of my favorites include *The Florida Panther, Blue Marlin and Papa Hemmingway, African Lion,* and *Whooping Cranes.*

Around 2018, I decided it was about time I included a painting of a pelican in my art collection, as it had been my symbol for many years. I asked Marcus Thomas if he would consider doing a commissioned piece. To my pleasure, he responded, "It would be an honor."

I immediately replied, "Stop right there. It would be *my* honor."

I humbly requested he paint a pelican, and he gladly obliged. I offered no other parameters, leaving him to use his imagination and creative talents to design the piece. I was not sure how the finished work would look, but I knew anything Marcus painted would be wonderful.

In a few months' time, Marcus Thomas graciously presented to me a piece that exceeded my wildest expectations. It was an oil painting, titled *The Pelican in Flight*, featuring a single, unbelievably-detailed pelican, coasting above the waters of the sea. I marveled at the intricate features of the bird and the fantastic use of color. The rich blues of the sea and sky and the chestnut browns of the feathers are brightened by a pop of saffron-yellow brilliance upon the pelican's crown. The depth of the scene, reaching beyond the bird in flight, draws the viewer into a world governed by the sea and the sky. The art piece left me awestruck.

Currently, the painting is proudly hung in the Mahaffey Apartment Company office conference room. The conference room is positioned near the front door of the main office, offering visitors a glance at the extraordinary art piece immediately upon entering. Every time I gaze upon *The Pelican in Flight*, I am amazed by the talent, I am inspired by the artist, and I am reminded of my own journey in life as a pelican—flying with a purpose, finding the right path.

Mark Mahaffey and Marcus Thomas at an art festival

342

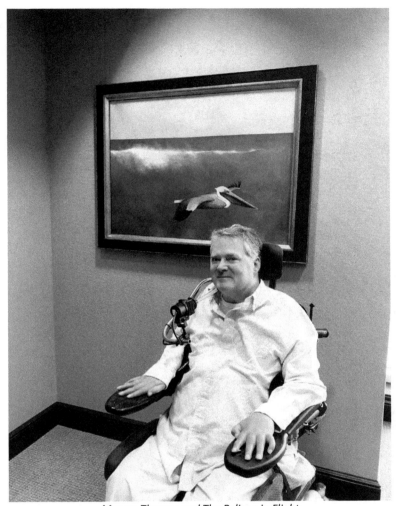

Marcus Thomas and The Pelican in Flight

The Florida Panther, by Marcus Thomas

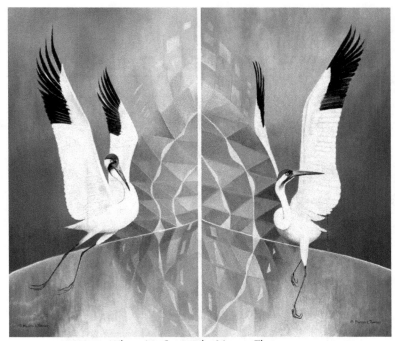

Whooping Cranes, by Marcus Thomas

African Lion, by Marcus Thomas

ABOUT THE AUTHOR

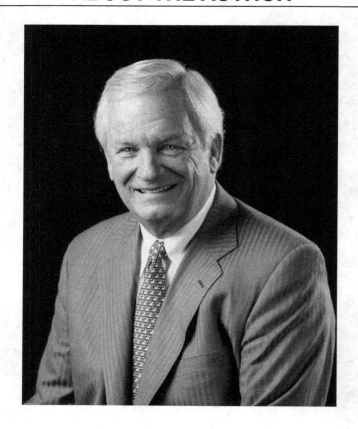

Mark T. Mahaffey has been a resident of Saint Petersburg, Florida, for over 50 years. Originally hailing from Indianapolis, Indiana, Mark graduated from the University of Notre Dame in 1966 with a degree in Business Administration and Finance. He is a United States Navy veteran, having served as a Lieutenant during the Vietnam War. After marrying his long-distance sweetheart, Marianne, in 1969, Mark and his young bride relocated to Saint Petersburg to help establish what, at the time, was an upstart family business — The Mahaffey Apartment Company. Mark and Marianne have three wonderful children, Tom, Kiley, and Colleen, who are all happily married and living in St. Petersburg. They are also blessed with five grandchildren.

Mark is the Chairman of the Board of The Mahaffey Apartment Company, which is now a well-established family enterprise, specializing in developing, building, managing and owning large rental apartment communities. Carlton Arms and The Carlton are familiar names across the State of Florida, with the company having continually served countless residents for over 60 years.

Mark and Marianne have been involved in many community organizations over the years, including Johns Hopkins All Children's Hospital, The St. Petersburg Museum of Fine Arts, The Dali Museum, Elon University, and the University of Notre Dame. In 1986, Mark and Marianne, jointly with Mark's parents, Tom and Jane Mahaffey, contributed significant funds toward the renovation of Saint Petersburg's former Bayfront Theater, which is now proudly known as The Mahaffey Theater.

It has long been a desire of Mark's to write a memoir of his life. The pages that precede are the culmination of the same forces that have served Mark well on his path in life – teamwork, determination, and maybe a little luck o' the Irish.

Printed in the USA
CPSIA information can be obtained
at www.ICGtesting.com
LVHW021157260823
756255LV00002B/32

Introducing Koine Greek by Jared August is the only work on the market written primarily for college undergraduates. It is, by design, understandable, practical, and accessible. August's goal is to provide the student only what he/she needs to know to learn the language. Here is a concise but complete first year grammar organized for maximum efficiency and effect. I highly recommend this great work.

DAVID L. ALLEN
Distinguished Professor of Preaching
Southwestern Baptist Theological Seminary

Comedian Jim Gaffigan compares raising multiple children to drowning ... and someone handing you a baby! So it is with first-year Greek. It is often overwhelming. Students begin with enthusiastic anticipation yet soon find themselves struggling to keep their head above the water, sometimes as early as chapter three! Those that manage to finish often find themselves intimidated instead of helped by the Greek text. Dr. Jared August's *Introducing Koine Greek* succeeds because it keeps first-year Greek accessible. From beginning to end, it is thoroughly confidence building. It does this by concentrating on the essentials, keeping memorization to a minimum, and always using examples from the Bible itself. While an excellent Greek scholar in his own right, Dr. August clearly teaches with the beginning student in mind. He comes alongside as a friend and mentor in the process and sets the student up for ongoing study and success. I cannot recommend his work highly enough.

TODD BOLTON
Professor of Biblical Languages
The Cornerstone Bible College and Seminary

I have often longed for a first-year Greek text that captured a little of the approach I enjoyed in my first exposure to Greek—personally encouraging and clearly communicated. Despite my search, I have always come up empty. When teaching the language, I have been forced to use one text or another and do my best to approximate the methods of my first instructors and tutor. Imagine my joy to read the textbook you hold in your hands. Finally! After all these years Dr. Jared August has captured this methodology and placed it in a textbook. In this volume, Jared August has given us the new standard textbook for first-year Greek students. It will likely enjoy the distinction of excellence for generations to come.

MARK H. BALLARD
President and Professor of Applied Theology
Northeastern Baptist College

Dr. August has written a Greek grammar for undergraduate students that is both practical and accessible. This textbook not only expedites the learning of Koine Greek, but also empowers students to apply the Scriptures to life. A manageable, straightforward resource that is pedagogically written with little complexity and greater intentionality toward the students' retention and understanding of God's revealed Word.

WAYNE T. SLUSSER
Seminary Dean and Professor of New Testament and Greek
Baptist Bible Seminary